PICTOGRAPHIC SCORE NOTATION

A Compendium

GARDNER READ

GREENWOOD PRESS
Westport, Connecticut • London

Library of Congress Cataloging-in-Publication Data

Read, Gardner, 1913–
    Pictographic score notation : a compendium / Gardner Read.
      p. cm.
    Includes bibliographical references (p.   ) and index.
    ISBN 0–313–30469–6 (alk. paper)
    1. Graphic notation (Music). I. Title.
  ML431.R34   1998
  780′.1′48—dc21   97–49480

British Library Cataloguing in Publication Data is available.

Library of Congress Catalog Card Number: 97–49480
ISBN: 0–313–30469–6

First published in 1998

Greenwood Press, 88 Post Road West, Westport, CT 06881
An imprint of Greenwood Publishing Group, Inc.

Printed in the United States of America

The paper used in this book complies with the
Permanent Paper Standard issued by the National
Information Standards Organization (Z39.48–1984).

10 9 8 7 6 5 4 3 2 1

CONTENTS

PREFACE

A pictogram, as one dictionary informs us, is "a symbol belonging to a pictorial graphic system; a diagram representing statistical data by pictorial forms." Pictographic musical notation, therefore, is a method by which not pitches, rhythms, or intensities are represented on the score page but, instead, the relevant instruments themselves are rendered in visual rather than verbal terms. By subscribing to this notation practice, many composers are evidently heeding Arnold Schoenberg's advice: "One should express [musical materials] as little as possible with letters, or even words, and make ever increasing use of signs (if possible, pictures . . .).[1]" This notational philosophy is one that has been embraced to a greater or lesser degree by many composers of the mid to late twentieth century. Pictographs, these musicians believe, are the most efficient devices by which their instrumental performance requirements can be unambiguously transmitted to their performers. They are also obvious space-savers for they require far less room on the score page than do written-out terms or instrumental nomenclature. They are, in addition, usually unequivocal in their meaning. In spite of this, however, some composers still believe that verbal instructions and the use of universally accepted nomenclature are the most precise notational methods for the average musician to comprehend. But at the same time written terminology and instrumental identifiers can sometimes be confusing to a performer lacking proficiency in foreign languages. The directives in many scores, of course, may be in French or in German; even Italian, the *lingua franca* of most musical publications, may cause problems for some musicians. Also, terminology and nomenclature can often take up an inordinate amount of space on the page, besides conflicting with other essential notational elements.

The most extensive use of instrumental pictograms in contemporary publications occurred between the 1950s and 1980s, after rather sporadic appearances in earlier published compositions. The reason for a subsequent slackening of their use might be attributed to a gradual disenchantment on the part of some composers with either the effectiveness or the necessity of such methodology. This development is perhaps also influenced by a certain lack of enthusiasm on the part of many performers of contemporary music, in particular percussionists, whose performance materials are the most directly affected.

It is an intriguing fact that many of the instrumental pictograms devised by twentieth-century composers have their antecedents in areas of endeavor far removed from music. As a matter of information—if not to satisfy one's outright curiosity—these earlier prototypes are identified in the pages to follow as they are illustrated in Walter Shepherd's *Glossary of*

Graphic Signs and Symbols.[2] It is doubtful if most composers are aware of even a fraction of the symbols listed in this reference volume, or of their original, often multiple, meanings. Of course, certain pictograms encountered in contemporary scores are immediately recognizable as being derived from a musical context; the symbol for a triangle △ , for instance, is perhaps the most obvious. Though this sign appears in the Shepherd glossary in at least nine non-musical categories,[3] it was hardly ever necessary for any composer to seek out these other instances of its earlier meanings, or to consider its potential as a useful symbol in music. Equally ubiquitous is the circular symbol ○ , the obvious choice for depicting a member of the drum family or one of the cymbals, whether suspended, crash, or sizzle. How to differentiate the one from the other becomes the problem for the orchestrator if pictographic representation is the preferred method of score notation.

To address this and other problems of contemporary notation, a conclave sponsored by the *Index of New Musical Notation* was held at the University of Ghent, Belgium, in 1974. The discussions included the pros and cons of symbol, or pictographic notation. Recommendations were advanced as to the most effective, least ambiguous pictograms for the various instruments, mainly the members of the percussion and keyboard sections of the orchestra. Although a general consensus was achieved on most issues at the conclave and the recommendations published and widely circulated, with typical stubbornness and resistance to conformity most composers continued to go their own way in notational matters, inventing and reinventing their own private pictograms from one work to the next. A source of gratification to the individual composer, perhaps, this practice was of little help to the performer of new music who had to learn a different set of symbols for each new work encountered.

Whether or not pictographic score notation will continue to be an integral part of the contemporary composers's arsenal of techniques is anyone's guess. For those composers convinced of its effectiveness it will undoubtedly show up in their future scores. For the nonbelievers, their works will just as surely continue to rely on the standard procedures of nomenclature and other verbal directives to identify both the instruments and their position in any performance set-up. But for advocates and non-advocates alike, this compendium at the very least will provide convincing proof of the resourcefulness and vivid imaginations of many twentieth-century orchestrators in their devising of individual instrumental pictographs and suggested stage diagrams, essential components of their published scores.

NOTES

1. Arnold Schoenberg: *Style and Idea.* Ed. Leonard Stein. 2nd ed. New York: Faber, 1975.
2. Walter Shepherd: *Shepherd's Glossary of Graphic Signs and Symbols.* New York: Dover Publications, Inc., 1
   1. *Electronics:* switchboard.
   2. *Electronics:* substation; *Engineering:* closed tank.
   3. *Electronics:* indirectly heated cathode.
   4. *Chemistry:* hydrogen; *Engineering:* terminating pipe; *Meteorology:* sunshine.
   5. *Electronics:* capacitor.
   6. *Astronomy:* Pluto.
   7. *Meteorology:* dew.
   8. *Engineering:* pressure vessel.
   9. *Electronics:* bell-push outlet.
   10. *Astronomy:* new moon; *Chemistry:* carbon; *Meteorology:* sky completely overcast.
   11. *Astronomy:* full moon; *Chemistry:* oxygen; *Electronics:* motor; *Mechanics:* polar axis; *Telecommunications:* cavity resonator.
   12. *Botany:* superior position; *Electronics:* negative charge; *Engineering:* surface weld; *Meteorology:* falling barometer.
   13. *Chemistry:* lime.

14. *Engineering*: stud weld; *Geometry*: perpendicular to.
15. *Telecommunications*: capacitive susceptance.
16. *Alchemy*: fire; *Botany*: evergreen; *Engineering*: projection weld; *Meteorology*: small hail; *Telecommunications*: single line discontinunity.
17. *Chemistry*: potash; *Electricity*: reinforced concrete support.
18. *Telecommunications*: tapering waveguide.
19. *Meteorology*: rain.
20. *Alchemy*: arsenic; *Chemistry*: nickle.
21. *Electronics*: support for conductor line.
22. *Engineering*: butt weld; *Meteorology*: lunar halo.
23. *Chemistry*: mercury.
24. *Engineering*: plug.
25. *Chemistry*: triple bond; *Meteorology*: fog.
26. *Engineering*: expansion joint.

3. *Alchemy*: fire, sand; *Astronomy*: distance from center of earth; *Botany*: evergreen; *Chemistry*: double bond between carbon atoms; *Electronics*: internal telephone point; *Engineering*: projection weld; *Meteorology*: small hail; *Physics*: heat drop; *Telecommunications*: single line discontinuity.

ACKNOWLEDGMENTS

Any author who undertakes a reference volume that requires extensive research is quite generally beholden to other individuals who assist one's labors by making many valuable suggestions and providing essential materials for the project at hand. I am, therefore, greatly in debt to the following persons, who in one way or another contributed to the successful compilation of this compendium of pictographic score notation:

John Beck (Eastman School of Music; Peter Tanner (University of Massachusetts, Amherst); Millard Irions (Loeb Music Library, Harvard University); Diane Ota (Music Division, Boston Public Library); Holly Mockovak (Music Library, Boston University); Daniel Dorf (Theodore Presser Co.); David R. Fuqua (Frog Peak Music); William J. Holab (G. Schirmer, Inc.); Pamela Miller (Margun Music, Inc.); Thomas Siwe (Media Press, Inc.); Sylvia Smith (Smith Productions); and Bruce Taub (C.F. Peters Corp.). Special thanks are due Patti Cardinale Cohen and Bonnie Bruce (Photo-Stop Shop, Manchester, Massachusetts) for their kind cooperation in the photocopying of materials for the book.

An expression of gratitude is owed to three members of the Boston legal firm of Ropes and Gray, who clarified for this writer the definition and interpretation of "fair use," a critical factor in the compiling of the present book: Richard W. Southgate, Gregory E. Moore, and Todd H. Shuster.

To Alicia Merritt, Acquisitions Editor and Lisa Reichbach, Production Manager of Greenwood Press, kindest thanks for encouragement and timely advice during all phases of this compendium. And last, but by no means least, I owe a special debt of gratitude to Jayson Rod Engquist, who undertook the daunting task of preparing the camera-ready copy of the book. With his enviable expertise in computer technology, he achieved what this computer-illiterate compiler could not hope to accomplish, and for that I am most grateful.

I. INSTRUMENTAL PICTOGRAPHS

Percussion Instruments

Because a reliance on pictographic notation in contemporary scores relates more to the instruments of the percussion section than to any of the members of either a chamber ensemble, the orchestra, or the symphonic band, they are given priority in the listings to follow. The tuned and the unpitched idiophones head the references, followed by the membranophones, tuned and unpitched. Under each category the pictograms are separated into instruments made of metal and of wood. Within each category the instruments are grouped according to their functional similarities. The same procedure is followed in the listings of both the traditional and the nonstandard members of the ensemble. But as no common denominator is discernable among the unusual objects included under the heading of *exotica*, the entries are arranged according to their basic materials--metal, wood, glass, and miscellaneous.

Percussionists, it must be said, are generally of two minds regarding pictographic representation of the various instruments at their disposal. There are some who are firmly convinced that the practice is not only logical but is eminently pragmatic as well. Pictograms, they believe, are the ideal solution for conveying essential information beyond normal notational contexts. In addition, they are convinced that their use greatly facilitates sight reading, a not inconsiderable advantage for any performing musician.

Many other percussionists, however, are either lukewarm about relying on pictograms when interpreting their parts in a new score, or are openly disdainful of either the need or their effectiveness. The problem for the percussionist, as for the composer, is compounded by the present lack of consensus as to the most serviceable and readily recognizable symbological representation of even a standard instrument like the snare drum or the tam-tam. When it comes to depicting such exotic and rarely requisitioned instruments as the African slit drum or the Arabic tabla, for instance, the issue becomes doubly compounded. One problem of paramount significance: there is no common usage of certain specific pictograms; composers tend to invent their own symbols for certain instruments. Thus both conductors and percussionists are forced to learn a new set of instrumental pictographs for almost every new score they confront, surely one reason why not all percussionists are enthusiastic about the practice of pictorial representation of their instruments. In addition, many composers have learned the hard way that it is not always possible to clearly and unambiguously depict the unique appearance of certain members of the percussion family--the wind machine or the boobam, for instance. This fact perhaps explains why so many orchestrators choose simple generic symbols, such as ○ and □ to identify a wide variety of instruments.

Although pictograms are especially pertinent in scores that require many different percussion instruments, plus a wide assortment of mallets and beaters, the frequently excessive abundance of these symbols can be intimidating for some percussionists. In addition, the choice of certain pictograms that are either too abstract or that are relied upon too readily by the composer to identity many different, even though related, instruments can end up being self-defeating. The sign ○, for instance, used to depict a large number of idiophones and membranophones, and the design □, called upon to specify any one or even all of the tuned metallophones and other idiophones, clearly lessens the overall effectiveness of these pictographic devices. Furthermore, these two abstract symbols are not truly pictograms as they do not unequivocally show the individual shape and dimension of the instrument they are intended to specify. But on the other hand, to be successful any pictogram should not be so overly detailed and fanciful, bordering on the merely decorative, that it defeats its stated intent.

To summarize: to achieve maximum effectiveness a pictogram must not be so abstract that its meaning is ambiguous or, on the other hand, so complex that it is impossible for the composer to draw easily by hand or on the computer. Instant visual recognition by the performer and ease of reproduction by the composer are criteria that cannot be ignored in the designing of universally accepted pictographic models for the percussion instruments.

It seems obvious, on scanning the following illustrations of percussion instrument pictograms, that composers on the whole are in no more agreement on the choice of such representational notation than are the players who must interpret these images. These examples demonstrate clearly both the disagreements as to the best choice among many possibilities and the often overly fanciful inventiveness of some composers in devising their personalized variant forms.

Many composers, however, are needlessly nonspecific in their choice of symbology for certain instruments. Too often they have relied on the same basic sign for sonically related, yet differently constructed instruments, such as suspended cymbal and tam-tam (*See:* Examples #10 and #15, for instance). Any orchestrator convinced of the pragmatism of percussion pictograms would do well to emulate the logic and distinctiveness of the symbols devised by Hans Werner Henze for one of his major published scores:

Example #1. Hans Werner Henze: *Tristan* (1974)

I	Appeau	III	Tom	V	Appeau
	Cymbales antiques		Grosse caisse		Tambour militaire
	Dobači		Tambour à friction		Quatre tam-tams
	Marimbula		Timbales		Deux water-gongs
	Marimbaphone		Corne de brume		Tonnerre
II	Appeau	IV	Appeau		Elephant bell
	Castagnettes		Quatre cymbales suspendues		Plaque métallique
	Wood-block		Paire de cymbales frappées		Cloches tubulaires
	Boo-bam		Quatre cow-bells		
	Jeu de timbres		Flexatone		
	Trinidad Steeldrum		Vibraphone		

The pictographic representations of the percussion instruments to follow are arranged in three categories: first, as they apply to the so-called standard percussion members--instruments that are commonly available to any professional ensemble. Second, as they refer to those nonstandard instruments that are only occasionally requisitioned yet are still readily available to the percussionist. In point of fact, some players might well dispute the inclusion of certain instruments in this category. maintaining that they are called for almost as frequently as those found in the listings of the more standard members. Brake drums, Chinese cymbals, sandblocks, and flexitones, for instance, have appeared in enough recent scores to qualify as at least a semipermanent adjunct to the section. Though the division of the listings into the two categories of standard and nonstandard is perhaps arbitrary, it is the prerogative of this present compiler of instrumental pictograms.

It might be noted that there are some instruments belonging to this secondary classification that do not appear at all in the following listings; although they were included by a few composers in their scores, no pictographic identification was given of the instrument, only terminology when it appeared. The keyboard glockenspiel is one such instance, as is the tabor and the puili-puili, the latter instrument a Hawaiian bamboo drum. The inquisitive reader can no doubt find other similar omissions, absent in the listings because the composer researched did not include a related pictographic symbol for the instrument.

Finally, under the extensive umbrella of exotica are listed those instruments or objects of unusual construction and potential sonic qualities that are only very rarely encountered in contemporary scores, even those patently experimental. Indeed, some items in this listing are not musical instruments at all. Coins, dice, egg-beaters, or flower pots cannot even remotely be classified as percussion instruments; yet these and other equally esoteric items have found their place in certain avant-garde compositions of recent times. Each has been identified with a uniquely designed pictogram, found only in the work at hand. The score reader should not look for any consensus on pictorial representation here; each instance displays only one composer's personal choice of symbol, applicable solely to that particular work. For an outstanding example of such invention see Mauricio Kagel's extensive list of in his *Repertoire* (*See:* Example #155).

In many of the listings in all three categories, alternative terms for some of the instruments are given in parentheses. Some composers may request antique cymbals in their scores while others may call for crotales; both instruments are one and the same. Likewise, a rasper and a guiro are identical, as are string drum and lion's roar. The choice of one or the other of the commonly available terms is the personal decision of each composer. Whatever the choice of nomenclature the pictorial symbol will almost always be the same, or at least one that is closely related in design.

Standard Percussion Instruments

Tuned Idiophones (Metal)

Example #2. *Vibraphone (Vibes; Vibraharp)*

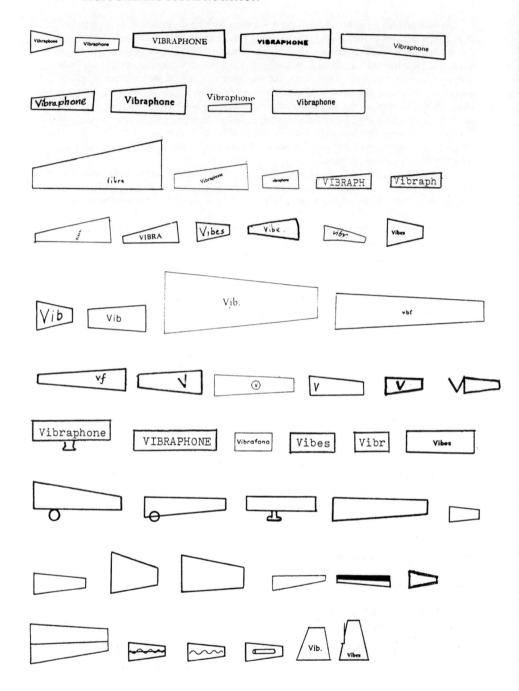

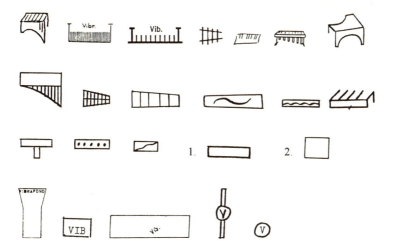

Example #3. *Glockenspiel (Orchestra Bells)*

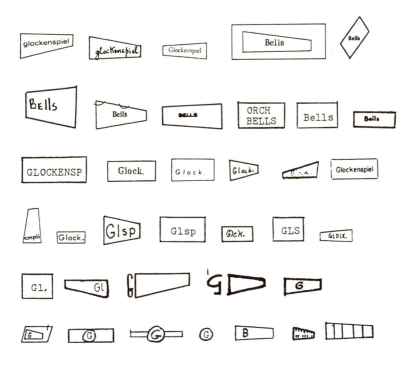

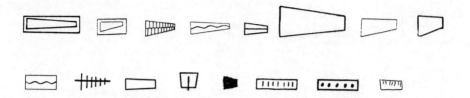

Example #4. *Chimes (Tubular Bells)*

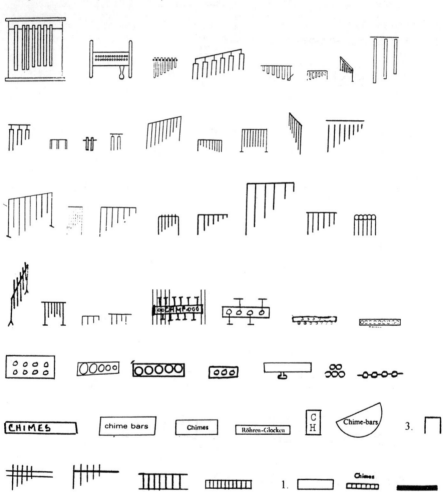

Example #5. *Antique Cymbals (Crotales)*

Example #6. *Almglocken (Alpine Herd Bells)*

Example #7. *Tuned Gongs*

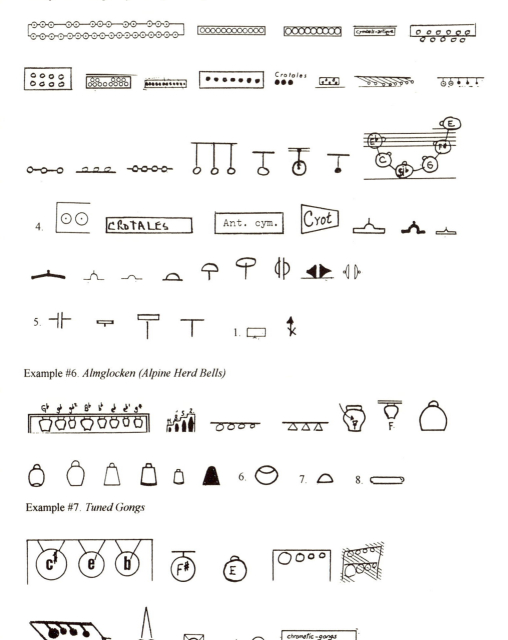

Tuned Idiophones (Wood)

Example #8. *Marimba (Marimbaphone)*

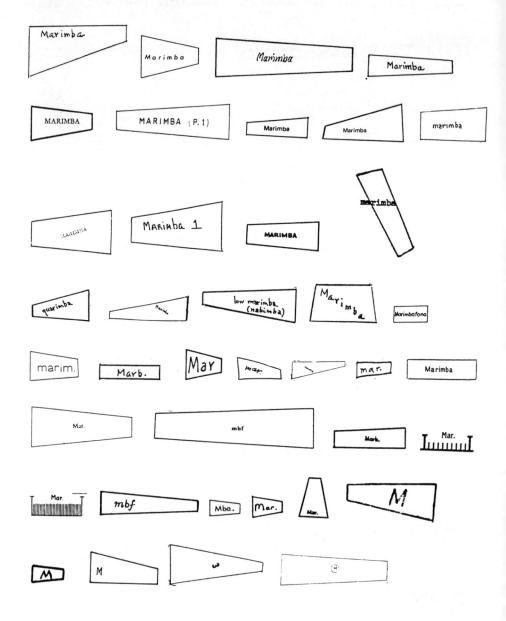

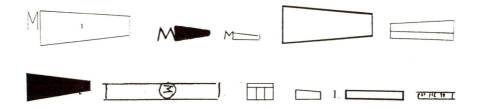

Example #9. *Xylophone (Xylorimba, Xylomarimba)*

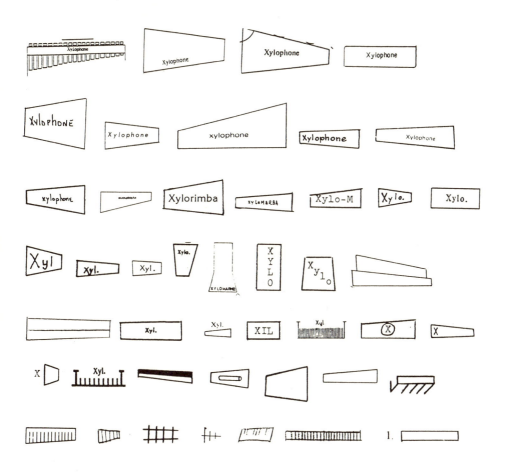

Unpitched Idiophones (Metal)

Example #10. *Tam-tam*

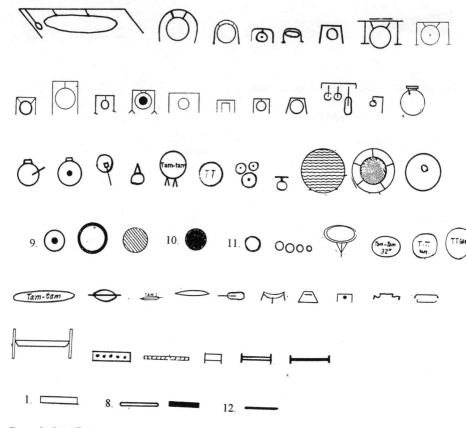

Example #11. *Gong*

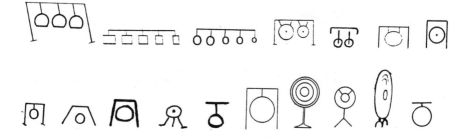

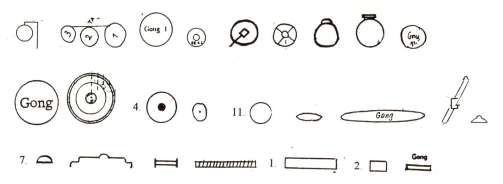

Example #12. *Button (Nipple) Gong*

Example #13. *Chinese Gong*

Example #14. *Muted Gong*

Example #15. *Suspended (Splash) Cymbal*

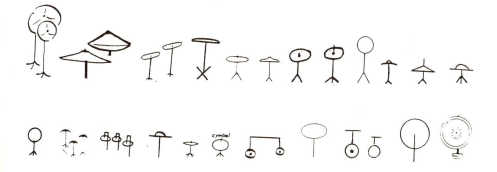

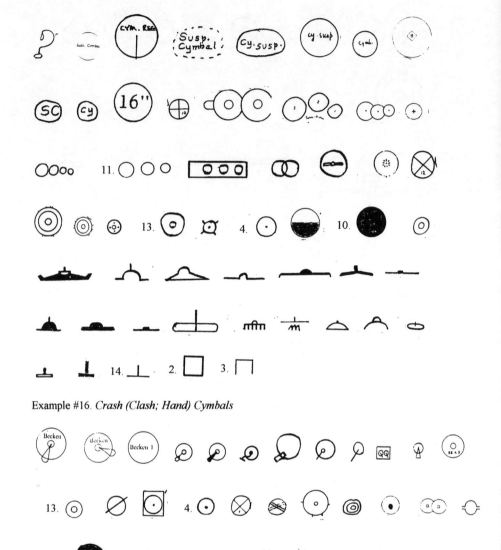

Example #16. *Crash (Clash; Hand) Cymbals*

Example #17. *Sizzle (Rivet) Cymbal*

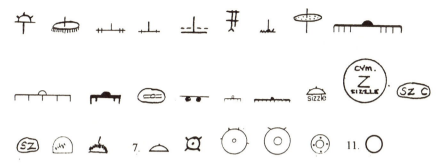

Example #18. *Hi-hat (Charleston; Pedal) Cymbal*

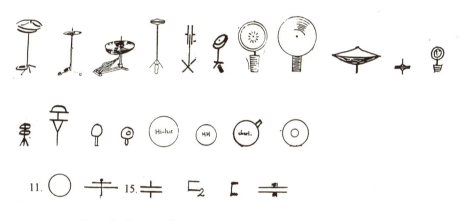

Example #19. *Cowbells (Cencerros)*

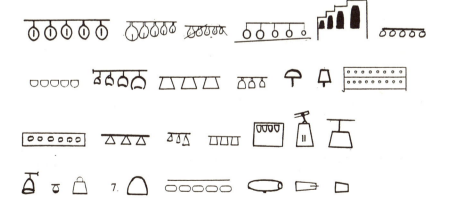

Example #20. *Triangle*

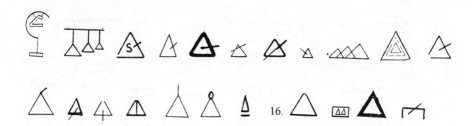

Example #21. *Sleigh bells*

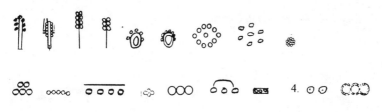

Example #22. *Thunder Machine (Sheet)*

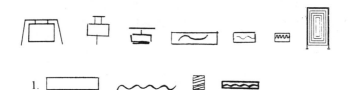

Unpitched Idiophones (Wood)

Example #23. *Temple (Korean) Blocks*

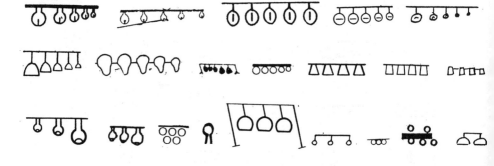

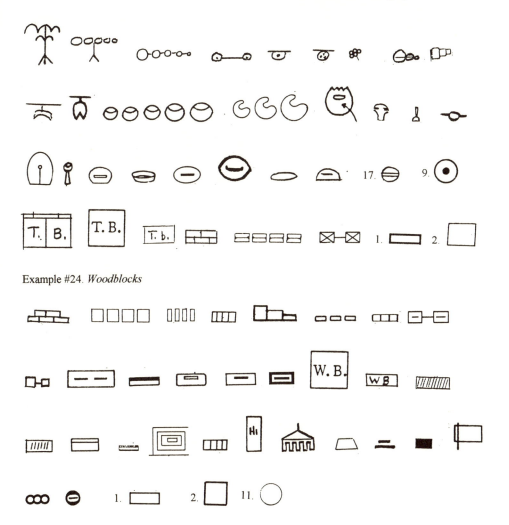

Example #24. *Woodblocks*

Example #25. *Chinese Block*

Example #26. *Maracas*

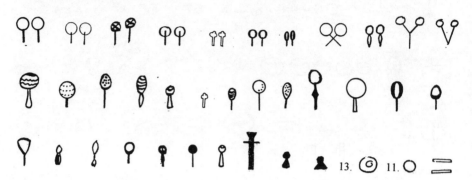

Example #27. *Castanets*

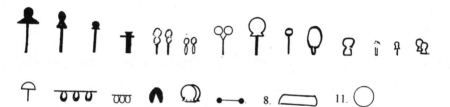

Example #28. *Board (Mounted) Castanets*

Example #29. *Handle Castanet (Matracca)*

Example #30. *Guiro (Gourd Scraper; Rasper; Scratcher)*

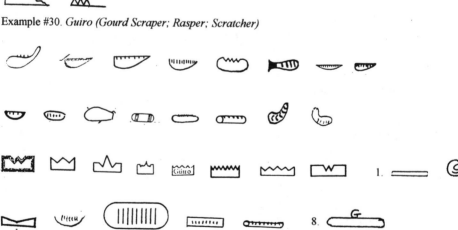

Example #31. *Claves (Bamboo Clappers)*

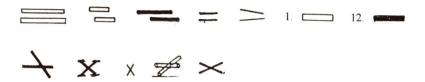

Example #32. *Ratchet*

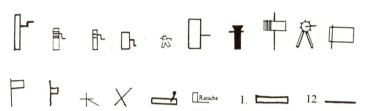

Example #33. *Slapstick (Whip; Wooden Clapper)*

Example #34. *Gourd Rattle (Cabaza)*

Example #35. *Wind Chimes - Brass (Metal)*

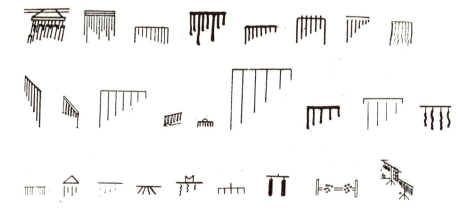

Example #36. *Wind Chimes - Bamboo (Wood)*

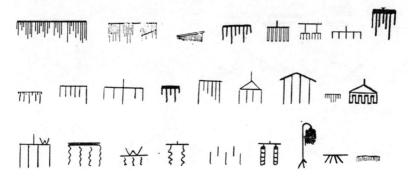

Example #37. *Wind Chimes - Glass*

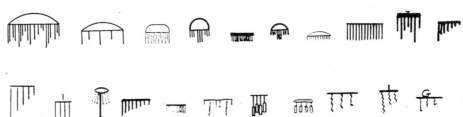

Example #38. *Wind Chimes - Ceramic*

Example #39. *Wind Chimes - Shell*

Membranophones (Tuned*)*

Example #40. *Timpani (Kettledrums)*

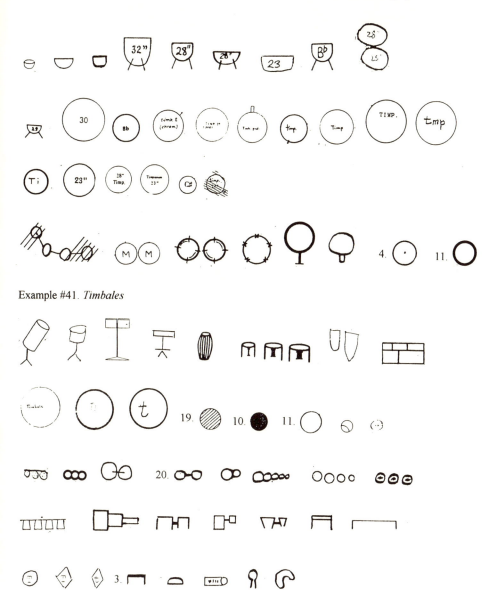

Example #41. *Timbales*

Example #42. *Roto-toms*

Example #43. *Tuned Drums*

Membranophones (Unpitched)

Example #44. *Snare Drum*

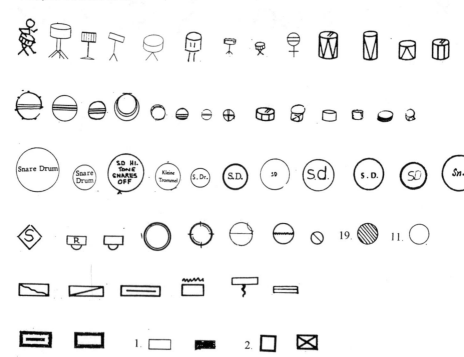

Example #45. *Bass Drum*

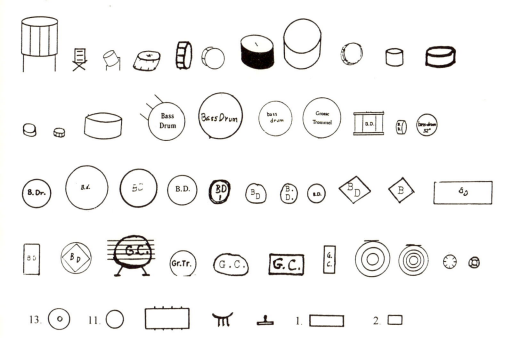

Example #46. *Bass Drum with foot pedal (or cymbal) attached*

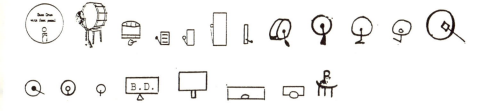

Example #47. *Bass Drum on side (dry tone)*

Example #48. *Tenor Drum*

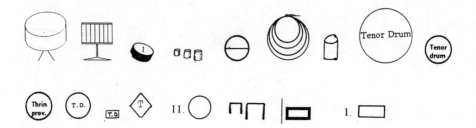

Example #49. *Field (Military; Side) Drum*

Example #50. *Small Drum*

Example #51. *Bongos (Bongo Drums)*

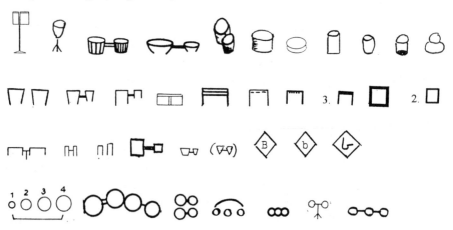

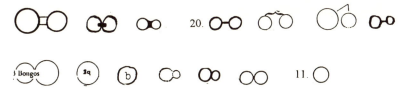

Example #52. *Tom-tom*

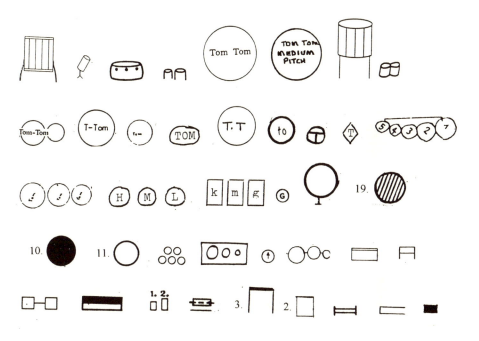

Example #53. *Conga Drum (Tumba)*

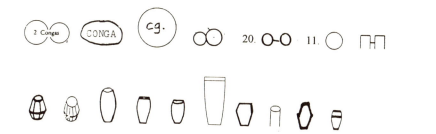

Example #54. *Tambourine*

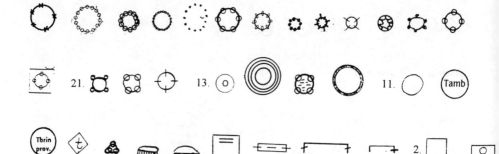

Nonstandard Percussion Instruments

Tuned Idiophones (Metal)

Example #55. *Suspended Bells*

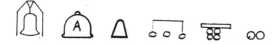

Example #56. *Church (Large) Bell*

Example #57. *Buddhist (Chinese; Japanese) Temple Bell*

Example #58. *Agogo Bells*

Example #59. *Brake (Calypso; Steel; Trinidad Gong) Drum*

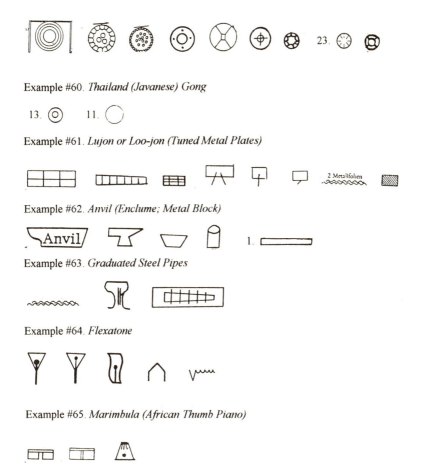

Example #60. *Thailand (Javanese) Gong*

13. ⊚   11. ◯

Example #61. *Lujon or Loo-jon (Tuned Metal Plates)*

Example #62. *Anvil (Enclume; Metal Block)*

Example #63. *Graduated Steel Pipes*

Example #64. *Flexatone*

Example #65. *Marimbula (African Thumb Piano)*

Tuned Idiophones (Wood)

Example #66. *Polychord*

25. ≡

Tuned Idiophones (Glass)

Example #67. *Crystal Glasses (Goblets; Tumblers)*

Unpitched Idiophones (Metal)

Example #68. *Jingle Bells*

Example #69. *Bell Plate*

Example #70. *Bell Tree*

Example #71. *Elephant (Sarna) Bell*

Example #72. *Goat (Sheep) Bell*

Example #73. *Persian Bell String*

Example #74. *Chinese Cymbal*

     13.

Example #75. *Greek Cymbal*

14.

Example #76. *Finger Cymbals*

Example #77. *Orff Cymbal*

Example #78. *Vietnamese Hat Cymbal*

Example #79. *Cymbal Tongs (Metal Castanets)*

Example #80. *Javanese Gong*

Example #81. *Water Gong*

Example #82. *Sistrum*

Unpitched Idiophones (Wood)

Example #83. *Sandpaper (Sandblock)*

Example #84. *Thai Buffalo (Wooden) Bell*

Membranophones (Tuned)

Example #85. *African Log (Wood) Drum*

Example #86. *Boobam (Bamboo Drum)*

Example #87. *Chinese Tom-tom*

Membranophones (Unpitched)

Example #88. *Wood Drum*

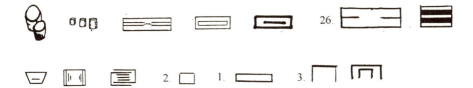

Example #89. *African Slit Drum*

26.

Example #90. *Dumbeg (Hand Drum; Tabla)*

11.

Example #91. *String (Friction) Drum (Cuica; Lion's Roar)*

Example #92. *Indian Drum*

11.

Example #93. *Chinese Clatter Drum*

Example #94. *Saharan Drum*

11.

Example #95. *Puili-puili (Hawaiian Drum)*

Example #96. *Wooden Tom-tom*

3.

Example #97. *African Tom-tom*

Example #98. *Pedal Tom-tom*

Exotica

Pitched (Metal)

Example #99. *Handbell*

C#

c#

Example #100. *Windup Bell*

Example #101. *Slide Whistle*

Example #102. *Bird Whistle*

Example #106. *Metal Saw*

Example #103. *Mouth Siren (Wind Whistle)*

Example #107. *Fog Horn*

Example #104. *Police Whistle*

Example #108.
Ondes Martenot (Electronic)

[côté clavier]

Example #109. *Harmonica*

Example #105. *Siren*

Pitched (Miscellaneous)

Example #110. *Auto (Bulb) Horn*

Example #112. *Music Box*

5.

Example #111. *Klaxon Horn*

Example #113. *Oscarina*

Unpitched (Metal)

Example #114. *Auto (Coil) Springs*

  22.

Example #115. *Chains*

Example #116. *Coins*

Example #117. *Washboard*

Example #118. *Peking Opera Cymbals*

Example #119. *Egg Beater*

Example #120. *Mixer*

Example #121. *Garbage Can Cover*

Example #122. *Pinwheel*

Example #123. *Tape Recorder*

Example #124. *Gun Shot*

Unpitched (Wood)

Example #125. *Abacus*

Example #126. *Bamboo Hanging Sticks*
(Tubes)

Example #127. *Bamboo Plates*

Example #128. *Bamboo Rattle*

Example #129. *Thin Bamboo Rod*

Example #130. *Wooden Board*

Example #131. *Wooden Box*

Example #132. *Large Crate*

   11. ◯

Example #133. *Ruler*

Example #134. *Tree Stump and Axe*

Example #135. *Barrel*

Example #136. *Chair (Siege)*

Example #137. *Wind Machine*

Unpitched (Glass)

Example #138. *Pyrex Bowls*

Example #139. *Glass Bottle*

Unpitched (Miscellaneous)

Example #143. *Dog Bark*

Example #144. *Duck Call*

Example #145. *Flower Pot*

Example #146. *Japanese Bowl*

Example #147. *Salad Bowl*

Example #148. *Mexican Bean*

Example #140. *Glass Tumbler*

Example #141. *Wine Glass*

Example #142. *Pane of Glass (to break)*

Example #149. *Dice and Case*

Example #150. *Stones*

Example #151. *Toy Noise Makers*

Example #152. *Hose (Vinyl) Pipe*

Example #153. *Jawbone (Quijada; Vibraflap)*

Example #154. *Zither*

Example #155. Mauricio Kagel: *Repertoire* (1970).

Steel globe

Cape

Styrofoam globe half

Double bass bridge

Rubber bands

Metal shoehorn

Steel spike

Styrofoam ball with handle

Tennis balls

Hand drum

Threaded balls

Metal support

Cotton bag

Infant pacifier

White smock

Wire brush

Slipper

Toy motor

Magnet

Plastic shovel

Kazoo

Wrist band

Foot mat

Bone

Iron band

Bellows

Rubber mallet

Cardboard tube

Coconut half

Toy wagon

Black bag

Recording

Nail

Bass drum foot pedal

Small measure

Tire pump

Carpet beater

Two wood slabs

Plastic mask

Voting Booth enclosure

Ashtray

Matchbox

Match

Enema bag

Rubber glove

Zipper

Pocket handkerchief

Cloth mitten

Whistle

Crossed hands

Bell push

Book

Military helmet

Tophat

Valve pump

Lid

Sprayer

Bottle with tubing

Roller

Looped rope

Wheel

Flagpole base

Plastic tubing

Stool

Footstool

Garment

Soundboard

Dark glasses

Plastic waistband

Metal rattle

Bamboo beaker

Wad of cotton

Spiral lassoo

Black tulle

Orthopedic shoe

Tin can

Alarm

Stapler

Guitar case

Filter mask

Crank

Hand drum

Dress coat

Brass tube

This just cited list of pictograms from Kagel's work represents only 84 of the total of 142 exotica invented by this prolific and imaginative experimentalist. A number of the omitted illustrations are variations, in one degree or another, of various of those pictures included here. Others left out are so arcane as to defy intelligent translation.

Keyboard Instruments

Next to those pictograms specifying the multifarious percussion instruments there are more comparable symbols for the several keyboard members to be found in mid to late twentieth-century scores thatn for any other instrumental group. Primarily, it is the grand piano that is most frequently depicted, and in amazingly varied forms. One would think that a single design might suffice, but contemporary composers have devised an almost infinite number of variations on the basic shape of the concert grand. Some have superimposed an identifying label on the instrument symbol (as if one were needed). Others have appended a simple representation of the instrument keyboard, while some have added the outline of the player's seat or bench. A few have indicated in their pictogram that the piano lid is to be up or else entirely removed from the instrument.

More specialized forms of keyboard pictographs, understandably few in number, include those for the electric piano, the upright or player piano, the spinet, or the child's toy piano. Another unique application of a keyboard instrument pictogram relates to the prepared piano, the interior strings detailed so as to show the various objects that are to be placed on or else attached to certain strings (*See:* Section III [Pictographic Performance Directives, Keyboard Instruments]).

The requisitions of harpsichord or cembalo and celesta have produced far fewer pictographic symbols than has the piano. This is not because there is little consensus on their best visual representation but only because these instruments are less frequently called for in the composers' scores. The harpsichord or cembalo are easier to depict, of course, than is the celesta, which does not have the distinctive shape of the other keyboard members. Usually this latter instrument is identified by a simple open rectangle: ⊂⊐ . Even less frequently utilized are the pipe organ and the harmonium, not to mention the modern accordion; hence there are very few pictographic examples of these instruments.

Frequently the keyboard pictographs in contemporary score publications reveal the composer's stipulation that the pianist is also to play on another keyboard member, this instrument usually placed at right angles to the piano so that both keyboards can be easily reached. The celesta is the secondary instrument most often designated, but the harpsichord and organ have also been requisitioned as alternatives. Occasionally a percussion instrument is placed adjacent to the piano, to be played by the pianist, as demonstrated in Example #320.

Following the same procedure used in the listing of the percussion instruments, the keyboard pictographs first show the most literal and detailed representations of each instrument, continuing progressively to the least orthodox, most abstract, pictographic symbol. Some will find the distinctions between one pictogram and another minor indeed; both are included to fulfill the requirements of any compendium, which is to make the listings of the visual representations as complete as possible. As a consequence the composer today can see what his or her peers have favored and thus make a personal choice among the many possibilities depicted.

Example #156. *Piano*

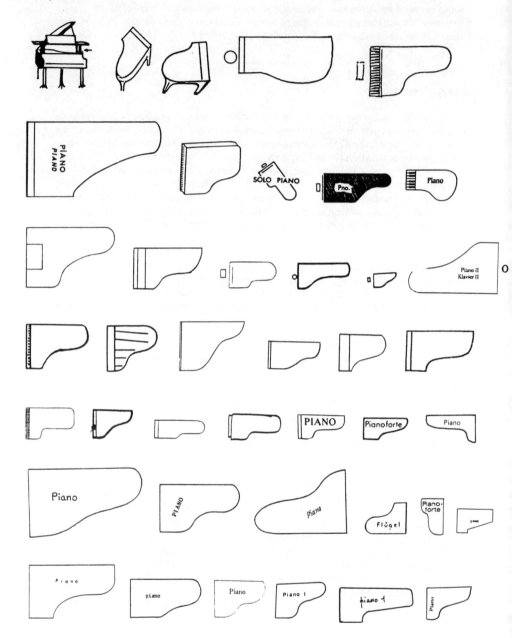

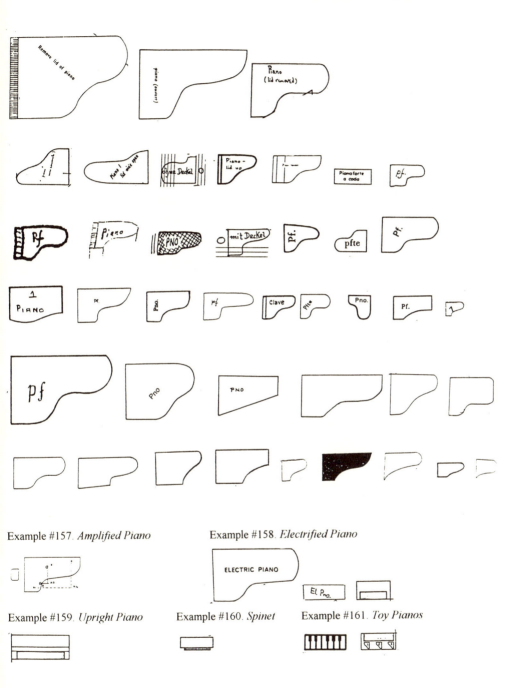

Example #157. *Amplified Piano*

Example #158. *Electrified Piano*

Example #159. *Upright Piano*

Example #160. *Spinet*

Example #161. *Toy Pianos*

Example #162. *Celesta*

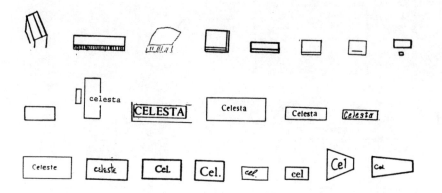

Example #163. *Piano/Celesta*

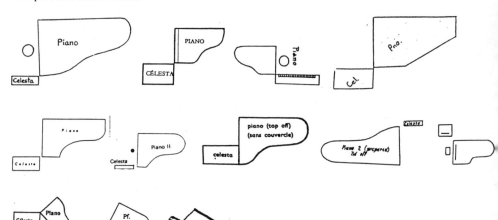

Example #164. *Harpsichord (Cembalo)*

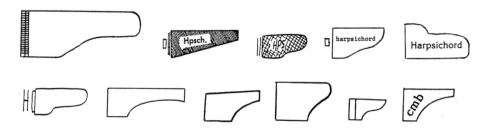

Example #165. *Piano/Harpsichord*

Example #166. *Harpsichord/Celesta*

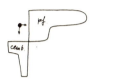

Example #167. *Pipe Organ*

Example #168. *Electric Organ*

Example #169. *Harpsichord/Organ*

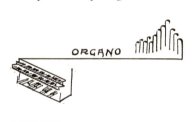

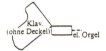

Example #170. *Harmonium*

Example #171. *Piano/Percussion*

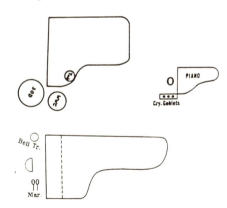

Plucked Instruments

Harp pictograms range from easily recognizable representations to curious abstract designs that give no clue to the instrument's true shape and dimension. Whereas composers might take great pains to accurately depict a percussion or keyboard instrument, at the same time they may be satisfied with a less than realistic image of the harp. Perhaps the challenge of rendering an authentic profile of this patrician instrument proved too great, and the composers only contented themselves with a more abstract symbol for its location in the ensemble.

As in the previous listings of the percussion and keyboard pictograms, those for the harp progress generally in order from the most to the least literal in design.

Pictograms for the guitar are notably few in number, and those for such instruments as the mandolin and ukelele are nonexistent, at least in those scores researched for this compendium. One example was uncovered for the electric guitar and one for "a plucked instrument," presumably the choice of the performer.

Example #172. *Harp*

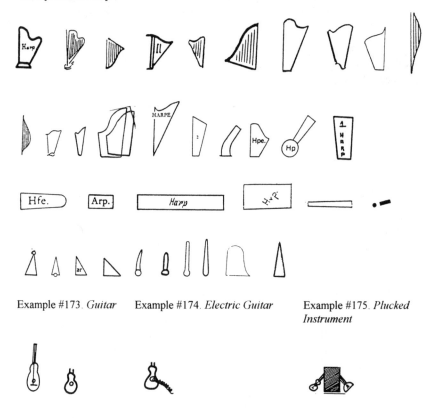

Example #173. *Guitar*   Example #174. *Electric Guitar*   Example #175. *Plucked Instrument*

Woodwind and Brass Instruments

Example #176. *Piccolo* Example #177. *Flute and Clarinet* Example #178. *Saxophone*

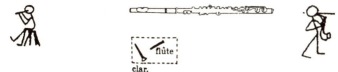

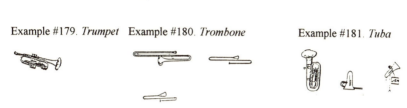

Example #179. *Trumpet* Example #180. *Trombone* Example #181. *Tuba*

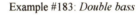

String Instruments

Even fewer in number that the pictographic symbols for woodwind and brass instruments are those for the stringed members of any ensemble. Violins and violas are not represented at all, those pictograms that have appeared being limited to the violoncello and double bass, used in a solo capacity or as the sole representative of the section.

Example #182. *Violoncello*   Example #183: *Double bass*

II. STAGE DIAGRAMS

Without a doubt the most ubiquitous manifestations of pictographic score notation to be found in mid to late twentieth-century published scores are the composers' suggested platform dispositions of the forces required in their works. These performance diagrams range from simple abstract markings to show the desired position of each instrument to quite elaborate depictions of each member of the ensemble. Many pictographic stage set-ups mix abstract with representational symbols; they will identify certain percussion and/or keyboard instruments in fairly literal outlines while at the same time relegating the remainder of the composer's forces to abstract representations (*See:* Example #328 and Example #366, for instance). Even in works for percussion ensemble alone there is a frequent mixture of the non-literal and the authentic in the composer's stage arrangement. The composer may, for example, depict some instruments, such as vibraphone, temple blocks, or piano in visually accurate terms, while at the same time relying on the same generic shape (○) for various of the membranophones such as timpani, snare drum, or bongos. In addition this same generic design is often used to specify other instrumental categories, such as chimes, crotales, or suspended cymbal.

Our contemporary composers have also favored many different, though clearly related, terms for the heading of their suggested or required instrumental positionings. Just as it was obvious that there is presently no discernable consensus on the best visual depiction of each instrument called for in the composers' scores, so there is no agreement on the best term that describes their appended pictographic disposition of the forces required.

The list that follows, arranged alphabetically for convenience, demonstrates the wide variety of related terminology to be found in the scores researched. It shows as well the almost perverse predilection on the composers' part to differ in their nomenclature from that employed by their peers. But when all is said and done, whatever form the terminology takes the basic reason for it and the corresponding result remains the same: a pictorial depiction of the instruments and their separate stage positions integral to the work at hand.

It should be pointed out that there are occasional inconsistencies in the spellings of an instrument name among the various stage diagrams to follow—i.e., woodblock (wood block), cowbell (cow bell), windchimes (wind chimes), bongos (bongoes), or Roto-toms (Roto Toms), for example. This is because not all composers invariably agree on uniform instrumental terminology or punctuation. Nor are the standard orchestration texts and treatises on percussion instruments always in agreement—i.e., guiro, guïro, or guíro, for instance. A certain tolerance on the reader's part, therefore, is required when perusing the extensive lists of instruments that accompany many of the stage diagrams.

Stage Diagram Headings

Approximate seating plan
Approximate set-up
Arrangements of (the) instruments
Diagram for set-up
Disposition
Disposition of instruments
Disposition of the orchestra
Disposition of the percussion instruments
Disposition of the performers
Distribution of instruments
Ensemble layout
Floor plan
The following floor plan is suggested
The following general set-up is suggested
The following seating plan is suggested
General seating plan
General set-up
Instrumental disposition
Instrumental layout
Instrumental placement
Instrumentation diagram
Layout for percussion
Layout of ensemble
Layout of orchestra
Orchestra seating plan
Percussion arrangement
Percussion layout
Percussion set-up
Performance layout
Placing of instruments
Placement of instruments
Placement of performers
Placement of the instruments on the platform
Position of the instruments
Position of the instrumentalists

Position of orchestra
Positioning of the instruments
Positioning of the orchestra
Positioning of the performers
Possible distribution
Possible seating plan
Positions
Recommended disposition
Recommended placement of (the) instruments
Seating arrangement
Seating chart
Seating diagram
Seating order
Seating plan
Seating arrangement for the performers
Stage position diagram
Stage positioning
Suggested arrangement of (the) ensemble
Suggested arrangement of instruments
Suggested disposition
Suggested ensemble set-up
Suggested floor layout
Suggested floor plan
Suggested orchestral set-up
Suggested percussion placement
Suggested percussion set-up
Suggested seating
Suggested seating plan
Suggested seating set-up
Suggested stage arrangement
Suggested stage plan
Suggested stage set-up
Suggestion for positioning the instruments
Topography

To display the pictographic stage diagrams that preface the composers' published scores, the following plan has been followed:

    A. Percussion ensembles

    B. Percussion ensembles with solo instrument(s) or voice(s)

    C. Chamber ensembles

    D. Chamber ensembles with solo instruments(s) or voice(s)

    E. Orchestra or band

    F. Orchestra or band with solo instruments(s) or voice(s)

G. Diagrams that include electronic components such as microphones, loudspeakers, and tape decks

Within each category the examples are listed chronologically in the following order:
1) all or the majority of the instruments are representational
2) only the percussion are pictured
3) the same for the keyboard instruments only
4) both the percussion and the keyboards are representational
5) keyboard instruments and/or harp are so depicted
6) the same for the percussion, keyboards and harp
7) all the forces required in the composer's score are nonrepresentational, indicated only by abstract symbols or with terminology

---

Percussion Ensembles

Our present century has witnessed a veritable avalanche of works for the percussion ensemble, comprised of both the traditional instruments common to the section and, as well, numerous exotic additions employed for their unique sonic capabilities. Percussion instruments have been essential components of chamber music instrumental resources as well as those of orchestra, wind ensemble, and band scores. They have also figured prominently in works designed for solo instruments or voices in combination with these same performing sources.

By far the greatest number of stage diagrams discovered in the twentieth-century scores examined have related to the percussion section, employed either as the sole entity or as a vital component of other forces. Undoubtedly, this is because the percussion—and the keyboard members, as well—are easier to depict pictorially than are any of the woodwinds, the brasses, or the strings. Even though there is at this moment no firm consensus among either composers or percussionists as to the clearest, most pragmatic design for any of the instruments in the percussion section, there are more pictographic layouts for these forces than for any other groupings of the orchestra or symphonic band.

Listed in chronological order in each of the subsections to follow, the composers whose works share a common date of composition are arranged alphabetically. The initial group of examples illustrate fairly accurate representations of all of the percussion instruments required in each composer's work.

Even when a generic form is used for certain members of the ensemble, such as ○ or ⊏⊐, it is usually sufficiently varied so that clear distinctions are evident between the instruments of like construction and sonic function. The display of each stage diagram, together with a listing of the instruments required when not evident in the composer's set-up, is followed by a brief commentary or further explanation of the particular platform design.

All Instruments Fully Representational

Example #184. Karlheinz Stockhausen: *Zyklus* (1960).

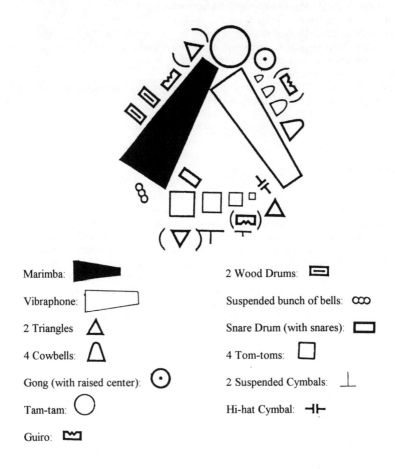

Marimba:	2 Wood Drums:
Vibraphone:	Suspended bunch of bells:
2 Triangles	Snare Drum (with snares):
4 Cowbells:	4 Tom-toms:
Gong (with raised center):	2 Suspended Cymbals:
Tam-tam:	Hi-hat Cymbal:
Guiro:	

Detailed instructions in the score refer not only to performance procedures (order of sections, timings, and so on) but to the instruments themselves. For instance: the guïro is to be attached to a music stand, the suspended bells of various sizes are to be Indian, while the cowbells with flat bells are to be suspended without their clappers, to be struck with iron beaters. The wood drums are African tree-drums, each having two pitches. Stockhausen specifies two high-pitched triangles, and furthermore suggests that the tam-tam usually be struck with a hard stick.

Example #185. Karlheinz Stockhausen: *Kontakte* (1960).

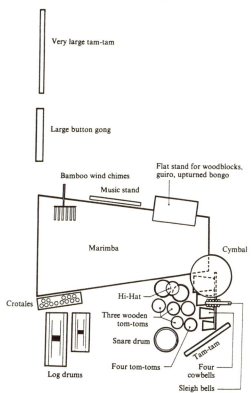

This, the second of the two versions of Stockhausen's *Kontakte (Nr. 12)*, is for electronic sounds on a 4-track tape, piano, and percussion. The stage pictogram illustrated does not appear in the composer's published score but was designed by an analyst of the work. Furthermore, the different instrumental symbols do not conform to those used by the composer in his score.

Example #186. Mauricio Kagel: *Match für drei Spieler* (1964).

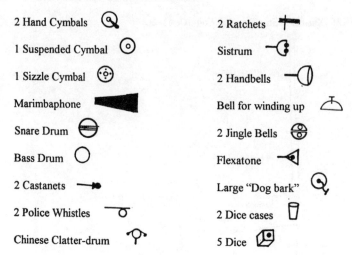

2 Hand Cymbals		2 Ratchets	
1 Suspended Cymbal		Sistrum	
1 Sizzle Cymbal		2 Handbells	
Marimbaphone		Bell for winding up	
Snare Drum		2 Jingle Bells	
Bass Drum		Flexatone	
2 Castanets		Large "Dog bark"	
2 Police Whistles		2 Dice cases	
Chinese Clatter-drum		5 Dice	

Two cellists and a single percussionist are the three players specified in Kagel's score. The cellists are separated from each other at the front of the platform, in profile to the audience, while the eighteen percussion instruments occupy the rear center.

Example #187. Larry Austin: *The Maze* (1965).
    Station A—METAL (4 stands)

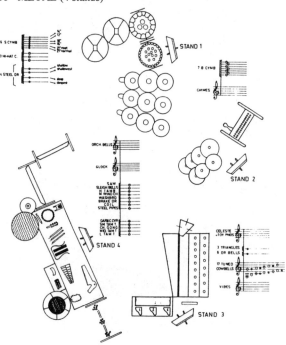

Stand 1:	5 Suspended Cymbals; Rivet Cymbal; 3 Hi-hat Cymbals; 4 Steel Drums.
Stand 1:	5 Suspended Cymbals; Rivet Cymbal; 3 Hi-hat Cymbals; 4 Steel Drums.
Stand 2:	7 Suspended Cymbals (bowed); Chimes.
Stand 3:	Celesta; 3 Toy Pianos; 3 Triangles; 6 Goat/Sheep Bells; 17 Cowbells; Vibraphone.
Stand 4:	Orchestra Bells; Glockenspiel; Saw; Sleigh bells; Tambourine; 3 Metal Windchimes; Washboard; Brake Drum; Coil; Steel Pipes; Barrel; Garbage Can Cover; Small Gong; Chinese Gong; 2 Tam-tams.

Station B—WOOD (4 stands)

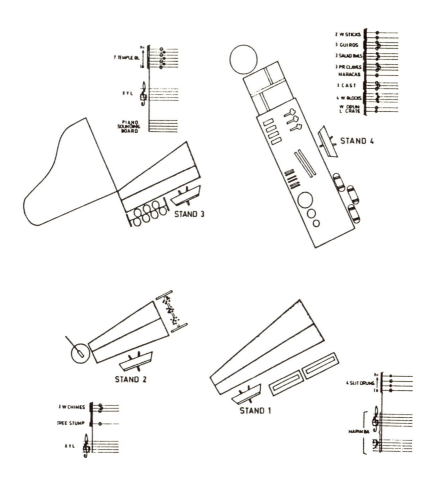

Stand 1:	4 Slit Drums; Marimba.
Stand 2:	2 Bamboo Windchimes; Chair; Tree Stump with Axe; Xylophone.
Stand 3:	7 Temple Blocks; Xylophone; Piano Sounding Board.
Stand 4:	2 Wooden Sticks; 3 Guïros; 3 Salad Bowls; 3 Pairs of Claves; 3 Castanets; 4 Woodblocks; Wooden Drum; Large Crate.

Station C—SKIN (2 stands)

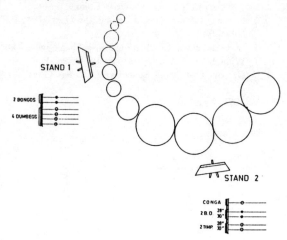

Stand 1:   2 Bongos; 4 Dumbegs.
Stand 2:   2 Conga Drums; 28" Bass Drum; 30" Drum; 2 Timpani (26" and 28").

Station D—GLASS (2 stands)

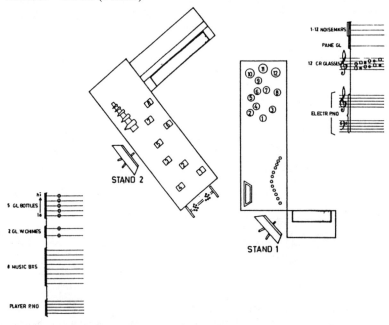

Stand 1:   12 Toy Noise Makers; Pane of Glass; 12 Tuned Crystal Glasses; Electronic Piano.
Stand 2:   5 Bottles; 8 Music Boxes; Player Piano; 2 Glass Windchimes.

According its composer—who is one of our most notably experimentally-minded advocates—this is a "Theatre Piece in open style for three percussionists, dancers, tapes, machines, and projections . . . [It] should envelop the audience and performers in sound, light, and movement." The score is unique in its quadruple division of percussive categories required: metal, wood, skin, and glass. The letters *X*, *Y*, and *Z* identify the three players in the score, at times one percussionist being responsible for managing two stations at a time. Three stereo tapes of electronic sounds are synchronized with the percussion output, relayed to the audience over three pairs of speakers (not shown in the diagram). The "machines" called for are properties for the dancer and are an essential part of the work's theatrical atmosphere; pinball and slot machines are suggested as likely candidates.

Example #188. Bobby Christian: *Danza Española* (1968).

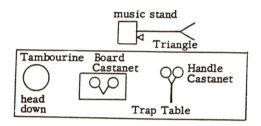

Example #189. Bobby Christian: *Rondino* (1968).

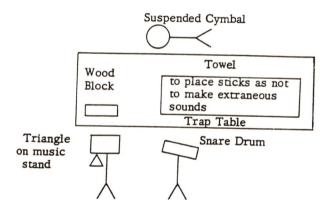

These two works and their accompanying stage set-ups are typical of many mid-century works for a small percussion ensemble. A curious aspect of both diagrams is the horizontal position of the music stand with attached triangle and the suspended cymbal, whereas the other pictograms are vertically positioned, as is normal.

Example #190. Siegfried Fink: *Alternation* (1968).

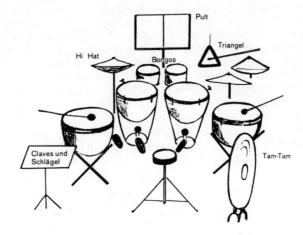

Subtitled *Scene and Variations for Percussion Solo*, the instruments required consist of 4 timpani (2 with pedals), a pair of suspended cymbals, tam-tam, triangle, 2 bongos, claves and hi-hat cymbal—all given representational pictograms.

Example #191. William Hibbard: *Parson's Piece* (1968).

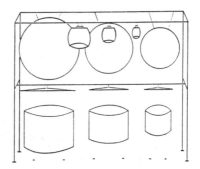

Percussion: 3 Tam-tams; 3 Cowbells; 3 Suspended Cymbals; Bass Drum; 2 Smaller Drums.

While using distinctive pictographs for each of the four kinds of instruments called for in the score, the composer clearly distinguishes their relative sizes. The work is just as clearly designed for only a single percussionist, with all of the instruments conveniently placed in one location.

Example #192. Norman Lloyd: *Night Piece* (1968).

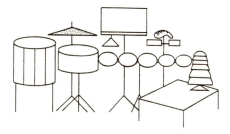

Triangle; Suspended Cymbal; Bell Tree; Scratcher; 5 Temple Blocks; 2 Woodblocks; Snare Drum; Tom-tom.

This is one of the few citations to include the bell tree. It is a wooden handle or metal ring on which are mounted a number of small bells, to be struck with a beater or shaken like a tambourine.

Example #193. William Schinstein: *Etude for Metal Idiophones* (1968).

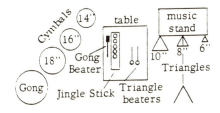

Example #194. William Schinstein: *Etude for Wooden Idiophones* (1968).

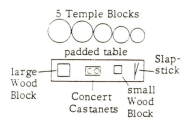

What sets the first of these two stage diagrams apart from other similar set-ups for small percussion ensembles are the exact dimensions specified for suspended cymbals and triangles.

Example #195. André Boucourrechliev. *Archipel III* (1969).

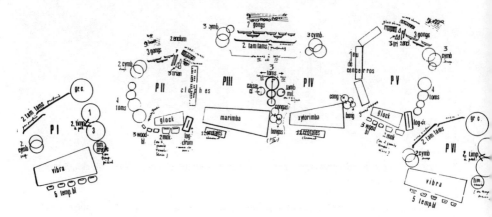

The elaborate percussion set-up in this work rivals the number and variety of the forces required in Liciano Berio's *Circles* (Example #275) and Austin's *The Maze* (Example #187), as well as Nguyên-Thiên Dao's *Máy* (Example #236). As is evident, a number of different instruments, both of metal and of skin, are served by the common O-symbol. All instruments, however, are clearly identified by means of terminology.

Example #196. Sheldon Elias: *Suite for Three Drumsets* (1969).

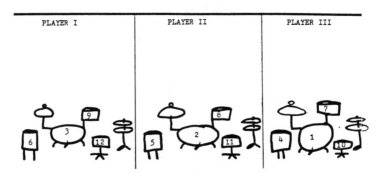

In this diagram the numbered instruments denote a scale of pitches, from 1 (the lowest) to 12 (the highest). Numbers 1, 2, and 3 are bass drums; 4, 5, and 6 are small tom-toms; 7, 8, and 9 are larger floor tom-toms; while 10, 11, and 12 are snare drums. Player I strikes the highest pitched, Player II the medium pitched, and Player III the lowest pitched of the cymbals. Two questions for the composer: what is the rationale for reversing the normal order of the pitch numerals? And could not Players I, II, and III interchange their positions? These queries are perhaps unimportant, but are motivated only by curiosity.

Example #197. Jean-Pierre Guézec: *Coulers juxtaposées* (1969).

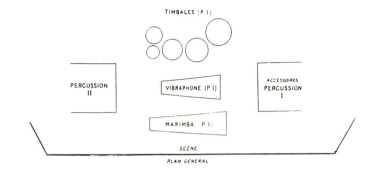

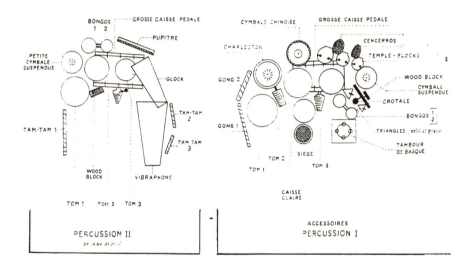

For two percussionists, this work was composed as a test piece at the Conservatoire National Superieur in Paris. The two stage diagrams show, first, a general plan for the entire ensemble, and second, detailed pictograms for the individual instruments. In the score itself, however, standard nomenclature identifies all the instruments. This is a procedure, of course, that is followed by many other orchestrators. Some composers, nonetheless, resort to both nomenclature and pictograms in their stage diagrams, as just shown in Example # 197 and in Example #199, for instance. In the case of Example #197, this practice is quite helpful, particularly for one whose knowledge of French is limited.

Example #198. Anne Boyd: *As far as crawls the toad* (1970).

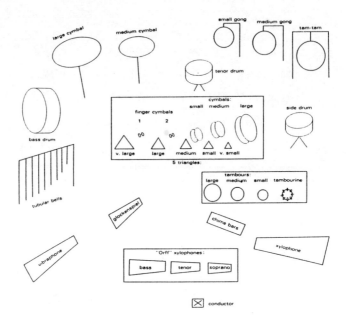

A notable feature of this score is the requisition of three "Orff" xylophones, sometimes called "trough" xylophones, whose combined range here extends from G in the F (bass) clef to g³ in the G (treble) clef. Also unusual is the inclusion of chime bars as well as a set of tubular bells.

Example #199. Paul Steg: *Targets* (1970).

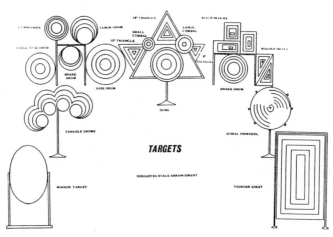

In addition to the standard percussion instruments indicated in the composer's stage pictogram, this experimental score calls for: an oval mirror on pivots (lower left), the target symbol on the reverse; a circular pinwheel with attached sleighbells (on the right); several desk bells; a blank pistol; a bow and arrow or buggy whip; a toy sub-machine gun; some powdered roisin; and various lighting facilities, including several slide projectors. Quite obviously, a notable visual effect is of paramount interest in any performance of this work.

Example #200. Marta Ptaszyńska: *Space Model* (1971).

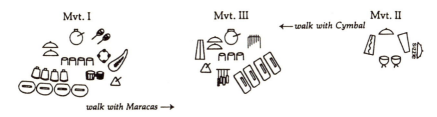

Movement I:
Triangle
4 Almglocken
Guïro
4 Temple Blocks
2 Bongos
4 Tom-toms
Tambourine
2 Suspended Cymbals
Tam-tam
Maracas

Movement III:
Triangle
Glockenspiel
4 Woodblocks
3 Tom-toms
Glass Windchimes
2 Suspended Cymbals
Chimes
Deep Tam-tam

Movement II:
Marimba
Vibraphone
Sizzle Cymbal
2 Timpani
Crash Cymbal

A singular feature of this percussion work is the different instrumental set-up for each of its three movements. The composer's pictograms are admirably distinctive.

Example #201. Howard Risatti: *Quartet No. 2* (1971).

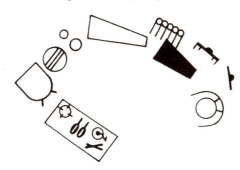

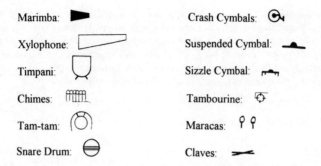

Marimba:	Crash Cymbals:
Xylophone:	Suspended Cymbal:
Timpani:	Sizzle Cymbal:
Chimes:	Tambourine:
Tam-tam:	Maracas:
Snare Drum:	Claves:

As its title proclaims, this work is for four percussionists. From the layout of the instruments one assumes that Player I is in charge of timpani, snare drum and bongos; Player II, tambourine, maracas, crash cymbals, and claves (placed on a table); Player III, xylophone, marimba, and chimes; while Player IV is responsible for suspended and sizzle cymbals and tam-tam.

Example #202. Dennis Eberhard and Annette Grieve: *Chamber Music* (1972).

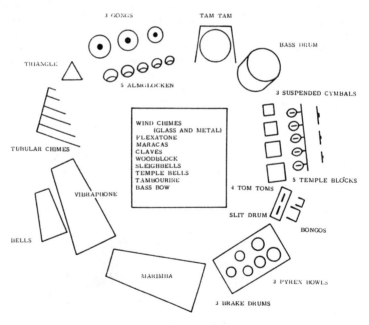

A unique feature of this dually-composed work is the score's format: each page can be read from either of two positions by reversing the separated pages. Consequently each pitch carries two accidentals (♯ ♮ or ♭ ♮, for instance).

Example #203. Charles DeLancey: *The Love of L'Histoire* (1973).

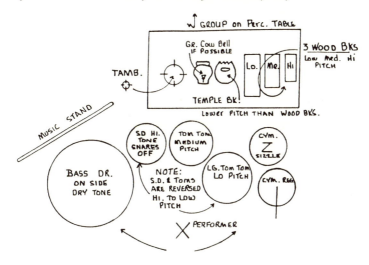

The composer of this work is very specific in his indications of relative pitch among certain of the instruments, a practice not encountered in contemporary percussion scores as frequently as one might expect.

Example #204. Gordon Stout: *Diptych No. 1* (1973).

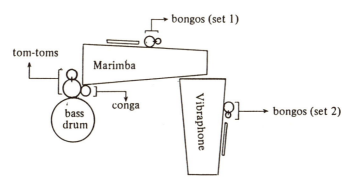

All the instruments called for in this work are arranged for easy access by the solo percussionist. Because of the opposing positions of the tuned idiophones, two music stands are required (⊂⊃). Although a common small O-symbol serves for the tom-toms, two sets of bongos, and the conga drum, their relative sizes recognize their individual pitch distinctions.

Example #205. Harold Weiss: *Rotation for Percussion Solo* (1976).

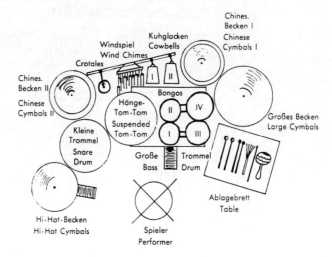

Dual nomenclature to identify each percussion instrument is a practice of many European publishers, a welcome boon for score readers not notably adept in foreign languages.

Example #206. John Beck: *Episode for Solo Percussion* (1977).

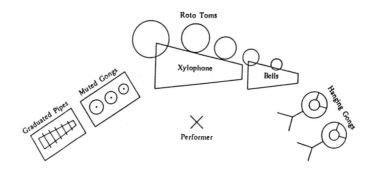

Two of the instruments in Beck's work are nontraditional: muted gongs and graduated pipes, although both do show up from time to time in more recent scores for percussion. It has only been in recent years that the roto-toms (sometimes called tuneable-toms) have become standard rather than occasional members of the percussion section. Their inclusion in a composer's stage diagram may also be seen in Examples #246 and #286.

Example #207. Mauricio Kagel: *Dressur* (1977).

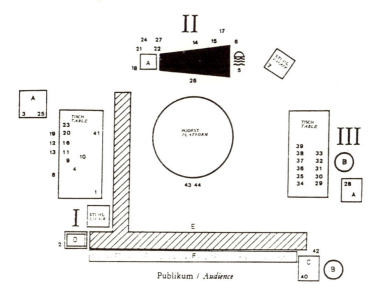

Player I:	*Player II:*	*Player III:*
1. Claves	14. Marimbaphone	28. Castanets
2. Pounding Tube	15. Cloth Sack	29. Coconuts
3. Carpet Beater	16. Wooden Tongues	30. Maracas
4. Giant Woodblock	17. Bamboo Rattle	31. Bamboo Sticks
5. Jug of Water	18. Scraper Stick	32. Swingers
6. Cleft Bamboo Tube	19. Angklungs	33. Guïros
7. Bound Wood Sheets	20. Elephant Bell	34. Nutcracker
8. Clapper-box	21. Coconut Rattle	35. Nuts
9. Rubbed Stick-Drum	22. Switch	36. Temple Blocks
10. Guïro	23. Castanets	37. Rattle
11. Wooden Mortar	24. Rattle	38. Ratchets
12. Wooden Bells	25. Whip	39. Claves
13. Wasamba Rattle	26. Woodblocks	40. Wooden Shoes
	27. Wooden Whistle	41. Same
		42. Nut Rattle (Sistrum)
		43. Slit Drum
		44. Bouncing Ball Box

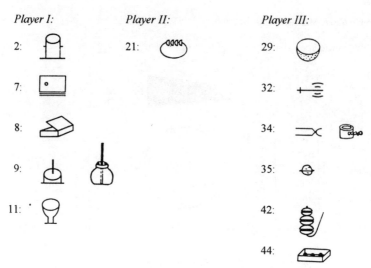

Player I: *Player II:*   *Player III:*

2:      21:   29:

7:      32:

8:      34:

9:      35:

11:      42:

44:

With his typically lively imagination, Kagel has here included a number of highly unusual instruments and objects in this experimental work that complement the more common members of the percussion ensemble. In addition to the requisitions listed above, together with their unique pictograms, see Player I's numbers 3, 5, 6, 12, and 13; Player II's numbers 15, 16, and 27; and Player III's numbers 40 and 41. It should be obvious that any performance of this composition might well intrigue an audience visually as well as sonically.

An even more extensive and exotic list of objects required in a Kagel score can be seen in Part I (*See:* Example #266), an illustration of pictographic notation that surely represents the *ne plus ultra* of this contemporary technique.

Example #208. John Downey: *Crescendo* (1978).]

Percussion: 5 Vibraphones; Glockenspiel; Marimba; Xylophone; Celesta; Large Tam-tam; Bass Drum; Claves; Large Cymbal; Very Large Suspended Cymbal; Triangle; Pearl Windchimes; Very Large Cowbell; 5 Temple Blocks; Low Bongo; Deep Conga Drum; Tambourine; 5 Timbales; Snare Drum; 2 Pianos.

Written for fifteen percussionists, including two pianists, this work is unusual in that it requires five vibraphones. Each player of these instruments is also responsible for another mallet member, glockenspiel, marimba, and xylophone, and the fourth player handles the celesta part. The fifth vibraphonist also plays the timbales (and snare drum?).

Example #209. James R. Riley: *Stick-Games* (1980).

Each of the nine percussionists in this work have relatively few instruments to manipulate. Riley's pictograms are simple but precise.

Example #210. Bill Douglas & Michael Udow: *Rock Etude No. 7* (1980).

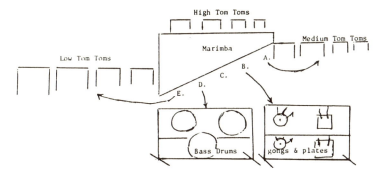

Five percussionists are entrusted with the five groups of instruments, as shown by the arrow-signs. Player B is responsible for the two gongs and two suspended metal plates. Although the same ⌐¬ -symbol is used for all 12 tom-toms in this diagram, their sizes are varied according to their relative tessituras.

Example #211. Eugene Novotney: *Intentions* (1983).

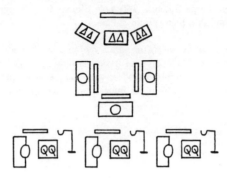

*Percussion:*6 Triangles (High and Low); 3 Tambourines; 3 pairs of Crash Cymbals; 3 Large Bass Drums (with attachment).

The composer's intentions here are clearly to arrange his instruments in a duplicate and triplicate pattern; two each of triangles and crash cymbals placed in threefold positions, in addition to the grouping of the instrumental categories in threes. Music stands are indicated as

Example #212. Stanislaw Moryto: *Vers Libre* (1987).

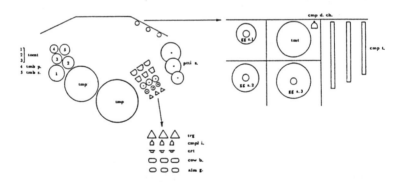

Percussion: Church Bell; 3 Chime Tubes; 3 Suspended Gongs; Tam-tam; 3 Triangles; 3 Crotales; 3 Cowbells; 3 Almglocken; 3 Suspended Cymbals; Small Snare Drum; Tenor Drum; 3 Tom-toms; 2 Timpani.

The duplication of symbols, different as they are, for the crotales, cowbells, and almglocken, is puzzling in this diagram, no explanation being offered by the composer as to the reason for his procedure.

Example #213. John Alfieri: *Fanfare for Tambourines* (1989).

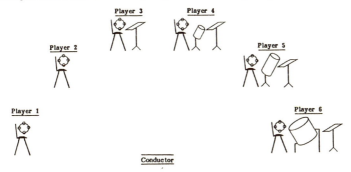

Obviously a tongue-in-cheek composition, not only the tambourines but the player's chairs and music stands also receive pictographic representation in this composer's stage set-up.

Many pictographic stage diagrams—in fact, the majority of those researched—are only partly representational in their depiction of the various percussion instruments. Certain members of the ensemble are clearly identified (the four mallet instruments in particular) while others are specified only with generic symbols such as $\bigcirc$ and $\square$. Thus instruments belonging to the membranophones and members of the cymbal and gong families are frequently represented by the same basic design, even though the instrument's overall size, unique material, and sonic function differ widely from one instrument to another. It cannot be maintained, therefore, that these symbols are truly pictograms as they do not always unequivocally distinguish between several similarly constructed members of the ensemble or between others completely different in both their basic materials and their sonic properties. Example #223, for instance, identifies various suspended cymbals, tom-toms, snare drums, bongos, conga drums, and Chinese cymbal all with the same pictogram $\bigcirc$-symbol, while Example #218 depicts both bongos and timbales with this symbol, even though the two instruments can vary considerably in their relative dimensions. The same applies to Example #220, where timbales, tom-toms, and snare drum are identically proportioned.

One might argue, of course, that this habit of some composers hardly presents an intractable problem for either the percussionist or the conductor of the ensemble. It remains, then, an individual decision of each composer as to how specific one should be in visually identifying several dissimilar instruments with the same basic symbol.

One the other hand, it will be noted that many composers not only adjust the relative sizes of their generic pictogram but indicate as well the exact dimension in inches of the drum or metallophone surface, as in Examples #193, #233, #242, and #251; by merely indicating high, medium, or low (Examples #203, #210, #215, #222, and #243); by super-imposing pitch letters on the symbol, as seen in Examples #253 and #421.

The other most widely prevalent generic pictogram, used for many diverse percussions, is $\square$ or $\sqsubset\sqsupset$; these may be seen, for instance, in Example #230 where they represent instruments as unlike as chimes, xylophone, gong, and woodblocks. A truncated form of this symbol, ⊓, is favored by some composers to identify members of the membranophone family, as shown in Examples #210 and #217. ☐ depicts tubular bells, antique cymbals, and bass drum in Example #241—an odd assortment of instruments to share a common pictographic sign. More logical, even though not truly representational, is the choice of [▭] to identify all four mallet instruments in Examples #242 and #249. Many composers, however, have preferred a more literal, if simplified, mallet instrument design ([▱]), but without making any distinction in their relative sizes (*See:* Examples #218 and #232). Some orchestrators, nonetheless, have stressed the relative dimensions of these instruments by varying both the size and the shape of the four symbols, as demonstrated in Examples #237 and #256.

Example #214. William Kraft: *Theme and Variations for Percussion Quartet* (1956).

Kraft's pictograms are commendably distinctive, and the division of labor between the four percussionists is clearly delineated. The composer's *Theme* is scored only for timpani, cymbals, bass drum and xylophone. *Variation 1* is for timpani, snare drum, bass drum, and cymbals; *Variation 2* is for metallophones, plus woodblock, castanets, temple block, and xylophone; *Variation 3* calls for membranophones only, while *Variation 4* enlists chimes, glockenspiel, cowbell, xylophone, timpani, siren, slide whistle, bulb horn, and ratchet—a curious mixture of sound agents. This composer's long experience as a professional percussionist, plus his equally fruitful association with jazz performance and arranging, has understandably influenced his many writings for the percussion ensemble. The *Theme and Variations* is the first in his lengthy catalog of percussion essays.

The following diagramatic example, taken from a work by this compiler, presented some special problems. Because the suite involved different instrumental concentrations for each of the movements, it was necessary to devise a comprehensive set-up that minimized any rearrangement of players and instruments.

Example #215. Gardner Read: *Los Dioses Aztecas* (1959).

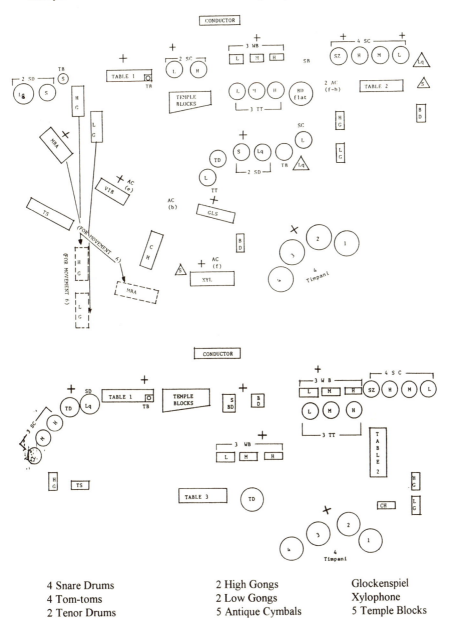

4 Snare Drums	2 High Gongs	Glockenspiel
4 Tom-toms	2 Low Gongs	Xylophone
2 Tenor Drums	5 Antique Cymbals	5 Temple Blocks

2 Bass Drums	Thunder Sheet	4 Timpani
3 Tambourines	Chimes	2 Raspers
3 Woodblocks	Sandpaper Blocks	2 Pair of Claves
7 Suspended Cymbals	3 Triangles	Maracas
1 Sizzle Cymbal	Marimba	Crash Cymbal
	Vibraharp	

Six percussionists play a total of sixty instruments in this work; consequently, it was essential that all moves of the players from instrument to instrument be carefully planned. Because of the special requirements in the seventh, final movement of the suite, it was necessary to suggest a somewhat different arrangement of the ensemble members.

Example #216. Robert Stern: *Adventures for One* (1961).

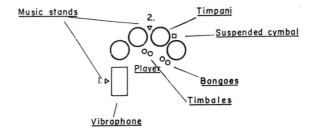

Stern depicts both bongos and timbales with the same-sized O-symbol, even though the two instruments can vary considerably in their relative dimensions. The □-symbol is a curious choice to portray the suspended cymbal, which after all is a circular instrument.

Example #217. Leo Brouwer: *Variantes* (1962)

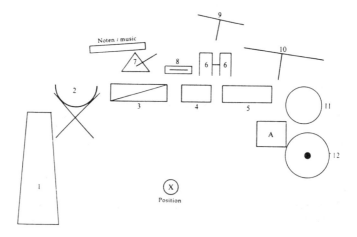

Percussion: 1) Xylophone; 2) Timpano; 3) Side Drum; 4) ; 5) Tom-toms; 6) Bongos; 7) Triangle; 8) Woodblock; 9) ; 10) Cymbals; 11) Tam-tam; 12) Gong.

One assumes that the symbol ⊗ , marked *Position*, indicates where the solo percussionist is to stand.

Example #218. Richard Fitz: *Chamber Sonata for Percussion Sextet* (1963).

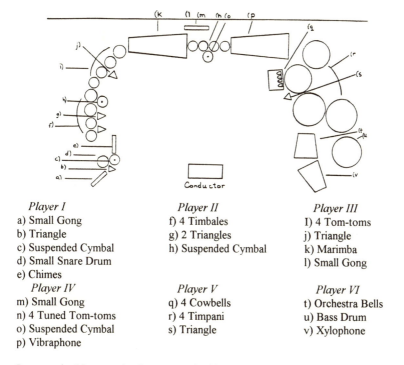

Player I	*Player II*	*Player III*
a) Small Gong	f) 4 Timbales	I) 4 Tom-toms
b) Triangle	g) 2 Triangles	j) Triangle
c) Suspended Cymbal	h) Suspended Cymbal	k) Marimba
d) Small Snare Drum		l) Small Gong
e) Chimes		
Player IV	*Player V*	*Player VI*
m) Small Gong	q) 4 Cowbells	t) Orchestra Bells
n) 4 Tuned Tom-toms	r) 4 Timpani	u) Bass Drum
o) Suspended Cymbal	s) Triangle	v) Xylophone
p) Vibraphone		

Because the 38 percussion instruments in this work are not positioned according to their clear visual separation between the six players, the composer has wisely labeled each instrument that is identified in his listing of the ensemble members.

Example #219. Pelle Gundmundsen-Holmgreen: *Chronos* (1964).

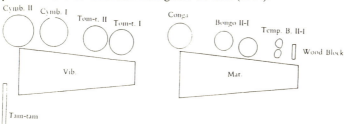

The ubiquitous O-symbol represents nine different instruments in the composer's diagram: two each of suspended cymbals, tom-toms, bongos, and temple blocks, and a single conga drum. Also to be noted is the same generic symbol (⊂⊃) shared by tam-tam and woodblock.

Example #220. George Andrix: *Concert for Percussion* (1965).

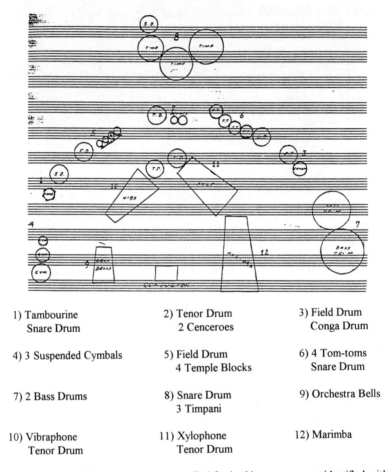

1) Tambourine
   Snare Drum
	2) Tenor Drum
	   2 Cenceroes
		3) Field Drum
		   Conga Drum

4) 3 Suspended Cymbals	5) Field Drum
	   4 Temple Blocks
		6) 4 Tom-toms
		   Snare Drum

7) 2 Bass Drums	8) Snare Drum 3 Timpani	9) Orchestra Bells

10) Vibraphone
    Tenor Drum
	11) Xylophone
	    Tenor Drum
		12) Marimba

Only six of the thirty-two instruments called for in this score are not identified with the generic O-symbol. The composer has supplemented the instrumental abbreviations with numerals relating to his listing of all the percussion. This diagram illustrates one problem a composer may encounter when superimposing instrumental symbology on a manuscript page of staff lines: the accompanying terminology can sometimes be rather obscured by the lines, as shown above.

Example #221. Klaus Hashangen: *Meditation für Schlagzeug* (1965).

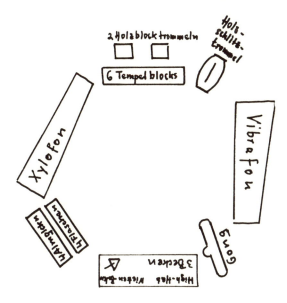

Percussion: Vibraphone, Xylophone, Gong, 3 Suspended Cymbals, Hi-hat Cymbal, Triangle, 4 Almglocken, 4 Goblets, 2 Woodblocks, 6 Temple Blocks, Slit Drum.

For one percussionist only, the composer of this work puts all the instruments within easy reach of the player.

Example #222. Rickey Tagawa: *Inspirations Diabolique* (1965).

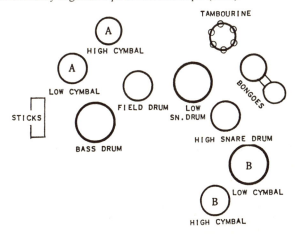

The O-symbol again does manifold service in this composer's diagram, representing both metal and skin percussion. Only the tambourine and bongos are given distinguishing features. The required number of players is not indicated here by the composer.

Example #223. Gilles Tremblay: *Kékoba* (1965).

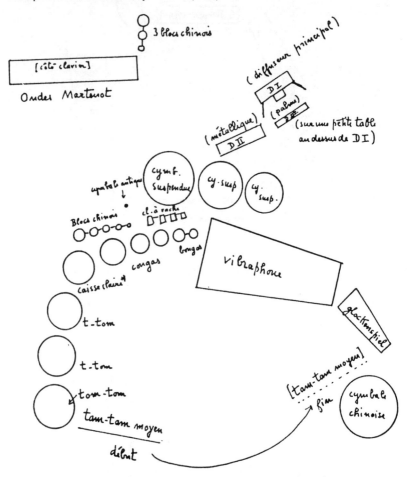

Percussion: 4 Cowbells; 5 Temple Blocks; 3 Woodblocks; Maracas; 2 Bongos; 3 Conga Drums; 3 Tom-toms; Snare Drum; Antique Cymbal; Small Turkish Cymbal; 3 Suspended Cymbals; Large Chinese Cymbal; 3 Gongs; 2 Tam-tams; Glockenspiel; Vibraphone; Tubular Bells; Ondes Martenot. *Also:* 3 Singers (Soprano, Alto, Tenor).

This is one more stage diagram that makes extensive use of the O-symbol to represent a number of disparate instruments. Curiously, stick and beater pictograms appear only sporadically in the score, while the instruments themselves are consistently indicated by nomenclature rather then with the symbols shown in the diagram.

Example #224. Al Payson: *Die Zwitschermaschine* (1967).

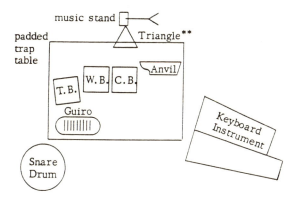

By the designation *Keyboard Instrument*, according to the shape of the pictogram, one assumes that a mallet instrument such as marimba or vibraphone is intended.

Example #225. Reginald Smith Brindle: *Orion M.42* (1967).

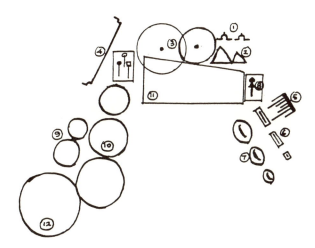

1) 2 Crotales; 2) 2 Triangles; 3) 2 Suspended Cymbals; 4) Large Tam-tam; 5) Bamboo Windchimes; 6) Woodblocks; 7) 3 Temple Blocks; 8) Castanets; 9) 2 Timbales; 10) 3 Tom-toms; 11) Vibraphone; 12) 1 Timpano.

Like the *Zyklus* of Stockhausen (*See:* Example #184) this work is for a solo percussionist responsible for twelve different instruments. The composer includes directions for shaking the windchimes or clapping them together with both hands; also playing on the membranophones with fingers, knuckles, and palms, as well as with the fingernails on vibraphone.

Example #226. Thomas L. Davis: *Spanish Dance* (1968).

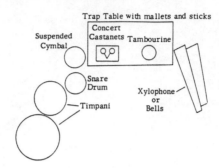

Example #227. Thomas L. Davis: *Sounds of the Kabuki* (1968).

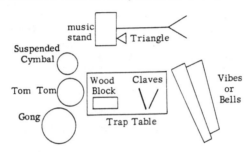

Vibes, of course, is the familiar and common term for the vibraphone; *Bells* would here seem to indicate glockenspiel (orchestra bells), also suggested in the composer's second quoted stage diagram.

Example #228. Reginald Smith Brindle: *Auriga* (1968).

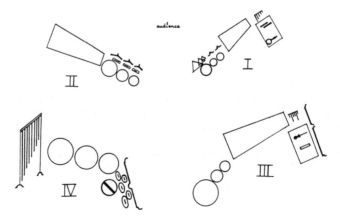

Percussion I: Glockenspiel; Crotales; 3 Triangles; 2 Bongos; Timbale; Glass Windchimes; Maracas; Claves.

Percussion II: Vibraphone; 3 Suspended Cymbals; 3 Woodblocks; 3 Tom-toms.

Percussion III: Marimba; 2 Tam-tams; Wood Windchimes; 2 Conga Drums; Small Bass Drum; Anvil; Castanets.

Percussion IV: Tubular Bells; Large Gong; 5 Temple Blocks; 3 Timpani; Small Snare Drum.

A note below this platform diagram informs us that "the above layout is designed so that the author's *Auriga* and *Crux Australis* can be played together as a group." Not all of the instrumental pictographs of the forces required and displayed on a preliminary page are exactly reproduced in the composer's layout just shown. For instance, tom-toms are first represented by □ and next as ○; conga drums first as ◯ and then by ○, while timpani first appear as ♡ and then with the O-symbol—a puzzling inconsistency on Smith Brindle's part. Throughout the score proper the initially presented pictograms are combined with symbols for the various beaters to be used.

Example #229. Duane Thamm: *Etude No. 40* (1968).

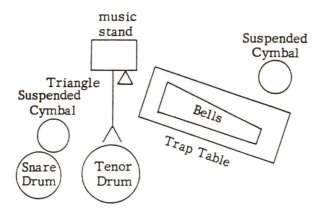

As in Example #226, illustrated previously, *Bells* refers to the glockenspiel. The music stand here does double duty; it supports the hung triangle as well as holding the player's part. Oddly, there is no pictogram for the piano, an integral member of the ensemble. The trap table is the obvious repository for the sticks and mallets used for striking the various instruments. Other instances of this requirement can be seen in Examples #215, #266, and #299, to cite but a few such depictions.

Example #230. Marcel Farago: *Rhythm and Colors* (1969).

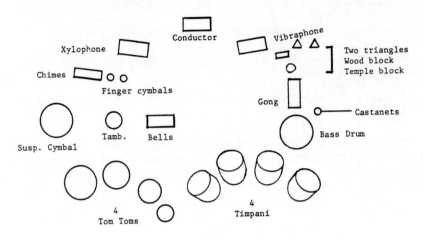

Not evident from the composer's diagram is the fact that the work requires six percussionists. Also, the division of labor between the players is not indicated. The four mallet instruments are given abstract representation rather than more realistic profiles.

Example #231. James F. Latimer: *Motif for Percussion* (1969).

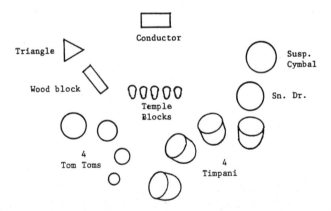

Seven players are specified by the composer for this work, their individual responsibilities more clearly indicated here than was evident in the previous example quoted. As a professional percussionist, Latimer would naturally be expected to favor concise and accurate depictions of his instruments.

Example #232. Stanley Leonard: *Symphony for Percussion* (1969).

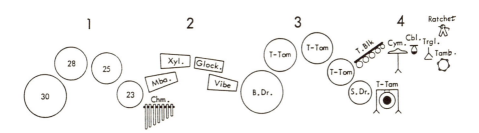

Leonard's *Symphony* is in four movements, each subtitled: I. *Drum Tune*; II. *The Bells*; III. *Xylem*; IV. *Evolutions.* Nine players are required, but the division of labor between them is not indicated in the stage diagram.

Example #233. H. Owen Reed: *Scoring for Percussion* (1969).

Percussion 1: 4 Timpani.
Percussion 2: Xylophone; Glockenspiel; Marimba; Vibraphone; Chimes.
Percussion 3: Bass Drum; 3 Tom-toms; Snare Drum.
Percussion 4: 5 Temple Blocks; Suspended Cymbal; Cowbell; Triangle; Ratchet, Tambourine; Tam-tam.

A feature of this suggested stage arrangement, included in Reed's book on percussion scoring, is the specification of timpani dimensions, from the largest (30") to the smallest (23").

This practice is evident in many other stage diagrams, applied to such other membranophones as tom-toms, roto-toms, and timbales, as well as to certain of the metallic idiophones.

Example #234. Gary M. Bolinger: *Symphony No. 1 for Percussion* (1970).

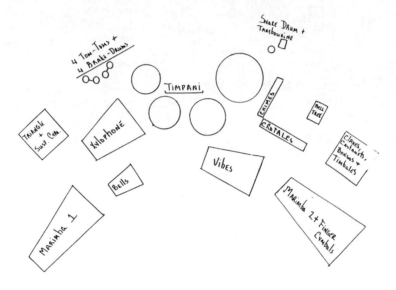

The composer's pictograms are fairly plain yet entirely adequate in identifying each instrument, even without the added terminology.

Example #235. Alvin Etler: *XL Plus One* (1970).

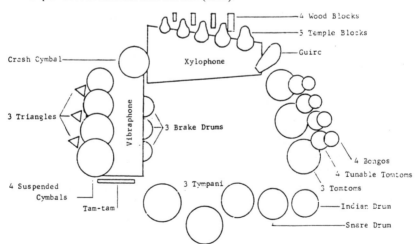

Interpreting the four-sided groupings of the instruments in this stage set-up logically, one can assume that at least four players are required. The ubiquitous O-symbol serves seven different instruments, both metal and skin.

Example #236. Nguyên-Thiên Dao: *Mây* (1972).

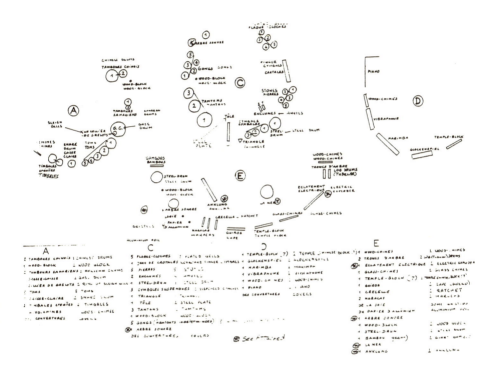

This is one of the most elaborately planned and executed pictographic diagrams encountered, not to mention the fact that the total number of instruments required (78) far exceeds the requirements of such other composers as Berio (*See:* Example #275), Kagel (*See:* Example #207), Bernard Rands (*See:* Example #333), or Stockhausen (*See:* Example #463). Furthermore, Dao calls for such exotica as stones, aluminum foil, anklung, and electric exploder to amplify his more standard resources.

The groupings *A*, *C*, *D*, and *E* designate categories of instruments: *A*, for instance, is comprised of wood and membrane instruments, while *D* includes keyed or plated instruments plus a single temple block. Strangely, there is no grouping of B, for reasons left unexplained by the composer.

Example #237. Zbigniew Wiszniewski: *Kadenzen für drei Schlagzeuger* (1972).

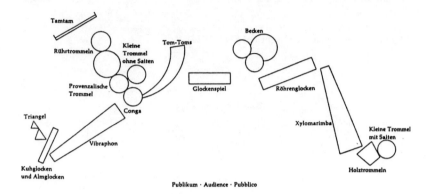

Percussion: Tam-tam; Tenor Drum; Snare Drum with snares; Snare Drum without snares; Tom-toms; Tabor; Conga Drum; Triangles; Vibraphone; Cowbells; Almglocken; Glockenspiel; Suspended Cymbals; Tubular Bells; Xylomarimba; Wood Drum.

In addition to the instruments listed in this stage diagram, *Kadenzen* also requires a pair of large castanets, finger cymbals, antique cymbals, guïro, 6 tom-toms, conga drum, whip, and flexitone. It is odd that the composer did not include these extras in the pictographic set-up.

Example #238. Larry Spivack: *Fip Fop Fuppe* (1973).

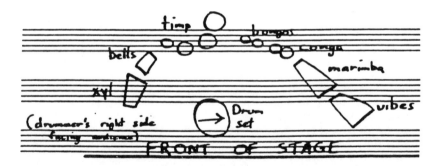

Eight players are required for this work, although one would not find this fact evident from the given layout and number of instruments involved. Unless required to be played upon simultaneously, xylophone and orchestra bells could easily be handled by one member of the ensemble, as could marimba and vibraphone. The drum set shown at stage front is obviously treated as a solo entity.

Example #239. Allen Brings: *II. Kitchen Sounds* (1974).

To enhance the antiphonal effects in this piece, performers should be arranged in two groups at either end of a long table, as shown in the diagram below.

At each end of the table are the kitchen instruments, and, if possible, a microphone to amplify their sounds. The mixer, if used, should be placed in front of (therefore hidden by) the conductor, so that its sound will come as a surprise.

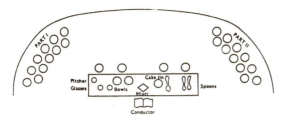

An apt symbol for the conductor in this visual-auditory piece is the open pages of the score, a device that also appears in Example #399.

Example #240. Niel DePonte: *Celebration and Chorale* (1974).

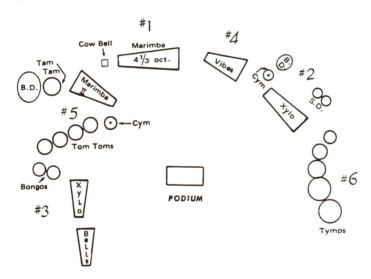

#1: Marimba; Cowbell
#2: Xylophone; 2 Snare Drums; Bass Drum; Suspended Cymbal
#3: Bells; Xylophone; Bongos
#4: Vibraphone; Bass Drum; Suspended Cymbal
#5: Marimba; 4 Tom-toms; Bass Drum; Suspended Cymbal; Tam-tam
#6: 5 Timpani

All the pictograms in this stage diagram are appropriate save for that identifying the cowbell (□), also seen in a previous set-up to specify a suspended cymbal (*See:* Example #217).

Example #241. Robert Campana: *Roto for Percussion Quartet* (1975).

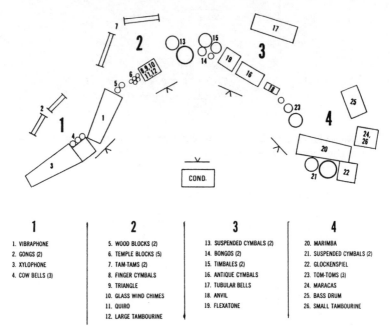

1	**2**	**3**	**4**
1. VIBRAPHONE	5. WOOD BLOCKS (2)	13. SUSPENDED CYMBALS (2)	20. MARIMBA
2. GONGS (2)	6. TEMPLE BLOCKS (5)	14. BONGOS (2)	21. SUSPENDED CYMBALS (2)
3. XYLOPHONE	7. TAM-TAMS (2)	15. TIMBALES (2)	22. GLOCKENSPIEL
4. COW BELLS (3)	8. FINGER CYMBALS	16. ANTIQUE CYMBALS	23. TOM-TOMS (3)
	9. TRIANGLE	17. TUBULAR BELLS	24. MARACAS
	10. GLASS WIND CHIMES	18. ANVIL	25. BASS DRUM
	11. QUIRO	19. FLEXATONE	26. SMALL TAMBOURINE
	12. LARGE TAMBOURINE		

Most stage diagrams seen so far have relied on self-evident pictograms or simplified nomenclature to identify the various percussion instruments. A few such set-ups combine numerals with the instrument symbols, illustrated in this score example.

Example #242. Jere Hutcheson: *3 Things for Dr. Seuss* (1975).

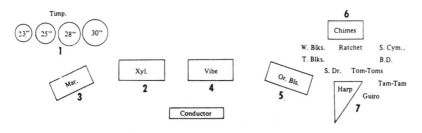

Displayed here is one more stage diagram that substitutes the abbreviation "Or. Bls." (Orchestra Bells) for the more common term "Glockenspiel."

This work is among the first to include the harp as a member of the percussion ensemble; its pictogram is, of course, only partially representational. On the other hand, the four mallet instruments are represented abstractly, only the timpani being shown with the generic O-symbol. In company with many other percussion works, their exact dimensions are specified.

Example #243. Robert Suderburg: *Chamber Music IV* (1975).

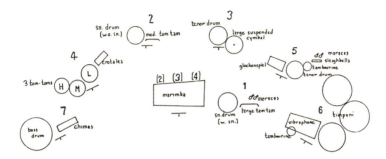

The division of labor for the seven percussionists is clearly delineated, even to the shared responsibility of three players at the marimba. Music stands also receive representation, a custom not encountered as frequently as one might expect.

Example #244. David Loeb: *Nocturnes and Meditations* (1975).

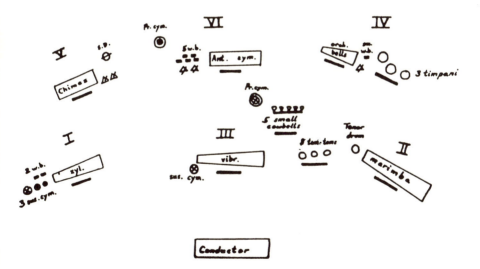

I) Xylophone; 2 Woodblocks; 3 Suspended Cymbals
II) Marimba; Tenor Drum; 3 Tom-toms; 5 Small Cowbells
III) Vibraphone; Suspended Cymbal
IV) Glockenspiel; 3 Timpani; Woodblock; Triangle
V) Chimes; Snare Drum; 2 Triangles
VI) Antique Cymbals; 5 Woodblocks; 2 Triangles; pair of Cymbals

Indicating the positions of various music stands is a practice only occasionally carried out by composers in their stage diagrams. Loeb's symbols (—) are simple and perfectly adequate for their purpose.

Example #245. James Tenney: *Three Pieces for Four Drums* (1975).

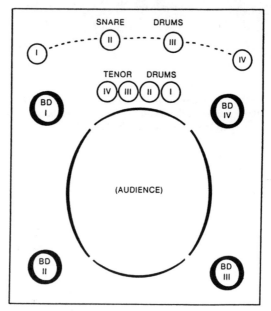

A different configuration of drums is used for each of the three sections of this work. In the first, *Wake for Charles Ives*, only tenor drums play. The second, *Hocket for Henry Cowell*, is for four bass drums, which surround the audience. The final section, *Crystal Canon for Edgard Varèse*, is for snare drums only, widely separated at the rear of the platform or auditorium.

Tenney's tribute to Varèse is in response to his early study with that noted avant-gardist. Tenney's subsequent work with John Cage no doubt inspired the 1971 composition entitled (with obvious tongue-in-cheek) *Having never written a note for Percussion*. Two earlier computer-genereated scores, *Ergodos I* and *Ergodos II* (1963 and 1964), may be combined with either a string or a percussion complement. Because these additions are optional, the composer evidently did not feel the need to provide any diagramatic set-ups for these instruments.

Example #246. William Mickelsen: *Percussion for Five Players* (1976).

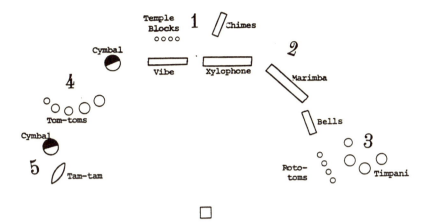

Strangely, the five mallet instruments in this diagram are not given pictorially accurate representation, although the remaining members required are more realistically depicted.

Example #247. Wilfried Hiller: *Katalog V für Schlagzeug* (1977).

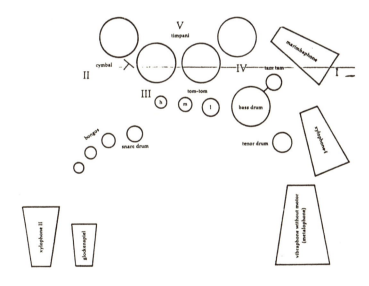

Only the size of the pictogram and its accompanying nomenclature, and not its shape, distinguish one mallet instrument from another in this stage diagram. It is not evident from the spacing which of the five percussionists is responsible for which one, or more, of these ensemble components.

Example #248. Thomas Gauger: *Nomad* (1979).

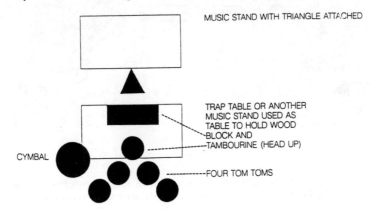

MUSIC STAND WITH TRIANGLE ATTACHED

TRAP TABLE OR ANOTHER
MUSIC STAND USED AS
TABLE TO HOLD WOOD
BLOCK AND
TAMBOURINE (HEAD UP)

CYMBAL

FOUR TOM TOMS

This is only the first of two stage diagrams included in this compendium that render the instruments in blackened symbols (*See:* Example #425). Occasionally a composer will resort to representing one or two of the percussion or other instruments in this fashion but rarely will all the components be so depicted. The genesis of the blackened circle will be recognized, of course, as the astronomical symbol for the new moon. As a professional percussionist (he is a member of the Boston Symphony Orchestra), one would assume that Gauger would favor more authentic depictions of the instruments in this score, rather than rely on symbols that are essentially neutral.

Example #249. Karel Husa: *Three Dance Sketches* (1979).

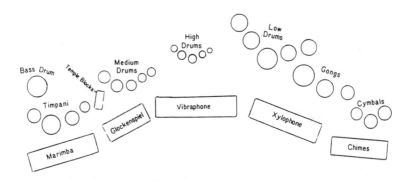

Husa has here relied exclusively on the generic O-symbol to identify seven skin and metal instruments. His mallet instruments receive the same abstract forms that have appeared in a number of other stage diagrams, such as in Example #242.

Example #250. Eugène Bozza: *Rag Music* (1981).

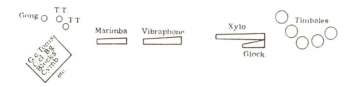

Although a piano is prominent in this work, its pictogram is strangely missing in the composer's diagram. One assumes that it is placed in front of the percussion line-up. Five timbales appear to substitute for timpani here, and are widely separated from the pair of bongos, their sonic cousins. Curious is the coupling of glockenspiel with xylophone rather than with the more expected vibraphone.

Example #251. Satoshi Ohmae: *Polymer for Solo Percussion and Assistant Players* (1980-84).

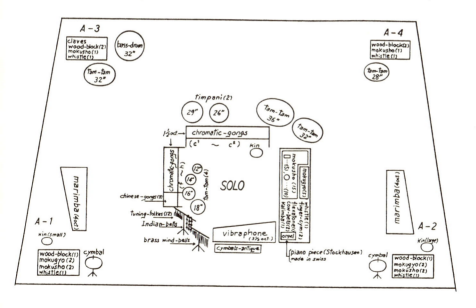

Four assistants (A-1; A-2; A-3; A-4) are required for this work in addition to the solo percussionist, each positioned in a corner of the performance platform. Specific dimensions are indicated for bass drum, timpani, tom-toms, and tam-tams, and all are clearly identified. Two instruments indigenous to Buddhist music are called for by the composer: the *kin*, a bowl-shaped bell that is struck on its rim with a mallet, and the *mokugyo*, a slit gong known in our Western music as a Chinese temple block. Two other native Japanese instruments are components of the percussion, the *mokusho* and the *kalimbo*.

Example #252. Per Nørgård: *I Ching* (1982).

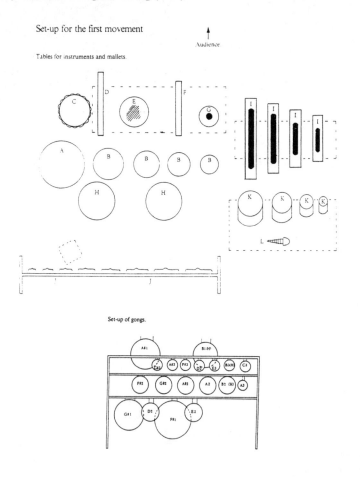

Percussion: A) Large Roto-tom; B) 4 Tube Drums (Boo-bams); C) Tambourine; D) Long Metal Pipe; E) Peking Opera Gong; F) Little Metal Pipe; G) Peking Opera Woodblock; H) 2 Roto-toms; I) 4 Slit Drums; J) 8 Suspended Cymbals; K) 4 Temple Cup Cells; L) Bell Tree.

I Ching (Book of Changes), the ancient Chinese manual of divination (circa 1000 B.C.), has been the compositional inspiration for several twentieth-century composers, most notably John Cage and Per Nørgård. The suspended cymbals are hung from a metal support, arranged from small to large, the same layout applied to the tube drums, slit drums, and temple bells.

Example #253. Arne Mellnäs: *Rendez-vous 2* (1983).

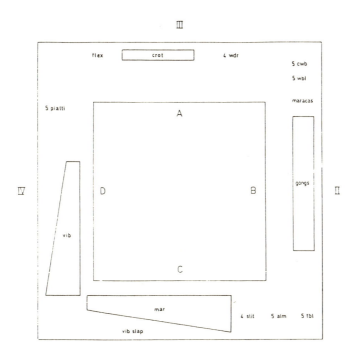

Percussion: Crotales; 5 Cowbells; 5 Suspended Cymbals; 5 Almglocken; Gongs; Flexatone; 4 Wood Drums; 4 Slit Drums; 5 Woodblocks; Maracas; 5 Temple Blocks; Marimba; Vibraphone; Vibraslap.

This is one more example of a work for percussion that positions the players around the audience space. Thus both sight and sound exist on equal terms. Although the instruments assigned to each of the percussionists appear to be widely dispersed, in reality they are closely positioned, so that no player is required to over-reach while striking an instrument. Vibraphone and marimba both receive accurate representation here, but the remaining instruments in the ensemble are identified only by terminology, a practice seen in other stage diagrams.

Example #254. Irwin Bazelon: *Fourscore* (1985).

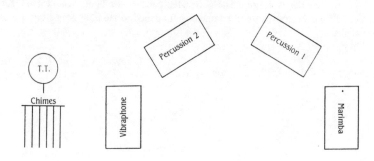

Percussion 1: High (Piccolo) Wood Block; Large Cowbell; Scratcher (Guïro) (on stand); Suspended Finger Cymbal; Suspended Cymbal (medium size); Triangle; Bell Tree; Japanese Wood Chimes; Claves; Snare Drum; Temple Blocks (set of five).

Percussion 2: High (Piccolo) Wood Block; Tam-tam; Log Drums (High & Low); Snare Drum; Bongos (High & Low); High Tom-tom (9 X 13); Tenor Drum (no snares); Bass Tom-tom (16 X 16); Bass Drum (laid flat).

Percussion 3: Vibraphone; Chimes (Tubular Bells); Tam-tam.

Percussion 4: Marimba.

It is odd that the composer chose to picture only two out of a total of 30 instruments in his score. It may be granted, of course, that pictograms for those instruments played by percussionists 1 and 2 would have complicated the visual aspect of the composer's diagram.

Example #255. Lawrence Weiner: *Perspectives for Percussion Ensemble* (1986).

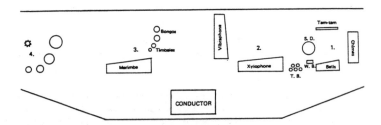

Curiously, only half of the required percussionists in this score are included in the composer's stage diagram. The pictograms that are shown are relatively simple, relying as they do on generic symbols for the majority of the instruments.

Example #256. István Márta: *Doll's House Story* (1987).

Percussion I: 4 Timpani; Small Bass Drum; Marimba; Tenor Drum; Snare Drum; Wood Drum; Suspended Cymbal.

Percussion II: Large Bass Drum; Tenor Drum; Wood Drum; 3 Tom-toms; Chimes.

Percussion III: Tenor Drum; Wood Drum; 2 Tom-toms; Suspended Cymbal; Whip; Marimba.

Percussion IV: Xylophone; 6 Thai Gongs; Tenor Drum; Tam-tam; Triangle; 3 Chime Tubes.

A curious feature of this stage set-up is the positioning of the two bass drums (G.C.) at the very front of the ensemble. Presumably, the six tuned Thai gongs are suspended from a metal rack.

Example #257. Jan Oleszkowicz: *Mare Imbrium* (1987).

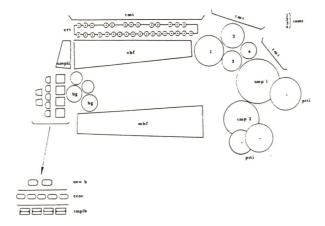

Percussion: Glockenspiel; Marimbaphone; Vibraphone; 2 Cowbells; Crotales; 4 Temple Blocks; 4 Bongos; 3 Suspended Cymbals; 3 Tam-tams; 4 Tom-toms; 2 Timpani.

It is unclear as to why there are two pictograms each for the cowbells, cenceros, and temple blocks, indicated by the arrow sign. The inclusion of a two-and-one-half octave set of crotales is unusual in a percussion ensemble work.

Example #258. Lori Dobbins: *Chamber Music* (1988).

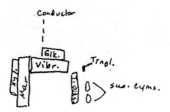

Like several previously illustrated diagrams (*See:* Examples #188 and #189, for instance), this is quite typical of a small percussion ensemble set-up for one performer. A more elaborate depiction of the few instruments involved here would be quite unnecessary, simplicity in this instance meriting its own reward.

Example #259. Phil Faini: *Highlife* (1988).

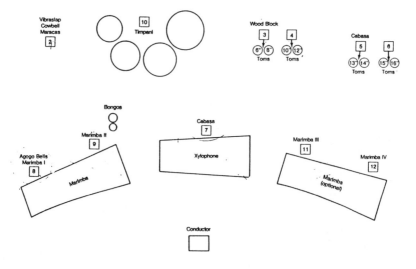

As shown, there are four marimba players for the two instruments depicted. Not often encountered in composers' pictograms for tom-toms are the exact dimensions of each; in this work they create a scale of relative pitches from high to low.

Many twentieth-century works that feature a percussion ensemble include the piano, the celesta, and/or the harp among their complement of instruments. The piano in particular is by now a standard member of the section, and is quite generally depicted in fairly literal form in the composers' stage diagrams. A few composers are careful to indicate that the piano lid is to be up, or even in some instances to be removed entirely from the instrument, as in Examples #261, #262, #266, and #267.

Keyboard Instrument(s) Only Representational

Example #260. James H. Sutcliffe: *Two Pictures for Percussion* (1957).

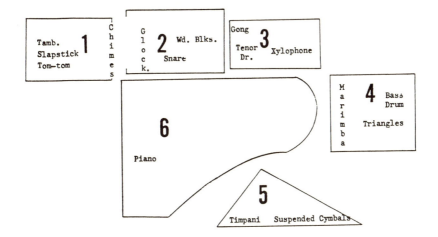

Many composers favor the practice of identifying their percussion instruments only by means of terminology, while at the same time using pictograms to show the keyboard instruments (in this case, the piano) as components of the total ensemble. The division of labor in this work is clearly delineated, although the positioning of the instruments within each box is obviously left to the discretion of the individual players. Even when such arrangements of the instruments are indicated by the composer, percussionists frequently feel free to reorganize their order. A composer's stage diagram frequently invites speculation as to why a particular configuration of instruments is requested. In Sutcliffe's set-up, one wonders why such forceful members as timpani and suspended cymbal are placed in front of less dominating instruments as triangles, woodblocks, tambourine, and the four mallet idiophones.

Example #261. Werner Heider: *Le Saint esprit* (1986).

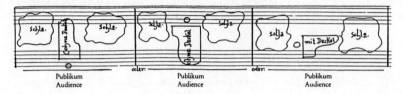

Three possible stage arrangements are provided here by the composer, all relating to the positioning of the piano. The first two require the piano lid to be removed. It will be noted that the shape of the piano varies from one position to another, for reasons left unexplained.

Percussion and Keyboard Instrument(s) Representational

The two previous examples were notable for their absence of any percussion pictograms, only the piano being pictured. Next are shown the stage diagrams that illustrate pictographically both the percussion and the keyboard instrument(s). Included among the latter are the celesta and harpsichord as well as the piano.

Example #262. Shin-ichi Matsushita: *Canzona da Sonore No. 1* (1960).

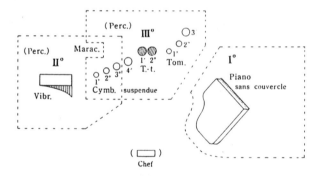

Percussion I: Piano without lid.
Percussion II: Vibraphone; Maracas; 3 Suspended Cymbals.
Percussion III: Suspended Cymbal; 2 Tam-tams; 3 Tom-toms.

The dotted lines in this Japanese score diagram serve only to enclose the positions of the three instrumental groups, showing that the suspended cymbals are to be struck by both players II and III.

Example #263. Peter Schat: *Signalement* (1961).

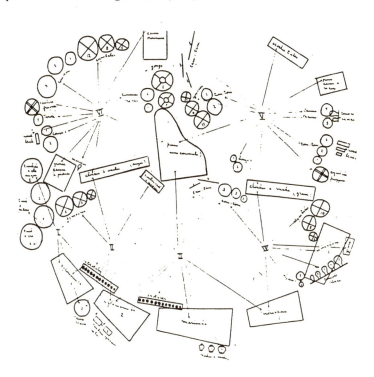

Percussion: 2 Xylorimbas; Marimba; 2 Vibraphones; Chimes; Crotales; 4 Timpani; 9 Suspended Cymbals; 3 Sizzle Cymbals; 2 Pair Crash Cymbals; 6 Tam-tams; 4 Tom-toms; 2 Conga Drums; 2 Timbales créceles; 4 Bongos; 4 Snare Drums; 2 Slapsticks; Tarole; 2 Pedal Bass Drums; 7 Temple Blocks; 3 Cowbells; Triangle; Claves; Maracas; 2 Log Drums; Piano.

Each percussionist in Schat's work is accountable for a number of dispersed instruments, shown in the diagram by the lines radiating from the players' identifying number. The piano, with lid removed, is treated like another percussion instrument, its interior strings to be struck by player III. This is a prime example of a platform set-up whose instrumental terminology is almost illegible, due to minuscule printing on the part of the composer, plus the publisher's further reduction of the diagram in the printed score.

Example #264. William Bolcom: *Dream Music No. 2* (1967).

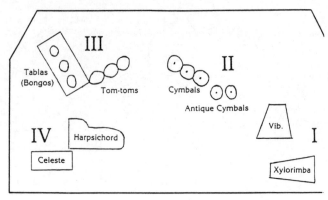

Apron

Bolcom's composition was written in memory of the influential poet Frank O'Hara. Although the O-symbol is used to depict both skin and metal instruments, the latter are distinguished by the dot at the center of the sign. Both the harpsichord and the celesta are to be lightly amplified, but the composer does not show any electronic components in the diagram.

The keyboard pictogram in this stage set-up is the first encountered to show the normal instrument profile to be reversed: the treble register is on the left side rather than on the right (and see also Examples #316, #323, #387, #390, and #458).

Example #265. Walter Ross: *Five Dream Sequences* (1968).

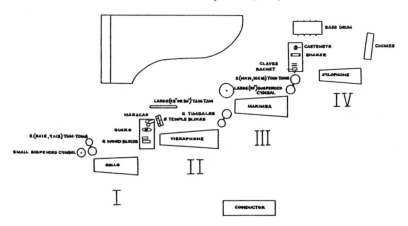

This work requires a pianist and four percussionists, their division of labor indicated by the numbers, although some instruments might possibly be shared by several players.

Example #266. Alain Louvier: *Duel pour 2 à 5 percussions* (1970).

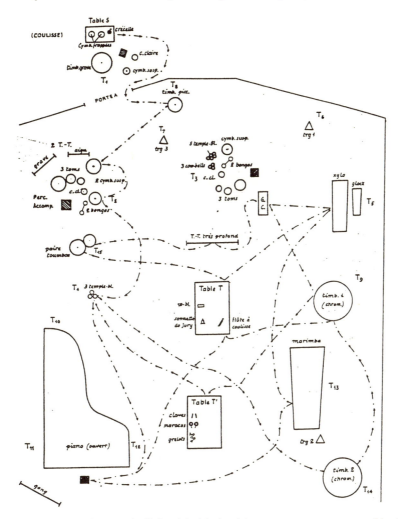

This percussion pictogram is distinguished by its elaborate stage arrangement and by the dotted-line tracks that specify the movement of certain players from instrument to instrument. Even the pianist is required to leave the keyboard to play on some percussion at a remove from the normal position at the piano. The notational device of tracking the movements of some percussionists during the performance of the score has appeared in several other stage diagrams illustrated in this compendium, such as Examples #223, #263, and #269, for instance. It is an effective means of indicating essential performer actions during the traversal of a score.

Example #267. Herbert Brün: *"At Loose Ends:* (1974).

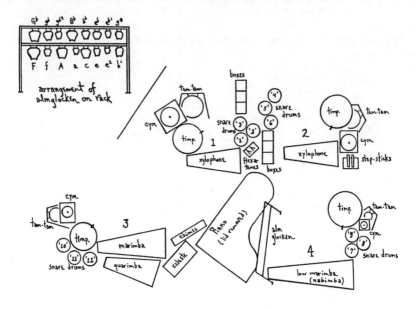

A notable feature in this set-up is the detailed pictogram of the tuned almglocken hung on a rack next to the piano. The division of labor among the four players is carefully indicated in the diagram. Of special note are the numbered snare drums, twelve in all, with three assigned to each percussionist.

Example #268. James Reichert: *Prelude and Double Fugue* (1978).

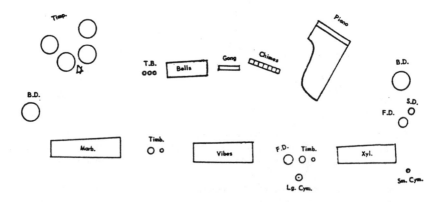

Percussion: 4 Timpani; 2 Bass Drums; Temple Blocks; Gong; Chimes; 4 Timbales; 2 Field Drums; Snare Drum; Large and Small Suspended Cymbals; Marimba; Vibraphone; Xylophone; Glockenspiel; Triangle.

Five percussionists are specified by the composer (in addition to the pianist), but their individual responsibilities are not made clear as there appear to be six groupings of the instruments.

Example #269. Steven Mackey: *The Big Bang and Beyond* (1984).

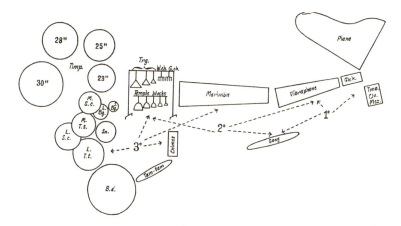

Percussion 1°: Glockenspiel; Marimba; Vibraphone; Large Gong; Tambourine; Claves; Maracas.

Percussion 2°: Marimba; Vibraphone; Large Gong; Glass Wind Chimes; Wood Wind Chimes; Temple Blocks; Triangles.

Percussion 3°: Marimba; Wood Wind Chimes; Temple Blocks; Triangles; Suspended Cymbals; Tam-tam; Bongos; Snare Drum; Tom-toms; Bass Drum.

4 Timpani; Piano; Harp.

Although a harp is included in the composer's listing of required instruments, it receives no pictographic or other representation of its position in the ensemble. The diagram constitutes one more example of its author specifying the dimensions of each of the four timpani requisitioned. In addition, bongos, tom-toms, and suspended cymbals are indicated as small (S.), medium (M.), or large (L.). Furthermore, triangles and temple blocks are graduated in size, thus providing relative scales of tessitura in all of these ensemble members.

Example #270. Maurice Ohana: *Études d'interpretation XI et XII* (1985).

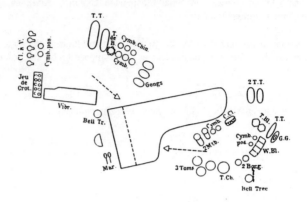

Percussion Étude XI: 3 Suspended Cymbals; 3 Chinese Gongs; 2 Tam-tams; 2 Crash Cymbals; Bell Tree; Crotales; 3 Chinese Cymbals; 5 Cowbells; Tambourine; Vibraphone.

Percussion Étude XII: 4 Woodblocks; 2 Temple Blocks; Snare Drum; 2 Bongos; 3 Tom-toms; 2 Tumbas; Contrabass Tom-tom; Maracas; Claves; 2 Tam-tams; 2 Crash Cymbals; Tambourine; Bell Tree; Piano.

These two "interpretive" etudes are the final sections of a collection of pieces by Ohana for piano, enlarged to include an extensive percussion ensemble. The composer warns that the piano lid is not to be removed as the sound is enhanced by the lid's surface.

All Instruments Non-representational

Example #271. Robert Buggert: *Introduction and Fugue* (1954).

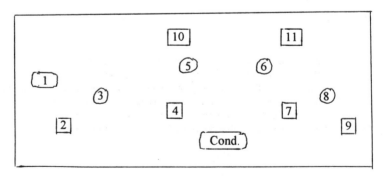

Player 1: Marimba; Piano.   *Player 2:* Snare Drum

Player 3: Small Tom-tom   *Player 4:* Bongos

Player 5: Large Tom-tom   *Player 6:* Xylophone; Woodblock.

Player 7: Maracas   *Player 8:* Tenor Drum; Triangle.

Player 9: Suspended Cymbal   *Player 10:* Timpani; Chimes.

Player 11: Bass Drum; Gong.

Only rarely has a composer suggested a stage floor plan for his percussion ensemble in which the individual instrumental symbology is completely abstract, with no attempt made to distinguish the instruments through pictographic symbols. In Buggert's score the instruments are identified only by numerals relating to the percussionist who is to play certain specified members of the ensemble. It is obvious that the great majority of composers utilizing suggested stage set-ups in their scores prefer more literal and clearly identifiable symbols for their percussion components.

Example #272. Finn Savery: *Like in Everyday Life* (1978).

<u>V</u>   <u>VI</u>
Congas   Tam-tam   Drums etc.
Roto-drums

<u>I</u>   <u>II</u>   <u>IV</u>   <u>III</u>
Steel drums   Vibraphone   Bass-marimba   Xylorimba
Gongs

From the foregoing stage set-up it is not clear as to which player is to strike the tam-tam at center stage rear; presumably it could be either Player II or IV, both being the closest to the instrument.

Example #273. Yoko Kurimoto: *Stolen Foot-Steps* (1984).

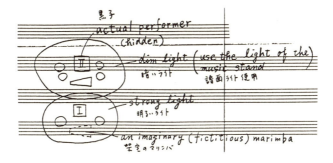

Percussion I: Imaginary Marimba; Cymbal; Woodblock; Tom-tom.

Percussion II: Marimba; Vibraphone; Cymbal; Tom-tom; Metal or Wood Windchimes; Shell Chimes; Triangle; Woodblock; Empty Tin Can; Boxing Match Chime.

Several singular aspects of this fairly recent Japanese work are the "fictitious" marimba among the instruments for *Percussion I,* and the opposing lighting effects for the two spaces, both requirements imparting a theatrical ambiance to the performance.

Percussion Ensemble and Solo Instrument(s) or Voice(s)

The percussion ensemble has been frequently entrusted with the assignment of accompanying a solo instrument or voice, even a full chorus. Pictographic signs present in the composers' stage diagrams have usually pertained only to the percussion, the solo players or singers represented by terminology or by abstract markings.

All Instruments Fully Representational

Example #274. Azio Corghi: *Stereofonie X 4* (1967).

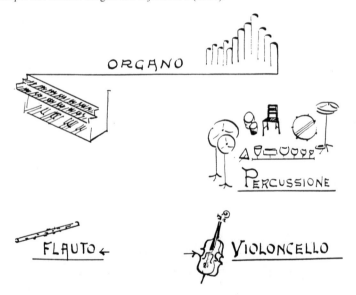

Percussion: Snare Drum; 2 Suspended Cymbals; Charleston Cymbal; 2 Bongos; 4 Temple Blocks; Woodblock; Triangle; Cowbell.

There are several singular aspects to this stage diagram: first, the electronic organ console and distant pipes, and second the literal depictions of the two solo instruments, flute and violoncello. Also quite literal are the percussion symbols and the performer's chair.

Percussion Instrument(s) Only Representational

Example #275. Luciano Berio: *Circles* (1960).

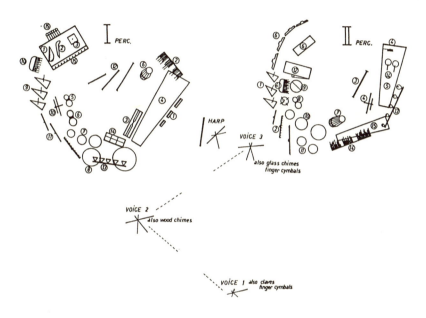

Percussion I: 1) 3 Woodblocks; Guïro 2) Mexican Bean; Wood Chimes 3) Log Drum; Sandblock 4) Marimbaphone 5) 2 Small Bongos 6) 2 Large Bongos; Tabla 7) 3 Tom-toms 8) 2 Small Timpani 9) 3 Triangles 10) Hi-hat Cymbal; Glass Chimes 11) 2 Suspended Cymbals; Sizzle Cymbal 12) 3 Tam-tams 13) 5 Cencerros 14) Lujon 15) 6 Suspended Chimes; Celesta

Percussion II: 1) 3 Triangles 2) 2 Suspended Cymbals; Sizzle Cymbal 3) Tam-tam 4) Hi-hat Cymbal; Glass Chimes; Clap Cymbals 5) Vibraphone 6) 4 Chinese Gongs; Glockenspiel 7) Tambourine 8) 2 Bongos 9) Snare Drum 10) 3 Tom-toms 11) 2 Conga Drums 12) Bass Drum (with foot pedal) 13) 5 Temple Blocks 14) Maracas; Wood Chimes 15) Xylophone

This seminal work of Berio has one of the most elaborate and detailed pictographic stage diagrams to be found in mid twentieth-century scores. For solo soprano and an extensive, two-part percussion ensemble, the vocalist moves to different positions in front of the percussion at various times during the performance, as shown by the broken lines. She also performs from time to time on the indicated auxiliary instruments.

Example #276. Edward Jay Miller: *Bashō Songs* (1961).

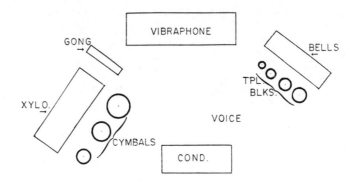

Gong, bells (glockenspiel), vibraphone, and xylophone all share the same simplified symbol (⊏⊐) in this diagram, while suspended cymbals and temple blocks also share another generic sign (⊙). The composer has reduced the technique of pictography to its bare minimum here.

Example #277. Ingolf Dahl: *Duettino Concertante for Flute and Percussion* (1966).

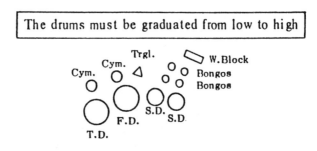

Percussion: Tenor Drum; Field Drum; Low Snare Drum; High Snare Drum; 4 Bongos; Woodblock; Small Triangle; Low and High Suspended Cymbals.

One percussionist is responsible for all the instruments in this score. The composer's pictograms rely on the exceedingly useful O-symbol to designate all but the triangle and woodblock.

Example #278. Carlos Roqué Alsina: *Trio 1967*

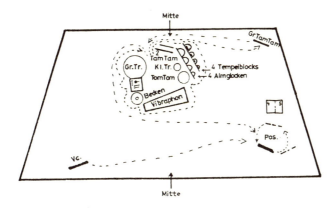

Percussion: Medium Suspended Cymbal; Small and Medium Tam-tams; Large Tam-tam; Sizzle Cymbal; 4 Temple Blocks; 4 Cowbells; Small Snare Drum; Tom-tom; Bass Drum; Vibraphone; Large Ratchet; 2 Dog Barks; 2 Trill Whistles; Small Greek Hand-Cowbell; Glass Marbles; Aluminum Paper.

The trombonist in this work also plays a small maraca and small trill whistle. He is to sit on a revolving stool, and at one point in the music must read from several pages of his part that lie on the floor behind him. The bass drum is to be laid at a slight angle so that marbles thrown on its head can easily roll about. Leaning against a chair leg, the sizzle cymbal is to be knocked over by the percussionist's foot. At the stage right rear the position of the large tam-tam is to give the impression that it is not actually needed in performance, although in fact it is to be struck.

Example #279. David Burge: *Sources III* (1967).

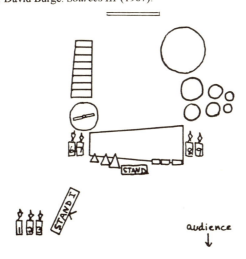

Vibraphone:	⬡	2 High Tom-toms:	○
Lujon:	▥	2 Low Tom-toms:	○
Sizzle Cymbal:	⊖	2 Conga Drums:	○
3 Triangles:	△	Bass Drum:	○
3 Woodblocks:	▭	Large Tam-tam:	▭▭

For solo clarinet and percussion, again only the latter is depicted pictographically. According to the composer his work is to be illuminated by ten candles, only seven of which are shown in the diagram. The eighth is located at the top left of the stage and the ninth and tenth on the right, more to the front. All ten are extinguished one by one by the clarinetist at designated moments in the score.

Example #280. William Kraft: *Encounters III: Duel for Trumpets and Percussion* (1971).

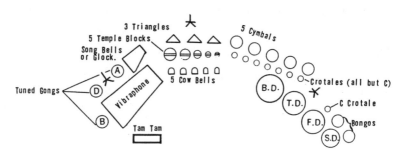

Both the percussion instruments and necessary music stands (✗) have representational symbols in this diagram. "Song Bells" seems to be a term coined by the composer as substitute for the glockenspiel.

Example #281. Richard Felciano: *Glossolalia* (1967).

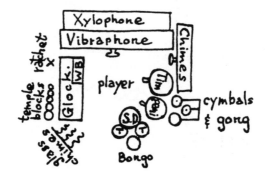

Felciano calls his work a "Ritual" for a baritone or dramatic tenor, organ, percussion, and electronic tape. As is evident, the percussionist is literally surrounded by his instruments so that all are easily reachable. Missing from the diagram is the suggested positioning of the soloist, tape deck, and loudspeakers.

Example #282. George Heussenstamm: *Poikilos* (1969).

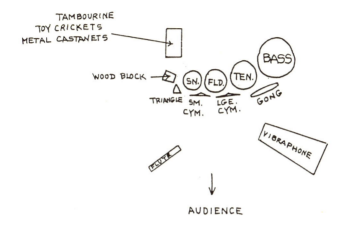

Percussion: Bass Drum; Tenor Drum; Field Drum; Snare Drum; Tambourine; Small Gong; Small and Large Suspended Cymbals; Triangle; Woodblock; Metal Castanets; 5 Toy Crickets.

All of the percussion instruments in this work, excepting the vibraphone, are non-pitched. As is the frequent custom in chamber music scores calling for flute, the player doubles on alto flute.

Example #283. Michael Udow: *African Welcome Piece* (1971).

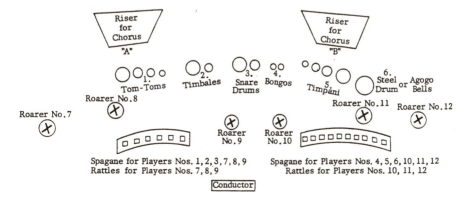

The familiar O-symbol serves to identify six different membrane instruments in this diagram. "Roarers" are string or friction drums (also known as cuica and lion's roar), while "spagane" are African idiophones—two flat wooden slabs that are clapped together. The two choral groups are optional, as the work may be performed solely as a percussion ensemble.

Example #284. Gardner Read: *Sonoric Fantasia No. 4* (1975).

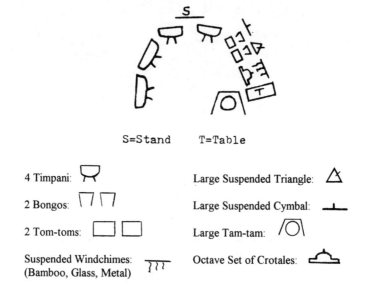

S=Stand   T=Table

4 Timpani:	Large Suspended Triangle:
2 Bongos:	Large Suspended Cymbal:
2 Tom-toms:	Large Tam-tam:
Suspended Windchimes: (Bamboo, Glass, Metal)	Octave Set of Crotales:

This work is designed for a large four-manual organ and a single percussionist. In the score both the instruments and beaters (nine different types) are indicated pictographically. The organist requires the services of an assistant, who manipulates the manual shades, stoptabs, and couplers.

Example #285. Erwin Chandler: *Duo for Bassoon and Percussion* (1976).

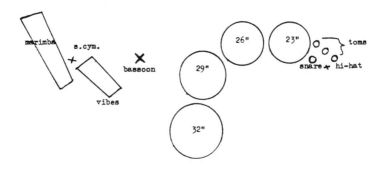

Percussion: 4 Timpani; Vibraphone; Marimba; Snare Drum; 3 Tom-toms; Suspended Cymbal; Hi-hat Cymbal.

From the visual layout of the instruments of this diagram it is evident that two percussionists are required, and we have one more timpani depiction that specifies their dimensions, from largest to smallest.

Example #286. Donald Erb: *Drawing Down the Moon* (1991).

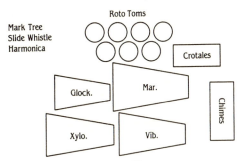

For the last movement, move the Vib. away.

Not shown in Erb's diagram is the position of the piccolo soloist, nor are there any pictograms given for the three auxiliary instruments to be played by the two percussionists.

Keyboard Instrument(s) Only Representational

Solo instrumentalists or vocalists have also been accompanied by a percussion ensemble in twentieth-century scores to which a keyboard instrument—usually piano—has been added. The latter sonic resource is most often depicted representationally, as is the organ console in Azio Corghi's work (*See:* Example #274).

Example #287. Alvin S. Curran: *Home-made* (1967).

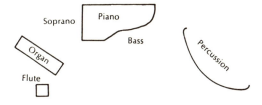

Among his varied instrumental resources only the piano in Curran's stage diagram is depicted in visual terms. Not shown are the auxiliary instruments to be played by the flutist (lion's roar, rubber crying doll, aluminum, pots, slide whistle, guïro, tambourine, bottle, and glass windchimes); the soprano (goat bells, toy frog, tin ratchet, shell chimes, maracas, dog whistle, small bell, electric buzzer, piano, electronic organ or harmonium); and the double bassist (sand block, dog whistle, claves, and hi-hat cymbal). The percussionist's array of instruments is extensive: vibraphone, xylophone, marimba, 3 triangles, 3 cowbells, 5 tin cans, 3 suspended cymbals, hi-hat and sizzle cymbals, 3 gongs, 5 temple blocks, 3 woodblocks, 5 wood drums, 4 bongos, 3 tom-toms, conga drum, snare drum, and bass drum with foot pedal. In addition to these standard members of the ensemble the composer calls for such exotica as a balloon, auto horn, 2 iron pipes, sand blocks, wood chimes, wooden ratchet, cap pistol, bottle, bicycle horn, police and dog whistles, duck horn, slide whistle, radio transistor, and two panes of glass. If all of these instruments had been shown pictographically the result might have induced visual trauma.

Percussion and Keyboard Instrument(s) Representational

Example #288. Maurice Ohana: *Signes* (1965).

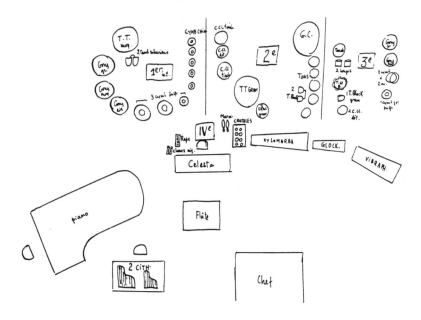

Percussion I: Large Tam-tam; 3 Gongs; 2 Saharan Drums; 3 Suspended Cymbals; 5 Chinese Gongs.

Percussion II: 3 Snare Drums; Deep Tam-tam; Large Hand Cymbal; Bass Drum; 5 Tom-toms; 2 Temple Blocks.

Percussion III: Tenor Drum; 2 Bongos; Tambourine; Large Temple Block; Snare Drum; 2 Gongs; 2 Crash Cymbals; Suspended Cymbal.

Percussion IV: Claves, Guïro; Maracas; Crotales; Celesta.

Shared: Glockenspiel; Vibraphone; Xylomarimba.

In addition to an extensive percussion section, including a piano and celesta, Ohana's score calls for two cithers, placed in a prominent position at the front of the platform. According to the diagram the glockenspiel can be played by either Player II or III, and the vibraphone, as well.

Example #289. Serge Garant: *Phrases I* (1967).

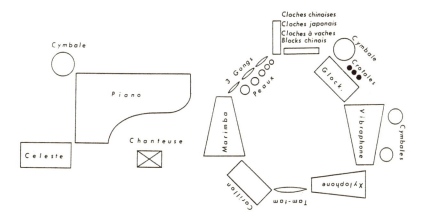

The contralto soloist in this work also plays windchimes, rattle, claves, and maracas, but these instruments are not depicted in the composer's stage set-up. The pianist also plays the celesta and a large suspended cymbal, which are represented. Percussion instruments and their beaters are identified in the score by nomenclature, a practice widely observed by other composers of percussion ensemble works. As shown, the percussionist is to stand in the center of the grouped instruments, which include a set of membranes (peaux), comprising snare drum, 2 or 3 tom-toms, bongos, timbales, and log and Basque drums. Also required are temple and sand blocks as well as a whip. The vibraphone bars are to be stroked with a double bass bow.

Example #290. Kazimierz Serocki: *Fantasmagoria* (1971).

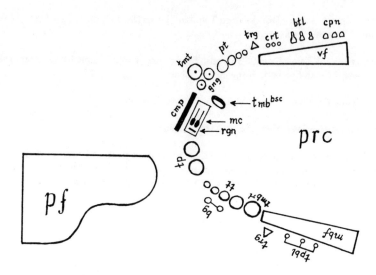

Percussion: Marimba; Vibraphone; Chimes; Tam-tam; 2 Gongs; 4 Suspended Cymbals; 2 Triangles; 3 Cowbells; Tambourine; Maracas; 2 Timpani; Bongos; 4 Tom-toms; Tenor Drum; 3 Temple Blocks; Claves; 3 Bottles.

In this work the piano is a solo instrument rather than a mere member of the ensemble. Although Serocki is quite precise on his instrumental designs shown in the stage diagram, like many other composers he identifies the instruments in the score itself by means of nomenclature, reserving any pictograms for the various beaters required.

All Instruments Non-representational

It was earlier demonstrated (*See:* pages 101-102) that very few scores for percussion ensemble have depended on completely non-representational stage diagrams to show the desired configurations of the instruments. The same is true with those chamber works that include a percussion complement; only three examples were uncovered in this compiler's research. In spite of their strakness and relative simplicity, however, these few examples are perfectly unambiguous in their depiction of the composers' preferences of instrumental arrangement.

Example #291. Henryk Gorecki: *III Genesis: Monodram* (1963).

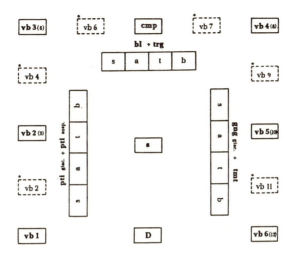

Percussion on left: 8 Crash Cymbals; 8 Suspended Cymbals; *Percussion on right:* 4 Gongs; 4 Tam-tams; *At top:* 12 Metal Blocks; Triangle; Chimes; *In Center:* Soprano Voice; *On all sides:* 6 Double basses.

This, the third section of Gorecki's *Genesis*, exhibits an unusual set-up of its instrumental forces. The soprano soloist is surrounded on three sides by an array of metal percussion instruments and by six double basses. Six additional double basses are optional, their positions indicated by the dotted-line boxes. The three percussion groups are arranged according to pitch, from high (s) to low (b).

Example #292. John Beckwith: *The Sun Dance* (1968).

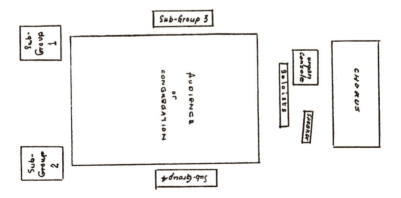

Sub-Group 1: SATB (4 to 10 voices); Pair of Small Cymbals; Small Gong; Low Tubular Chime; Deep Tam-tam.

Sub-Group 2: SATB (4 to 10 voices); Sleighbells; Large Cowbell; Tubular Chime.

Sub-Group 3: SATB (4 to 10 voices); Gourd Rattle; Claves; Castanets.

Sub-Group 4: SATB (4 to 10 voices); Large Hand Drum; Tambourine; Shell Wind Chimes.

Because the chorus, speaker, four groups of solo singers, and the percussion in this citation surround the location of the audience, the composer evidently felt that the presence of many pictograms in the diagram would have unduly complicated the visual appearance of his performing forces.

Example #293. Walter Hartley: *Concerto for Tuba and Percussion Orchestra* (1974).

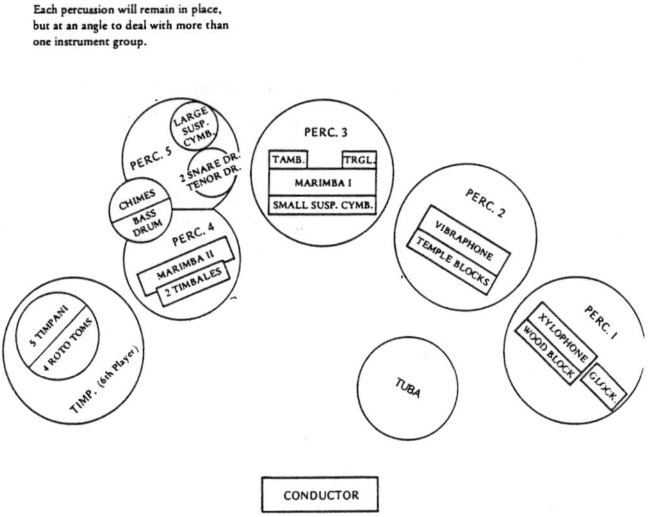

Six players, including the timpanist, are required for this tuba concerto, the separation of their parts clearly indicated. The composer's format for showing this is rather unique, the groupings being enclosed in circular designs.

Chamber Ensembles

Although twentieth-century scores for the percussion ensemble have exhibited the greatest number of pictographic stage diagrams as devised by their creators, by no means have other performing entities been overlooked by our contemporary composers in their pursuit of this particular notational concept. Chamber ensembles, with or without supplemental soloists, as well as the symphonic orchestra and concert band, have equally relied extensively on such pictographic representation of their instrumentalists and singers arrayed on the concert platform. Once again, the illustrated diagrams range from complete pictorial representation of the members requisitioned to an entirely abstract depiction of the players and vocalists chosen by the composer.

All Instruments Fully Representational

Because the number and variety of instruments normally included in a chamber ensemble composition usually preclude representing all the members pictographically, there are understandably few examples to cite. In fact, only two such instances were uncovered in the examination of hundreds of contemporary scores; both are illustrated below.

Example #294. Noam Sheriff: *"Destination 5'."* (1962).

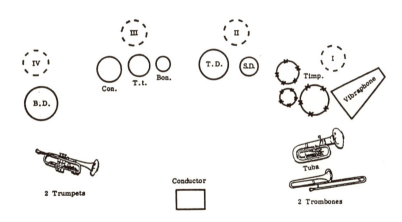

Percussion I: 3 Timpani; Vibraphone. *Percussion II:* Tenor Drum; Snare Drum. *Percussion III:* Conga Drum; Tom-tom; Bongo. *Percussion IV:* Bass Drum.

At first glance one might question whether the Sheriff citation is entirely pictographic, as only the generic O-symbol is used to identify six different membranophones (excepting timpani), but the accurate depictions of the three different brass instruments called for in the score are unique to this work; no other such instances were uncovered in this author's research.

Example #295. David Reck: *Blues and Screamer* (1967).

Instrumentation: Harmonium; Alto Saxophone; Double bass; Sock Cymbals; Large Suspended Cymbal; Shallow Snare Drum; Medium and Large Tom-toms; Bass Drum; Flute (Piccolo).

Thoroughly representational, as well as tongue-in-cheek, are the visual depictions of Reck's five instrumentalists. The ensemble functions as accompanist to a slide show projected on the screen behind the players.

Percussion Instrument(s) Only Representational

A more common approach for composers of chamber music works that include percussion instruments among their required resources is to use pictograms, either visually literal or else generic, only for the percussion, relying on abstract markings or nomenclature to show the location of the other ensemble members.

Example #296. Michael Colgrass: *Light Spirit* (1963).

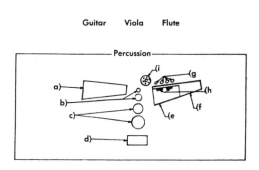

The stage diagram of Colgrass is a perfect example of this now common practice: the composer has made doubly sure that the symbols are clearly understood by identifying each pictogram in an appended listing of the instruments.

Example #297. Lawrence Moss: *Remembrances for Eight Performers* (1964).

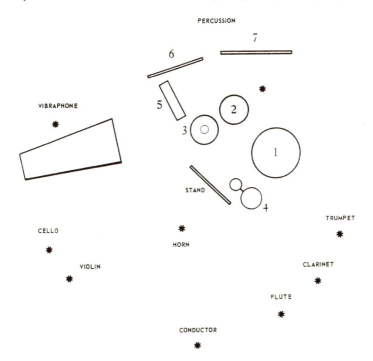

Instrumentation: 1) Tenor Drum; 2) Snare Drum; 3) Suspended Cymbal; 4) High & Low Bongos; 5) Tubular Bells; 6) Medium Tam-tam; 7) Low Tam-tam.

Two percussionists are required in this work, one for the vibraphone and the other for the remaining instruments. As is the custom for many other composers of similar works, only the different mallets called for are pictographically identified in the score itself. Unique to this score are the heavy asterisk-symbols (*) that identify the position of each of the eight performers. More frequently this procedure has been depicted with O's (as in Examples #320, #353, and #389, for instance), or by ⊏⊐'s (Examples #358, #374, and #405), by —'s (Examples #338, #342, and #366), with X's (Examples #285 and #317), or by ●'s (Examples #329 and #396). Once again we find no concensus among our composers on a common symbology for an ostensibly common stage requirement.

Example #298. Sydney Hodkinson: *Interplay* (1966).

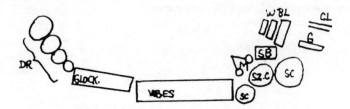

Instrumentation: Glockenspiel; Vibraphone; 3 Woodblocks; Maracas; Claves; Guïro; Sandpaper Blocks; 2 Timbales; 2 Bongos; 2 Suspended Cymbals; Sizzle Cymbal.

"A Histrionic Controversy" for four musicians, as the composer calls it, this work is scored for alto flute (piccolo), clarinet (alto saxophone), double bass, and one percussionist. The suggested pictographic platform set-up refers only to the percussion instruments; presumably these are placed behind the other three performers.

Example #299. Luc Ferrari: *Interrupteur* (1967).

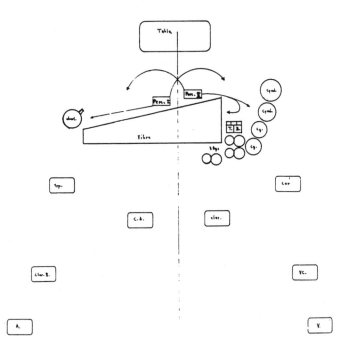

Percussion: Vibraphone; 3 Bongos; 2 Conga Drums; Guïro; 5 Temple Blocks; 2 Suspended Cymbals; Charleston Cymbal; Triangle; 4 Castanets; 2 Whips; 4 Maracas; 2 Tambourines; Crotales; Woodblock; 4 Claves. *Additional:* Trumpet; Horn; English Horn; Clarinet; Bass Clarinet; Violin; Viola; Violoncello.

The two percussionists in this work must exchange positions during the course of the music, shown by the arrow signs. Both play on the vibraphone, often at the same time and on the same pitch. Player I uses a double bass bow and Player II soft beaters. Like many other percussion compositions, the stage diagram symbols are not used in the score itself; only terminology identifies the instruments.

Example #300. Anthony Gilbert: *Brighton Piece* (1967).

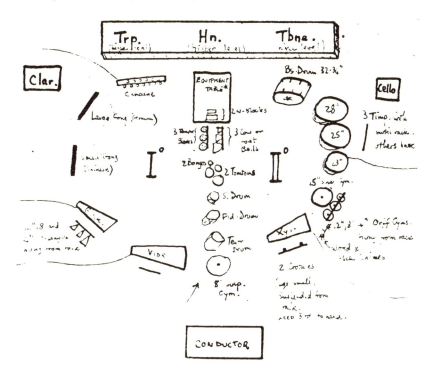

An unusual aspect of this stage set-up is the placing of the percussion ensemble at the front of the platform, with the five solo instruments behind them. The instruments aligned at the very center of the ensemble are to be played by percussionists I and II. It will be noted that the exact dimensions of triangles, suspended and Orff cymbals, bass drum, and timpani are specified. Mallets are shown pictographically in the score but not the instruments themselves, as one might expect.

Example #301. Hans-Joachim Hespos: *Keime und male* (1968).

schlgz. I   perc. I

symbol	description
	wood chimes (bambous suspendus)
	boîte en fer blanc (tôk)
	boîte en bois (tâk)
	caisse claire sans timbre
	grande cymbale
cymb. Dᵇ C⁵ B¹B²	cymbales antiques (crotales)
	bongos
s tom-tom)	tambourin (éventuellement tom-tom très petit)

schlgz. II   perc. II

symbol	description
▱/▱	caisse claire avec et sans timbre
	(dans : keime, détendue/dans : male, tendue)
	hi - hat
△	triangle
	petite cymbale
	tambour de bois (tronc creusé, africain)
✕	claves (moyennes)
cymb. Eᵇ F Dᵇ	cymbales antiques (crotales)

schlgz. III   perc. III

symbol	description
	cymbale moyenne
cymb. D E	cymbales antiques (crotales)
	tambour de basque
	sand block (papier de verre contre papier de verre)
	sand block (papier de verre contre velours)
	tom - tom (petit)
	tom - tom (grand)

Keim und male (translated as *Germes et signes*) is an ensemble of thirteen players: piccolo; flute; two clarinets; saxophone; horn; guitar; violin; violoncello; double bass; and three percussionists. Only the individual percussion are shown pictographically, their relative position in the ensemble outlined above each listing of the instruments. Curiously, under *Percussion II*, the symbol for an African wood drum is labeled as a cymbal.

Example #302. Reginald Smith Brindle: *The Death of Antigone* (1969).

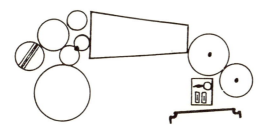

Instrumentation: Vibraphone; 2 Triangles; 2 Suspended Cymbals; Large Tam-tam; Maracas; 2 Woodblocks; 2 Bongos; 2 Tom-toms; Snare Drum; Large Bass Drum (laid horizontal).

The Death of Antigone is a mini-opera for mezzo-soprano and bass voices, two speakers (one a heavy male voice, the other a lighter male or female voice), flute (piccolo), violin (viola), piano, and one percussionist. The instrumental pictograms shown are entirely consistent with those used by Smith Brindle in other of his percussion works (*See:* Examples #225 and #228).

Example #303. Hans Werner Henze: *El Cimarrón* (1970).

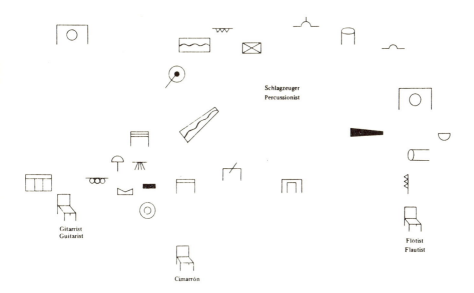

2 Tam-tams: $\boxed{\quad\bigcirc\quad}$ 2 Thunder Sheets: ⌐~⌐   Glass Windchimes: ͶͶͶ

Small Drum: ⊠   3 Suspended Cymbals: ‒⌒   Trinidad Gong Drum: 冂

Crotales: ⌒   Bass Drum (with foot pedal): ⊘   3 Bongos: 冖

Vibraphone: ⊏⊐   Marimba: ◄   3 Temple Bells: ▽

Bundle of hanging Bamboo Sticks: ⼪   Conga Drum: 𝖢

Afro-Cuban Marimbula: ⊞⊞   Shell Windchimes: ℧℧℧   Guïro: ⋈

Claves: ▬   13 Tom-toms: 冂.   8 Bamboo Drums: 冂

4 Log Drums: 冂.   Matraca: ⌇   Maracas: ◎   Bird Whistle: ‒◄‒‒

Henze calls this work a "Recital for Four Musicians." The spoken text is taken from the book of Miguel Barnet on the life of the runaway slave Esteban Montejo. Both the flutist and guitarist play various percussion instruments during the course of the music; both the instruments and their beaters are depicted pictographically in the score. The composer's symbols are quite imaginative and are notable for their depiction of such unusual oddities as African marimbula, bird whistle, matraca, and Trinidad gong drum.

Example #304. Donald Martino: *Notturno* (1974).

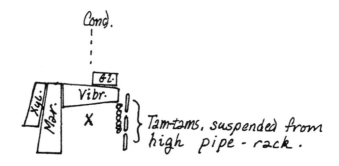

Percussion: Glockenspiel; Marimba; Vibraphone; Xylophone; 6 Temple Blocks; 3 Tam-tams; Piano.

Additional Instruments: Flute (Piccolo, Alto Flute); Clarinet (Bass Clarinet); Violin (Viola); Violoncello.

As in all of Donald Martino's scores calling for percussion, individual instrumental pictograms are consistent from one work to another. Although the composer does identify the various stick types by symbols in the score, the instruments are designated either by nomenclature (the four mallet members) or by staff position. Oddly enough, however, the piano is not depicted at all, nor are the woodwind and string members of the ensemble.

Example #305. David Maves: *Oktoechos* (1975).

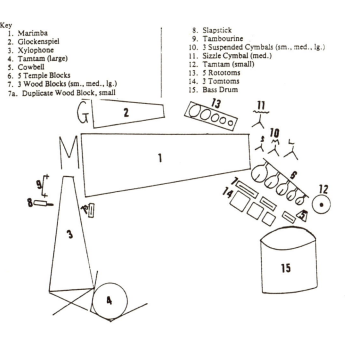

Few composers have been as precise in depicting music stands and chairs in their stage set-ups. The four "r.t." symbols specify roto-toms, while "s.d." represents a snare drum.

Example #306. Anne LeBaron: *Metamorphosis in Three Stages* (1980).

Key
1. Marimba
2. Glockenspiel
3. Xylophone
4. Tamtam (large)
5. Cowbell
6. 5 Temple Blocks
7. 3 Wood Blocks (sm., med., lg.)
7a. Duplicate Wood Block, small

8. Slapstick
9. Tambourine
10. 3 Suspended Cymbals (sm., med., lg.)
11. Sizzle Cymbal (med.)
12. Tamtam (small)
13. 5 Rototoms
14. 3 Tomtoms
15. Bass Drum

Lest the score reader be unsure of the composer's pictograms, LeBaron has included a numbered key to the various instruments, a notational device to be found in a number of other contemporary stage diagrams (*See:* Example #275, for instance).

Example #307. Donald Martino: *From the Other Side* (1988).

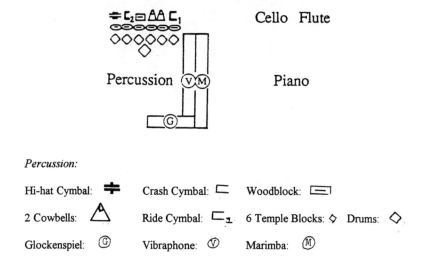

Percussion:

Hi-hat Cymbal: ✷   Crash Cymbal: ⊏   Woodblock: ⊏⊐

2 Cowbells: △   Ride Cymbal: ⊏₁   6 Temple Blocks: ◇   Drums: ◇

Glockenspiel: Ⓖ   Vibraphone: Ⓥ   Marimba: Ⓜ

Martino calls his work "A Divertimento for Flute, Violoncello, Percussion, and Piano." The flutist plays piccolo and alto flute as well as maracas. The cellist also manipulates one maraca, and the pianist plays on the interior strings with a bass drum beater. Pictograms identify both the percussion instruments and their beaters in the score pages.

Keyboard Instrument(s) Only Representational

A number of current stage diagrams for chamber music ensembles have depicted only the piano or other keyboard instruments in pictographic fashion, all other members being located in the performing area by means of nomenclature or abstract marks. Some composers favor placing individual instruments or related groups within boxes or rectangles (*See:* Examples #308, #311, and #325, for instance). Others prefer to use circles for this purpose (Examples #313, and #316), while yet other composers are content with positioning their instrumentalists in unconfined spaces, such as can be seen in Example #318.

Example #308. Rob du Bois: *Espaces à remplir* (1963).

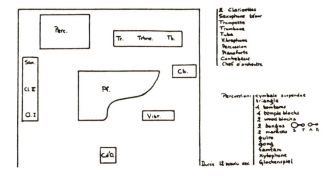

Not only are the ensemble members listed referring to the composer's stage plan, but the percussion instruments called for are specified as well in a supplementary column.

Example #309. Iannis Xenakis: *Eonta* (1964).

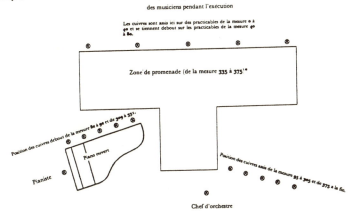

Eonta, meaning "beings" in Greek, is written for two trumpets, three tenor trombones, and piano; only the latter instrument is given pictographic representation in the composer's stage diagram. As indicated in the directions, the brass instruments move from their initial position at the rear of the platform to three other line-ups: twice behind the piano, twice at stage right, and once in the center, designated "zone de promenade."

A prolific composer of experimental works, both chamber and orchestral, Xenakis has not made a practice of including stage diagrams in his scores, the one in *Eonta* being an exception.

Example #310. Loren Rush: *Nexus 16* (1965).

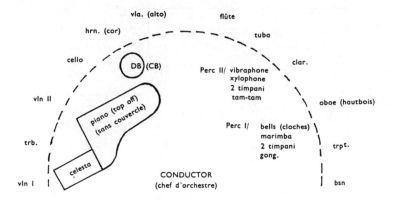

An unusual aspect of the composer's seating plan is the placing of a brass instrument between two string or two woodwind players. The diagram is also one of many that pair the piano and celesta, both played by one person.

Example #311. Wlodzimierz Kotonski: *a battere* (1966).

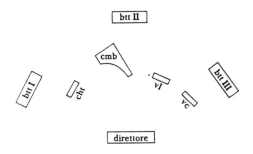

Percussion I: 3 Suspended Cymbals; Hi-hat Cymbal; Tam-tam; 2 Antique Cymbals; 4 Cowbells.

Percussion II: 3 Suspended Cymbals; Cowbell; Triangle; Large Almglocken; Gong; Cymbal (to lay on 1 Timpano).

Percussion III: 3 Suspended Cymbals; Hi-hat Cymbal; 4 Almglocken; 2 Antique Cymbals.

Kotonski's score is one of the few researched that includes a cembalo (harpsichord) among its chamber ensemble components. His pictogram is distinctive in the squared-off shape of the instrument's far end.

Example #312. Paul Méfano: *Interférences* (1966).

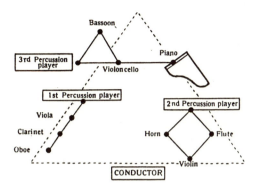

1st Percussion Player: Marimbaphone; Glockenspiel; 2 Suspended Cymbals; Woodblock.

2nd Percussion Player: Celesta; Tubular Bells; 2 Wood Drums; Side Drum.

3rd Percussion Player: Vibraphone; Tam-tam; 3 Chinese Gongs; Sleighbells.

Consisting of six fragments in all, the score at hand includes only the last three. The twelve players are divided into three groups of four players each, one of the three percussionists being a member of each group. The dotted lines do not represent any movement of the players, but only the rough triangular set-up of the instruments.

Example #313. Philippe Boesmans: *Correlations pour clarinette solo & 2 ensembles* (1967).

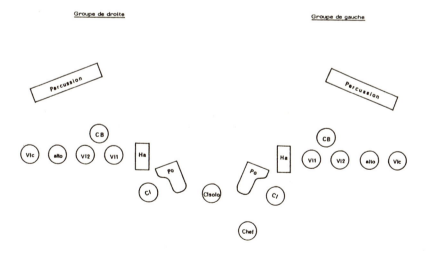

Percussion on Right: 4 Temple Blocks; 2 Bongos; 2 Snare Drums; 2 Tom-toms; Bass Drum; 3 Cymbals; Tam-tam.

Percussion on Left: 4 Woodblocks; 2 Bongos; 2 Snare Drums; 2 Tom-toms; Bass Drum; 3 Cymbals; Tam-tam.

Accessories: Wood & Glass Windchimes.

Percussion on Right and *Percussion on Left* signify their positions looking from the stage out to the audience. The stage diagram is reduced to its bare essentials, only the two pianos being given pictorial representation. Both ensembles are identical in make-up: clarinet; harp; piano; string quartet; and percussion. It will also be noted that the two percussion groups are identical, save for temple blocks substituting for woodblocks in one group.

Example #314. Roberto Gerhard: *Libra* (1968).

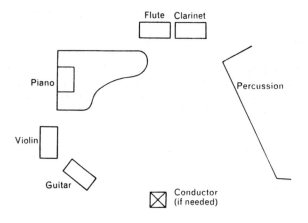

Percussion: Glockenspiel; Xylophone; Vibraphone; Timpani; Snare Drum; Bass Drum; Small Woodblock; Korean Block; 3 Suspended Cymbals; Castanets.

Libra, the seventh sign of the zodiac, happens to be Gerhard's own astrological symbol. In spite of this connection, however, the composer advises the listener to overlook any implied motivation for his work and just enjoy the music for its own appeal. The composer does not avail himself of any pictograms in this score; the percussion are consistently designated by means of terminology, as are the various beaters required. *Libra* is one of the few works by this composer to include a stage diagram in its preliminary pages.

Example #315. Elliott Schwartz: *Divertimento No. 2* (1968).

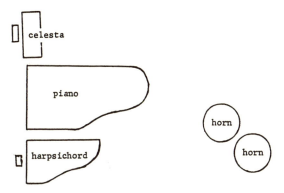

Two keyboard players are responsible for the three instruments indicated—celesta, piano, and harpsichord, as well as two music boxes (not shown). As the pianist plays only on the interior strings of the instrument, no seat is indicated in front of the keyboard.

Example #316. William Albright: *Marginal Worlds* (1970).

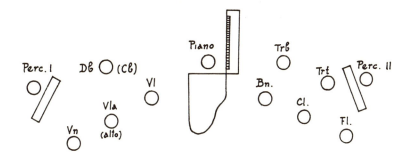

Percussion I: Tam-tam; 3 Tom-toms; Suspended Cymbal; Sizzle Cymbal; Maraca; Tambourine; Sand Block; Vibraphone.

Percussion II: Bass Drum; 3 Tom-toms; Suspended Cymbal; Hi-hat Cymbal; Maraca; Gong; Woodblock; 2 Triangles; Sleighbells; Antique Cymbals; Marimba.

Oddly enough, the pictographic representation of an upright piano, placed adjacent to the grand piano in this stage set-up, differs from the one accompanying the composer's performance instructions ('⊤⊤'). This latter symbol is also the one used in the score proper, as well as the more conventional design for the grand. Note also that the treble register is to the player's left rather than to the right as is customary. (*See*: Example #264, #387, and #390).

Example #317. Pauline Oliveros: *Aeolian Partitions* (1970).

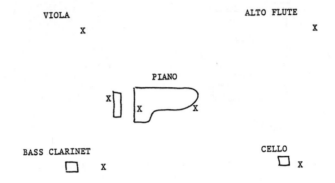

In this stage diagram seven-volt flasher lamps are shown as "x." Not included are a large variety of stage props required in the performance: six lanterns; a broom; transistor radio; megaphone; and a slide projector. All of these items are designed to enhance the visual ambiance of the composer's "Happening." These extra items requisitioned by the composer have a kinship in kind with those demanded by Elliott Schwartz in *Telly* (*See:* Example #465), in particular a transistor radio to be "played" by one percussionist.

Example #318. Jan W. Morthenson: *Labor* (1971).

Although its composer calls this work "Meta-Music for Chamber Orchestra," at no time are there more than eleven instruments playing, which would seem to qualify the composition more as a chamber than an orchestral essay. As is a common practice in many contemporary chamber music works, the flutist also plays alto flute, the oboist plays English horn, and the clarinetist plays bass clarinet. The composer does say, however, that two performers may be considered optional.

Example #319. Oliver Knussen: *Ophelia Dances* (1975).

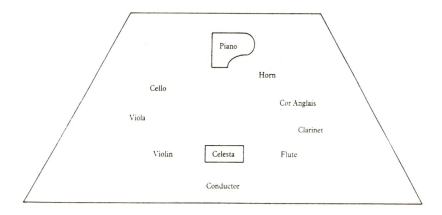

Only the piano in this instrumental nonet is pictographically identified, the diagram being a model of simplicity and succinctness. Three solo strings in this work (Book I of this title) are balanced by four solo winds, piano, and celesta.

Example #320. George Crumb. *Dream Sequence* (1976).

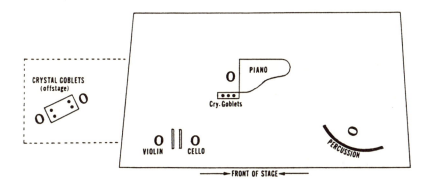

Percussion: 5 Japanese Temple Bells; 4 Crotales; Maraca; Sleighbells; 2 Suspended Cymbals; Thai Wooden Buffalo Bell; 7 Crystal Goblets.

Subtitled *Images II*, this score is notable for its inclusion of a Thai wooden buffalo bell (*See:* Example #84 for its pictogram), and seven crystal goblets which produce sounds simulating a glass harmonica.

Example #321. Elliott Schwartz: *Scatter* (1978).

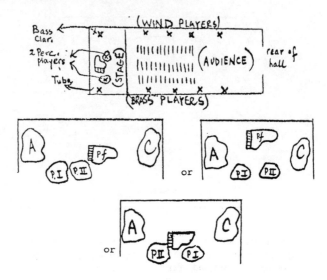

Percussion I: 3 Timpani; 5 Drums; Xylophone; Suspended Cymbal; Chimes

Percussion II: Bass Drum; Snare Drum; Large Tam-tam; 5 Woodblocks; Vibraphone; Glockenspiel; Piano.

Woodwind: 2 Flutes; Oboe; Clarinet; Bass Clarinet.

Brass: 2 Trumpets; Horn; Trombone; Tuba.

Four possible performance arrangements are indicated here. Only the first positions the wind and brass players at the sides of the hall; the other three set-ups place them on the platform with the piano and percussion.

Example #322. Oliver Knussen: *Coursing* (1979).

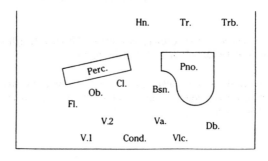

Percussion: Metallophone (Vibraphone); Triangle; Hi-hat Cymbal; Large Suspended Cymbal; Small Tam-tam; 2 Japanese Temple Bells.

Knussen states that the Metallophone may be replaced by a set of Orff chime bars and the Japanese temple bells by tubular bells or handbells at the same pitches.

Example #323. Simon Bainbridge: *Voicing* (1982).

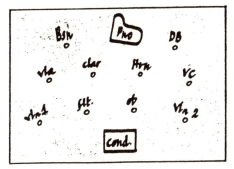

For a woodwind and a string quintet plus piano, the latter instrument is "prepared," a la John Cage, with rubber mutes on seven treble pitches.

Example #324. Wim Laman: *Pancabana* (1986).

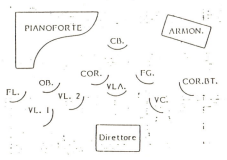

This is one of the few contemporary works researched to call for a harmonium, here pictured abstractly in contradistinction to that applied to the piano.

Both Examples #323 and #324, just cited, exhibit a problem sometimes encountered when photographing a stage diagram for inclusion in this compendium: the quality of the score paper and/or the printing itself can be quite poor, resulting in smudges and other imperfections in the copy used in these pages. The reader, therefore, must make allowances for these blemishes that are beyond the author's control.

Percussion and Keyboard Instrument(s) Representational

Example #325. Gunther Schuller: *Conversations for Jazz Quartet and String Quartet* (1959).

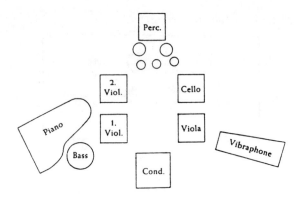

Percussion: 3 Suspended Cymbals; 3 Tom-toms; Triangle; Tambourine; Vibraphone.

To the standard jazz quartet of vibraphone, piano, double bass, and an assortment of percussion, Schuller juxtaposes the equally standard string quartet. Only his stage diagram makes use of instrumental pictograms, partially representational for the percussion. In the score, notehead differentiation and staff position, coupled with nomenclature, represent the percussion.

Example #326. Roger Reynolds: *The Emperor of Ice Cream* (1962).

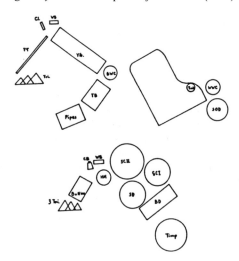

Percussion: Tambourine; Vibraphone; Tam-tam; Claves; Woodblock; Glass Windchimes; Temple Blocks; Metal Pipes; Piano; Small Oil Drum; Wood Windchimes; Triangles; Bottles; Cowbell; Hi-hat Cymbal; 2 Suspended Cymbals; Snare Drum; Bass Drum; Timpano.

This work calls for eight vocalists, piano, double bass, and the indicated percussion. In the score the instruments are identified by terminology, only the various beaters being shown pictographically. As is the custom in many experimental chamber works, the pianist must also play several percussion instruments. Not shown in the stage set-up are the positions of the eight vocalists and not included in the composer's listing of the instruments used is the vibraphone, as well as the tambourine placed on the piano.

Example #327. Francis Miroglio: *Phases* (1965).

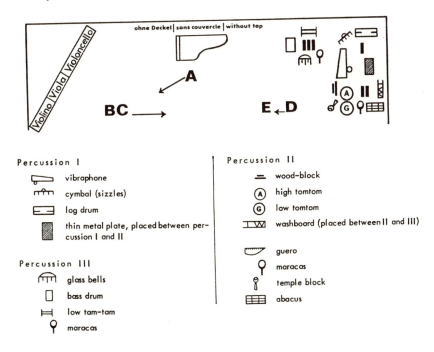

The order of the five sections of this work (A—E) may be varied at will by the performers. Furthermore, the instrumentation for each section may also be varied according to the four forms stipulated by Miroglio, based on different combinations of flute, piano, string trio, and percussion. Because the flutist is free to move about the stage in the fourth possible combination, the flutist's position in the stage diagram is not indicated. Out of the ordinary in the requisition of percussion instruments are washboard, abacus, and thin metal plate.

Example #328. Roger Reynolds: *Quick are the Mouths of Earth* (1965).

TT · WB · 4 TT · BD · TT · TIMP. · PIANO · 4 TT · PERCUSSION I · T · PERCUSSION II · SD · T · TB · BOT. · 3 SC · WB · GLOCK. · WC · T · VIB. · TRP. · OB. · FL. II · VC. II · TBN. · B. TBN · VC. I · FL. I · FL. III · VC. III

Percussion I: Tam-tam; 4 Woodblocks; Tambourine; Bottles; 3 Suspended Cymbals; Vibraphone; 3 Triangles; 4 Tom-toms; Bass Drum; 2 Crotales; Harmonica.

Percussion II: Timpano; Snare Drum; 5 Temple Blocks; Windchimes; Glockenspiel; 4 Woodblocks; 4 Tom-toms; Tambourine; Tam-tam; Harmonica.

Clearly labeled are all the instruments required in Reynold's score, with representative pictographs for the piano and individual percussion. Even though "T" represents both triangle and tambourine, and "TT" both tom-tom and tam-tam, there is no ambiguity in their depictions.

Example #329. William Albright: *Danse Macabre* (1971).

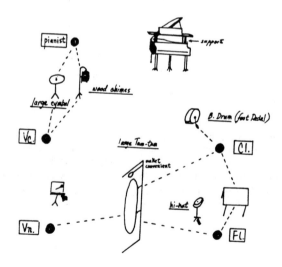

In this work the percussion instruments are played by each of the ensemble members, indicated by the dotted lines from one position to another. Not shown in the diagram are those instruments placed on a music stand (above "Vn."): single maraca (with attached sleighbells), and on a table (above "Fl."): a pair of maracas; claves; antique cymbals; woodblocks; and triangles. The indicated support on the piano consists of two heavy books or wooden blocks in the well of the instrument on which to place the music rack.

Example #330. Jorge Biarduni: *". . . de rumores el silencio"* (1971).

Para salas grandes

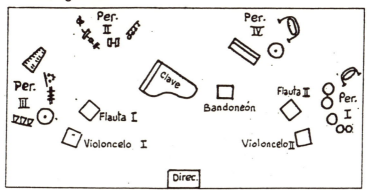

Para salas pequeñas

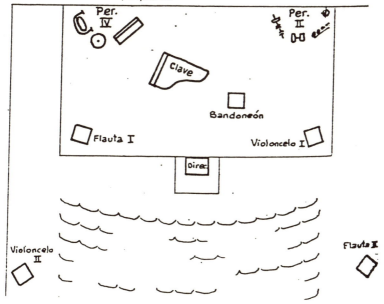

Percussion I: 2 Bongos; Snare Drum; Deep Tam-tam; *2 Tumbadoras; *Caracoles.

Percussion II: 2 Woodblocks; Guïro; Claves; *3 Cocos; *Semillas.

Percussion III: 3 Cenceros; Crotales; Glockenspiel; Suspended Cymbal; *Carcaboles; *Cuentas de Vidrio; *Pandereta.

Percussion IV: Celesta; Suspended Cymbal; Tam-tam; Claves; *Cadenas metalicas.

Many of the instruments called for in this work are of Latin-American origin; they are identified by "*." The term *clave* on the keyboard pictogram ought not to cause any confusion; it is the abbreviation for "clavecembalo," and not of course, the familiar percussion instrument. An unusual feature of the score is the two suggested set-ups, one for a large hall, the other for a smaller auditorium.

Example #331. Francis Miroglio: *Réfractions* (1973).

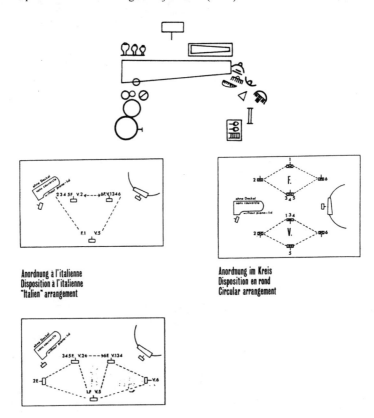

Anordnung à l'italienne
Disposition à l'italienne
"Italien" arrangement

Anordnung im Kreis
Disposition en rond
Circular arrangement

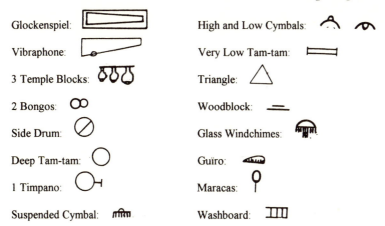

Glockenspiel:

Vibraphone:

3 Temple Blocks:

2 Bongos:

Side Drum:

Deep Tam-tam:

1 Timpano:

Suspended Cymbal:

High and Low Cymbals:

Very Low Tam-tam:

Triangle:

Woodblock:

Glass Windchimes:

Guiro:

Maracas:

Washboard:

Réfractions is for flute, violin, piano, and percussion. The composer indicates three possible stage arrangements of his instrumentalists: two versions of a so-called "Italian" set-up and one "circular" arrangement. Both flutist and violinist move to six different positions during the performance, shown by the dotted lines. Another instance of a composer's inclusion of a washboard among his percussion resources may be seen in Example #327.

Example #332. Henri Lazarof: *Suite for Solo Percussion and Five Instrumentalists* (1990).

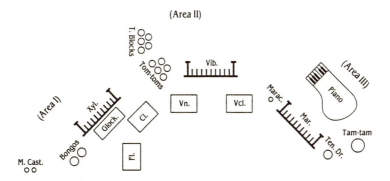

Four of the supporting instrumentalists in this work strike a mounted triangle (not depicted) and the pianist is to manipulate a pair of claves during the course of the music. The score itself uses no pictographs; the percussion are designated by terminology, staff position, and/or notehead shape. This researcher knows of few other keyboard instruments having such an odd profile as that shown here. Additional instances of this peculiar configuration may be seen in Examples #313, #316, #323, and #335, among others illustrated.

Percussion and Harp Representational

Example #333. Bernard Rands: *Actions for Six* (1963).

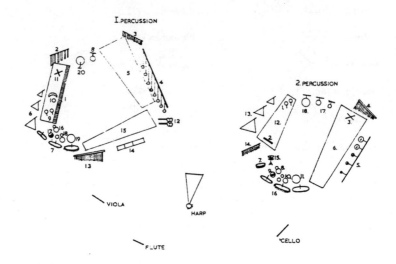

Percussion 1: 1) Celesta; 2) Bells; 3) Glass Windchimes; 4) Crotales; 5) Vibraphone; 6) Triangles; 7) Cymbals; 8) Tam-tam; 9) Maracas; 10) Mexican Bean; 11) Claves; 12) Castanets; 13) Wood Windchimes; 14) Woodblocks; 15) Xylophone; 16) Bongos; 17) Tenor Drum; 18) Tom-toms; 19) Timpani; 20) Bass Drum (with foot pedal).

Percussion 2: 1) Maracas; 2) Sandblock; 3) Claves; 4) Wood Windchimes; 5) Temple Blocks; 6) Marimba; 7) Tambourine; 8) Bongos; 9) Snare Drum; 10) Tom-toms; 11) Timpani; 12) Glockenspiel; 13) Triangles; 14) Glass Windchimes; 15) High-hat Cymbal; 16) Cymbals; 17) Tam-tam; 18) Gong.

No conductor is required for Rands' work as the six instrumentalists each serve in turn as "coordinators" during the performance, synchronizing entrances and timings by means of gestures. The composer's pictograms are quite detailed, even to noticeable distinctions for the two kinds of windchimes. His harp symbol is unique to this score. Six different mallet symbols accompany the stage diagram, and certain performing techniques, such as playing with the fingernails, also are indicated with special symbols.

The visual aspect of Rand's set-up bears a close resemblance to that of Luciano Berio for his *Circles (See:* Example #275), not only because of the separation of the two percussion groups, but also due to his meticulous depiction of many diverse instruments.

Percussion, Keyboard Instrument(s), and Harp Representational

Example #334. Roman Haubenstock-Ramati: *Ständchen* (1958).

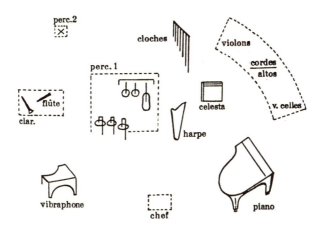

Percussion 1: 3 Suspended Cymbals; 2 Gongs; Tam-tam.

Percussion 2: Claves; Vibraphone; Chimes.

Together with Azio Corghi's stage diagram (*See:* Example #274), this score is one of the very few chamber works to depict a woodwind instrument in its pictographic set-up. This composer's representations of his piano, celesta, and vibraphone are as distinctive as those seen in Boulez's score illustrated in Example #360.

Example #335. Barton McLean: *Ritual of the Dawn* (1982).

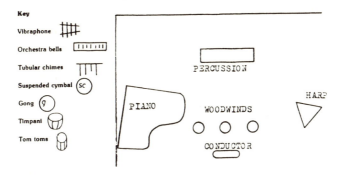

Save for the vibraphone and orchestra bells (glockenspiel), McLean's percussion symbols are quite precise. The same, however, cannot be said of the harp pictogram; it might have been more sensible to have represented the instrument's position by means of a generic symbol, such as ⌐⊐ or ○ .

All Instruments Non-representational

Example #336. Henryk Gorecki: *II Genesis: Canti strumentali* (1962).

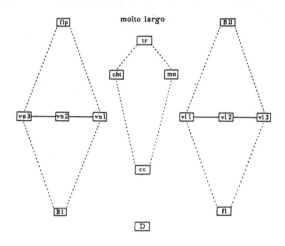

Instrumentation: Piccolo (flp); Flute (fl); Trumpet (tr); Mandolin (mn); Guitar (cht); Clavichord (cc); 3 Violins (vn); 3 Violas (vi).

Percussion I: 5 Wood Drums; 2 High Gongs (soprano, alto); Small Bass Drum; Very Deep Tam-tam.

Percussion II: 4 Bongos; 2 Low Gongs (tenor, bass); Large Bass Drum; High Tam-tam.

Gorecki's *Genesis*, of which this score is the second part, was composed long before his phenomenally successful *Third Symphony*. *Genesis* was written at the height of the avant-garde movement in Polish music, and although it employs no pictographs other than a generic ➤ symbol for various beaters, it makes extensive use of other performing signs widely favored by other European experimentalists. The designation *molto largo* above the stage diagram (rather than over the first measure) is the tempo distinction for the entire piece, which lasts ca. 8'4". No explanation is given as to the significance of the dotted lines connecting the three groups of instruments. The symbol ⊏D⊐ , of course, represents the conductor's position.

Example #337. Zbigniew Rudzinski: *Impromptu for Orchestra* (1966).

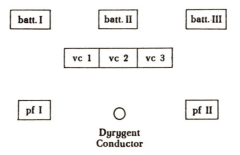

Percussion I: Chimes; 3 Tom-toms; Xylophone; Vibraphone; Sleighbells; Tambourine.

Percussion II: Chimes; 3 Tom-toms; Xylophone; Glockenspiel; Sleighbells; Tambourine.

Percussion III: 3 Tom-toms; 3 Woodblocks; Sleighbells; Anvil; Tambourine.

Eight tambourines and eight suspended metal bars are required in this score in addition to the specified percussion. All eight performers play these items at various times in the music, the metal bars to be struck with metal hammers.

Example #338. Jean-Yves Bosseur: *Un arraché de partout* (1968).

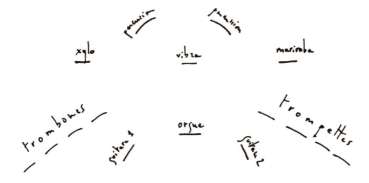

Percussion: Xylorimba; Vibraphone; Marimbaphone; 4 Cymbals; 4 Bongos; 2 Maracas; Snare Drum; Gong; Tam-tam; Pedal Timpano.

Both the stage diagram and the score itself of this composition illustrate the difficulties that one sometimes faces in deciphering a composer's manuscript. The problems can be compounded when the nomenclature is in a foreign language, although in this case the French is easily understood.

Example #339. Werner Heider: *Passatempo per 7 Solisti* (1968).

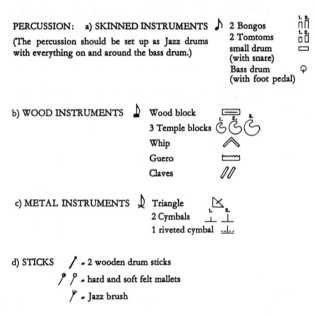

PERCUSSION: a) SKINNED INSTRUMENTS ♪ 2 Bongos

(The percussion should be set up as Jazz drums with everything on and around the bass drum.)

2 Tomtoms

small drum
(with snare)

Bass drum
(with foot pedal)

b) WOOD INSTRUMENTS ♩ Wood block

3 Temple blocks

Whip

Guero

Claves

c) METAL INSTRUMENTS ♩ Triangle

2 Cymbals

1 riveted cymbal

d) STICKS   / - 2 wooden drum sticks

𝄽 𝄽 - hard and soft felt mallets

𝄽 - Jazz brush

Although not shown in the stage set-up, Heider's percussion are arranged in three groups, as detailed in the appended listing, together with their individual pictographs. Four different stick types are also identified, and both instruments and beaters are pictographically represented in the score. The composer's list of instruments includes yet another variant spelling for the guïro (*See:* page 45), although his identifying symbol duplicates that to be found in several other scores. On the other hand, his pictogram for temple blocks seems to be unique to this particular score.

Example #340. Werner Heider: *Stundenbuch* (1972).

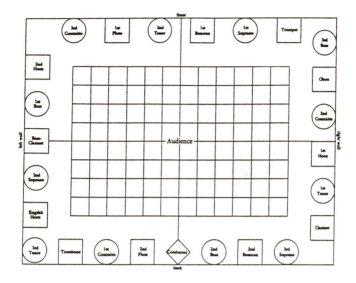

This "Book of Hours" is intended for a quadrophonic interpretation. The composer states that it is essential the indicated positioning of the twelve singers and twelve instrumentalists be strictly adhered to, so that the audience is completely surrounded by the performers, and hence the sounds. As shown, the conductor is stationed at the rear of the hall, behind the audience.

Example #341. Alan Stein: *Quintessence for Five Trombones* (1972).

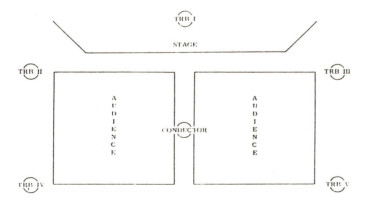

Trombones I, III, and IV are tenor instruments, while II and V are bass instruments. An odd feature of this set-up is the placing of the conductor in the middle of the audience.

Example #342. Toru Takemitsu: *Valeria* (1973).

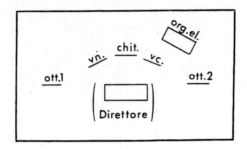

A note in Takemitsu's score specifies that the two piccolos (ott.1 and ott. 2) are to be placed as far apart as possible. No loudspeaker is indicated for relaying the sounds of the electronic organ.

Example #343. Donald Erb: *Fanfare for Brass Ensemble and Percussion* (1974).

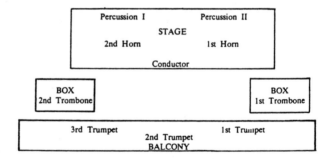

A distinctive feature of this score is the positioning of the trombones in the auditorium boxes and the trumpets in the rear balcony. Together with the horns and two percussion groups on the stage, the sonic resultant is meant to be quadrophonic. Other composers who arranged their stage musicians so as to produce related acoustical results include Elliott Schwartz (*See:* Example #321), Jorge Biarduni (Example #330), Werner Heider (Example #340), and Sydney Hodkinson (Example #374). These cited examples represent only a fraction of the total number of contemporary works that strive for multiple sound sources.

Example #344. Roger Reynolds: *The Promises of Darkness* (1975).

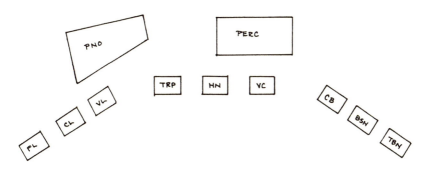

Percussion: Glockenspiel; Vibraphone; Crotales; Sizzle Cymbal; Large Tam-tam; Claves; Snare Drum; Large Bass Drum.

As indicated in Reynolds's score, the instrumentalists are arranged in five groups. According to the composer's stated plan, three concurrent streams of sound, each with its own distinctive musical character, are the objectives of this set-up.

Chamber Ensemble and Solo Instrument(s) or Voice(s)

It can easily be argued that all the players in any chamber ensemble are themselves the soloists. However, many twentieth-century chamber music scores that include a pictographic stage diagram among the composer's performance instructions, designate a specific instrument or voice as soloist, and so identify it in the set-up. The following section illustrates the various ways that such requirements have been pictured in the composers' layouts of resources.

Percussion Instrument(s) Only Representational

Example #345. Martin Gümbel: *Gesichte* (1969).

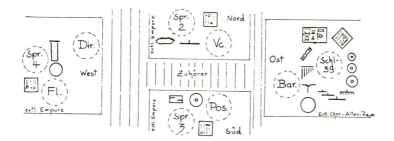

Designed for performance in a church, the four groups of instruments and speakers are positioned surrounding the congregation. On the east (right side) are the baritone, who is Speaker #1, and percussion (3 suspended cymbals, chimes, a number of percussion instruments); on the north (top center) are Speaker #2, violoncello, and two percussion; on the south (lower center) are Speaker #3, trombone, and two percussion; on the west (far left) are Speaker #4, flute, and two percussion. *evtl. Empore* indicates that all these groups may also be located in the church choir, while *evtl. Chor-Altar Raum* means that this group may be placed in the choir and altar room.

Example #346. Oliver Knussen: *Océan de Terre* (1972).

Layout for Percussion if one player:

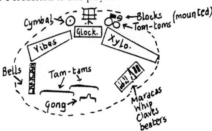

This composition is for soprano solo, flute (alto flute), clarinet (bass clarinet), one or two percussionists, violin, viola, double bass and piano. If a second person plays the celesta, they also double on extra percussion instruments. The composer specifies that the celesta should be amplified.

Example #347. Theodore Antoniou: *Parastasis II* (1977).

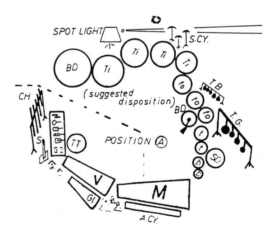

Percussion: Glockenspiel (Gl); Marimba (M); Vibraphone (V); Chimes (CH); Antique
Cymbals (A.CY.); 3 Triangles (TR); Tam-tam (TT); Musical Saw (S); Bass Drum (BD);
4 Timpani (Ti); 3 Suspended Cymbals (S.CY.); 3 Tom-toms (to); 5 Temple Blocks (T.B.);
4 Tuned Gongs (T.G.); Side Drum (SD); 2 Timbales (t); 2 Bongos (b); *On table:*
Woodblocks; Sleighbells; Flexatone; Castanets; Maracas; Claves; Windchimes.

A chamber ensemble consisting of any combination of flute (piccolo, alto flute), clarinet
(bass clarinet), horn, trombone, harp, piano, viola, and double bass, is combined with solo
percussion, tape, and optional dancer. Not shown in the stage diagram is a large gong set in
the center of the platform, but which provides only a visual contribution to the performance.
Neither the percussion instruments or beaters are pictographically indicated in the score.

Example #348. Ellen Taaffe Zwilich: *Passages* (1981).

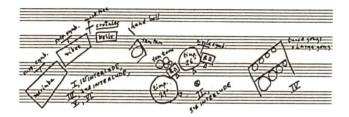

For mezzo-soprano solo and an additional ensemble consisting of flute (piccolo, alto flute)
clarinet (bass clarinet), violin, viola, violoncello, piano, and percussion (one player). Only the
latter instruments receive pictographic representation in the composer's stage diagram. The
Roman numerals refer to the sections of the work, the percussion grouped according to their
participation in certain of the sections.

Keyboard Instrument(s) Only Representational

For reasons that sometimes appear obscure, a few composers who usually favor detailed
pictographic score notation have chosen to bypass such comprehensive symbology in certain
of their scores that include the percussion and other orchestral instruments combined with a
keyboard part. The latter is then pictured realistically while the former appear only as abstract
symbols or nomenclature.

Example #349. Edison Denisov: *Die Sonne der Inkas* (1964).

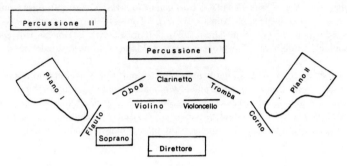

Percussion I: Marimbaphone; Vibraphone; Chimes; 2 Wood Drums.

Percussion II: 3 Suspended Cymbals; Tam-tam; 3 Tom-toms; Timpani.

Not shown in this stage diagram are the positions of the three male speakers who accompany the soprano soloist in the final section of Denisov's work. Presumably, they are placed at the conductor's right, in front of the horn. In the score itself there are no pictograms used, either for instruments themselves or for the percussion beaters; all are indicated by means of standard terminology.

Example #350. Harrison Birtwistle: *The Fields of Sorrow* (1971).

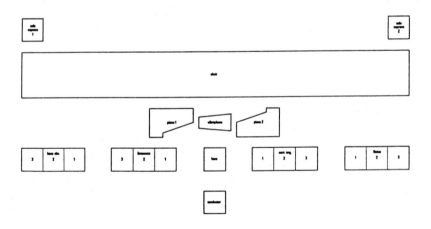

An unusual feature of this composer's stage arrangement is the placing of the two soprano soloists behind the spread-out choral forces instead of at the front, as one might expect. Also to be noted is the position of the vibraphone between the two facing pianos and the single horn separating the four groups of woodwind instruments.

Example #351. Bernard Rands: *Metalepsis 2* (1971).

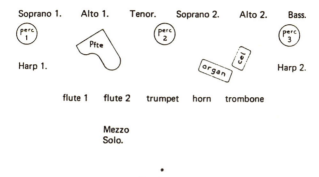

Percussion 1 & 3: 3 Triangles; Glockenspiel; 3 Suspended Cymbals; Gong; Mounted Tambourine; Bongos; Tam-tam; Vibraphone; 3 Almglocken.

Percussion 2: 3 Triangles; Tubular Bells; 3 Suspended Cymbals; 2 Gongs; Mounted Tambourine; Tam-tam; 5 Cencerros; 3 Tom-toms; Marimba.

The "choral" voices at the rear of the platform are to be amplified, each singer having an individual microphone (not depicted). In addition, the singers each operate a claxon horn at one point in the score. Pictograms of five types of percussion beaters are present on the score pages but not of any of the instruments.

Example #352. John Downey: *A Dolphin* (1974).

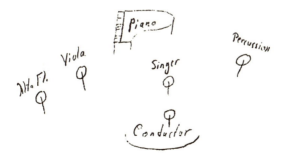

Percussion: Vibraphone; Suspended Cymbal; Bass Drum; Tam-tam; 5 Crotales.

For a high voice (either a soprano or a tenor), Downey's text is a poem by his wife, Irusha Downey. The alto flutist also plays on a tambourine, a requirement not often encountered in contemporary scores for chamber ensemble.

Example #353. Simon Bainbridge: *Concertante in moto perpetuo* (1983).

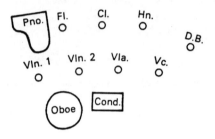

Nine instruments—three winds, five strings, and piano—are the concertante members of this ensemble—complementing the solo oboe, all depicted in simple fashion.

Percussion and Keyboard Instrument(s) Representational

It seems undeniably appropriate that a work of Mauricio Kagel should head this section of contemporary pictographic notation. This composer is one of the most prolific and imaginative of all the current practitioners of the technique, as his scores so extensively represented in this compendium can attest. Strangely enough, however, certain other composers we might expect to be frequently cited—Pierre Boulez, for one—do not appear here as often as one would anticipate. As is evident, the majority of the composers included in these pages have contributed only one or two instances of pictographic stage arrangements in their scores. For whatever reason these composers have not shared the commitment and flair for the elegantly conceived and executed pictographs that are so characteristic of Kagel's works.

On the other hand there are certain other contemporary orchestrators who have consistently applied the technique of pictographic notation to nearly all of their scores. These obviously include such composers as George Crumb (Example #355, for instance), Hans Werner Henze (most notably illustrated in Example #303), Henri Lazarof (*See:* Example #332 as a prime sample of his commitment), Donald Martino (probably the most consistent in using the same symbols in one work and the next), and Reginald Smith Brindle (Example #225 is typical). It can easily be said that these composers demonstrate a dedication to pictographic notation fully equal to that of Mauricio Kagel at his most creative.

Example #354. Mauricio Kagel: *Anagrama* (1958).

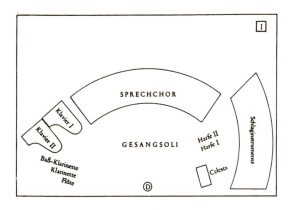

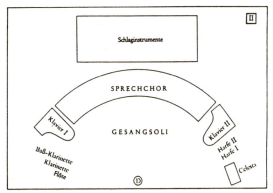

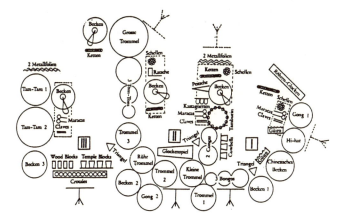

Kagel's score is for four solo voices, a speech choir, and a chamber ensemble consisting of piccolo, flute, clarinet, bass clarinet, celesta, two harps, two pianos, and percussion. Two seating possibilities are shown, plus an extremely detailed pictographic representation of the large percussion ensemble required. The dotted lines in this diagram merely indicate music stands or small table on which to place the smaller instruments and the various beaters called for in the score.

Example #355. George Crumb: *Night Music I* (1963).

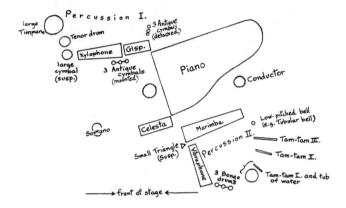

Four performers are required for this chamber work: soprano, pianist (who also plays celesta), and two percussionists. The singer also manipulates a pair of finger cymbals. Each instrument is clearly identified in Crumb's diagram and the exact position of singer and conductor carefully indicated. Neither the percussion instruments or the types of beaters to be used are shown pictographically in the score.

In addition to his being one of our most imaginative and innovative composers, George Crumb is also a staunch advocate of pictographic notation. There are few of his chamber or orchestral scores that do not exhibit detailed and precisely drawn instrumental symbols, such as those that can be seen in *Echoes of Time and the River* (Example #396), *Ancient Voices of Children* (Example #461), and *Dream Sequence* (Example #320). Together with Gilbert Amy, Werner Heider, Hans Werner Henze, Mauricio Kagel, Henri Lazarof, Donald Martino, Francis Miroglio, and Roger Reynolds, Crumb is one of the most persuasive defenders of the science and art of pictorial notation.

Example #356. Roger Reynolds: *Blind Men* (1966).

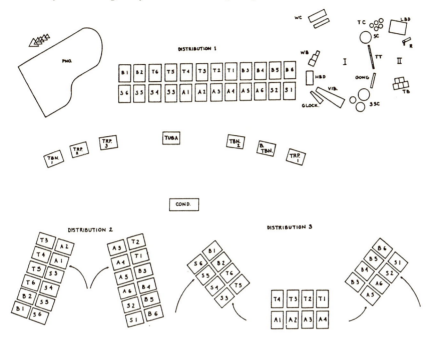

The 24 choral voices in Reynold's work may be grouped in the three possible distributions shown, the additional forces of brasses, percussion, and piano remaining unchanged. The tuba occupies a curious position in the set-up, placed as it is between the two groups of trumpets and trombones.

Example #357. Ronald Perera: *Chamber Concerto for Brass Quintet, Nine Winds, Piano, and Percussion* (1983).

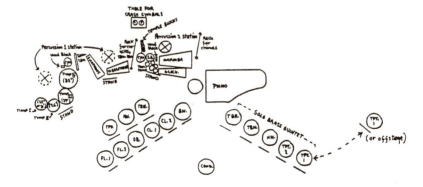

Percussion I: 4 Timpani; Vibraphone; Xylophone; Suspended Cymbal; 2 Tam-tams; Crash Cymbals; Woodblock; 5 Crotales.

Percussion II: Marimba; Glockenspiel; Suspended Cymbal; Crash Cymbals; 5 Temple Blocks; Snare Drum; Woodblock; 5 Tom-toms; 3 Chimes.

As shown in the diagram, Trumpet I is to move from off-stage (or the rear corner of the stage) to his normal position in the quintet. Arrows also indicate the change of position for the first percussionist.

Keyboard Instrument(s) and Harp Representational

Example #358. Friedrich Cerha: *Relazioni fragili* (1957).

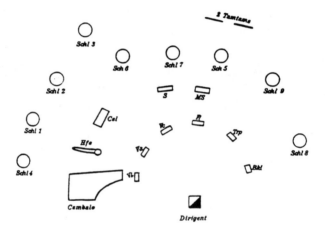

Percussion 1: 3 Suspended Cymbals; Crotales; Tambourine; Castanets; Claves.

Percussion 2: 3 Gongs; Crotales; 2 Glockenspiels; Bass Drum; Tambourine; Maracas.

Percussion 3: 3 Bongos; 3 Gongs; Whip; Small Cymbal; 2 Herd Bells; 2 Sleighbells.

Percussion 4: 4 Small Drum; Claves; Woodblock; Maracas.

Percussion 5: Bass Drum; Guïro; 3 Tom-toms; 2 Tam-tams; Small Cymbal; 2 Glockenspiel.

Percussion 6: Cowbells; Bass Drum; Woodblock; Castanets; 2 Temple Blocks; Claves.

Percussion 7: 2 Tam-tams; Bells; Crotales; Glockenspiel; Whip; 2 Metal Blocks; Bass Drum; Woodblock; 2 Temple Blocks; 2 Glockenspiel Bars.

Percussion 8: Marimba; Woodblock; Xylophone; 2 Temple Blocks.

Noteworthy are the stipulated positions of the nine percussionists in Cerha's diagram, surrounding as they do the other instrumentalists and solo female voices. Also curious is the isolation of the two tam-tams at the very rear of the concert platform. Although the cembalo is given a fairly accurate representation, the same cannot be said of the harp symbol.

Example #359. Gilbert Amy: *Echos XIII* (1976).

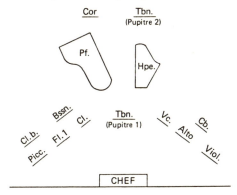

Horn, trombone, piano, and harp are solo instruments in this chamber score. The trombonist is to move to desk 2 (Pupitre 2) during the course of the music.

Percussion, Keyboard Instrument(s), and Harp Representational

Example #360. Pierre Boulez: *Improvisation sur Mallarmé: Une dentelle s'abolit* (1958).

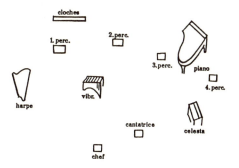

Percussion 1: Pair of Maracas, High Crotales; Claves.

Percussion 2: Pair of Maracas; Claves; Low Gong; Deep Tam-tam; Very Deep Tam-tam.

Percussion 3: Single Maraca; Claves; Large Suspended Cymbal.

Percussion 4: Pair of Maracas; Low Crotales.

Almost as ubiquitous as the inclusion of piano in many twentieth-century chamber ensembles is the presence of the harp. The pictograms favored by the composers in their stage diagrams are as varied as those for the keyboard members of the ensemble. A somewhat simplified silhouette of the instrument, however, has served for many of the composers surveyed, including Boulez in this voice and small instrumental ensemble. More detailed are his designs for piano, celesta, and vibraphone. Visually the layout in this score closely resembles that used by Roman Haubenstock-Ramati in his *Ständchen* (*See:* Example #334), in particular the designs for the piano and harp. There are only minor differences in the two composers' depictions of the celesta and vibraphone.

Example #361. Gilbert Amy: *Inventions* (1961).

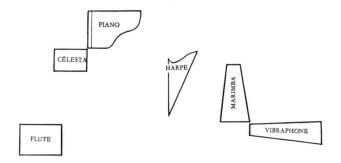

Like *Actions for Six* of Bernard Rands (*See:* Example #333), Amy's work does not require a conductor. The composer suggests that one of the instrumentalists may beat time in certain rhythmically difficult passages. To play the celesta, the pianist has only to turn the piano stool. Pictograms for three types of percussion beaters (hard xylophone, semi-hard vibraphone, and soft) are indicated in Amy's preliminary instructions and are present in the score itself. When four sticks are required simultaneously, the symbols conform to those shown in Example #536. The pianist is required to have two scores, one for the piano part, the other for the celesta. If the latter instrument is a large one, the composer says, the player may stand up to play, or else merely turn the piano stool.

Example #362. Jakob Gilboa: *The Jerusalem Chagall Windows* (1964).

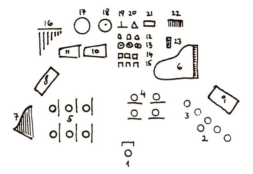

1) Conductor; 2) Solo Mezzo-Soprano; 3) 5 Singers; 4) 4 Violas; 5) 6 Recorders; 6) Piano; 7) Harp; 8) Celesta; 9) Harmonium; 10) Vibraphone; 11) Marimbaphone; 12) 3 Cowbells; 13) 3 Temple Blocks; 14) 3 Tom-toms; 15) 3 Bongos; 16) Bells; 17) Small Tam-tam; 18) Small Chinese Gong; 19) Cymbals & Crotales; 20) Triangle; 21) Side Drum; 22) Glass Windchimes; 23) Glockenspiel.

Tightly compressed as it is, this stage diagram is precise and admirably clear. The pictograms are individually designed and entirely unambiguous, in particular those for the harp, piano, and most of the percussion instruments.

Example #363. Jack Fortner: *S pr ING* (1966).

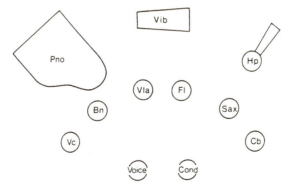

This work is for female voice and nine players, the singer's text based on poems by e.e. cummings. The seating arrangement of the instrumentalists is typical of many twentieth-century works: the string and woodwind or brass players are not grouped together but alternate their positions in the ensemble.

Example #364. Henri Lazarof: *Omaggio* (1968).

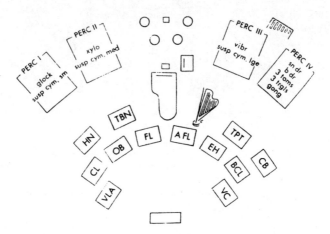

Not identified by means of terminology in addition to their symbols are the timpani, chimes, piano, celesta, and harp. Added labels would be superfluous as their distinctive shapes are self-evident.

Example #365. Henri Lazarof: *Third Chamber Concerto for 12 Soloists* (1974).

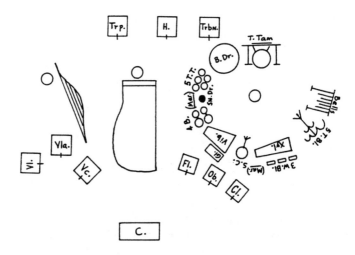

Percussion: Tubular Bells; 5 Temple Blocks; 3 Woodblocks; Maracas; Xylophone; Suspended Cymbal; Glockenspiel; Bass Drum; Vibraphone; 4 Bongos; 5 Tom-toms; Snare Drum; Tam-tam.

According to the composer's plan, the three solo strings, harp, and piano constitute one group; the three brass and three woodwinds, together with the percussion, form another entity. The discerning score reader will wonder why the right side of the piano bulges out rather than curves in. (*See also:* Examples #332 and #366).

Example #366. Gilbert Amy: *Seven Sites for 14 Players* (1975).

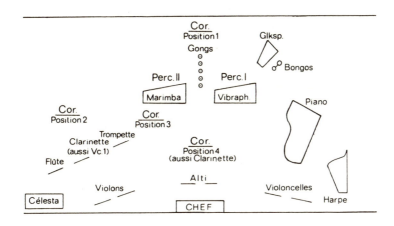

Percussion I: Vibraphone; Glockenspiel; 2 Bongos; 5 Gongs.

Percussion II: Marimbaphone (also Gongs).

Three of the soloists in this work (horn, clarinet, and violoncello 1) are to move to alternative positions during the course of the music. The placement of the celesta is curious, removed as it is from where the piano and harp are stationed.

All Instruments Non-representational

As the following section will illustrate, some composers of chamber works have chosen to simplify their suggested platform set-ups by bypassing all pictographic identification of the instruments involved in their scores. Instead, boxed or circled numbers and/or instrumental abbreviations suffice to locate the desired positions of the ensemble members. Logically enough, this practice has also been applied to compositions for solo instruments or voices with chamber ensemble.

Example #367. Francis Miroglio: *Magies* (1960).

Percussion: Snare Drum; Bass Drum; Timpano; Large Tam-tam; Chinese Block; Maracas; Whip; Tambourine; Guïro; Jazz Flute.

An early work by this composer, his stage diagram is not typical of his usual detailed depiction of the instrumental forces involved. The soloist in this work is a soprano, accompanied by ten instruments, hardly an orchestra as Miroglio has labeled it.

Example #368. Kenjiro Ezaki: *Moving Pulses* (1961).

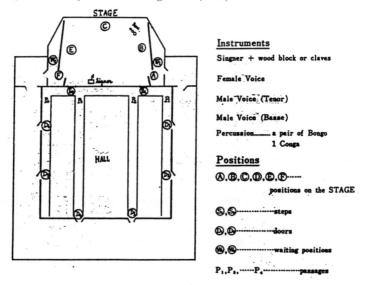

The "Signer" (*Note:* labeled "Singner" [sic] under "Instruments" in the pictogram) in this work is the conductor, who also plays a woodblock or pair of claves. The three vocalists must walk to various positions on the stage (A—F), or run off-stage to the doors leading into the auditorium (D), sometimes slowly, sometimes, noisily, through the passages (P) or aisles.

Example #369. Gunther Tautenhahn: *Double Concerto for Horn and Timpani* (1969).

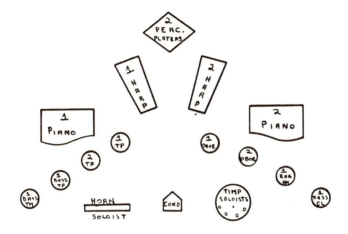

Percussion: Xylophone, Large Gong; Cymbals; Triangle; Snare Drum.

It cannot be claimed that either the piano or the harp pictograms in this diagram are truly representational. They do, however, serve their purpose without ambiguity. The timpani symbol is generic, but gives no indication of their individual sizes; four drums seem to be designated.

Example #370. Roque Cordero: *Musica Veinte* (1970).

Percussion I: Vibraphone; 5 Temple Blocks; Suspended Cymbal; Small Gong; Tenor Drum; Pair of Cymbals.

Percussion II: Xylophone; 2 Woodblocks; 2 Tom-toms; 2 Maracas; Large Gong; Snare Drum.

Five singers (two sopranos, two altos, and one baritone) are part of this ensemble of five woodwinds, two brass, six strings, and two percussionists, none of which are depicted literally in the composer's stage diagram.

Example #371. Enrique Raxach: *Paraphrase* (1971).

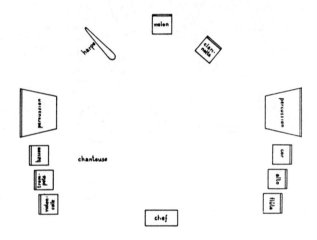

Percussion (Stage Right): Marimba; Vibraphone; Snare Drum; Chinese Suspended Cymbal; Large Suspended Cymbal; 4 Tom-toms; Bamboo Windchimes.

Percussion (Stage Left): Glockenspiel; Tubular Bells; Hi-hat Cymbal; 2 Bongos; Suspended Cymbal; Tam-tam; 2 Conga Drums.

A second stage diagram, not included here, shows the six instrumentalists stationed just below the two percussion sections, but this time they are arranged in a semi-circle at the front of the stage, and the vocalist is positioned in the direct center of the platform. A supplementary list of mallets and beaters is accompanied by pictographs for each; in the score they appear in conjunction with the instrument name. Two double bass bows are also required, one for each percussionist, but minus symbolic representation.

Example #372. William Hellerman: *Stop/Start* (1973).

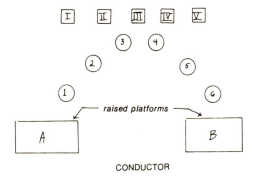

This work is designed for two soloists (A, B), six players of any instruments, but each within a specified range (1—6), and a five-part sectional group of instruments (I—V), such as a woodwind, a brass, or a string quartet.

Example #373. Simon Bainbridge: *People of the Dawn* (1975).

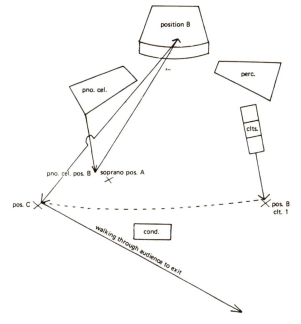

Percussion: Chimes; 4 Chinese Tom-toms; 4 Tuned Burmese Gongs (optional); Vibraphone; Marimba; 2 Tam-tams; Finger Cymbals.

The above ensemble consists of two clarinets, bass clarinet (shown at right), piano, celesta (on the left), and soprano voice. Clarinet 1 also plays soprano saxophone while Clarinet 2 plays another bass clarinet. The pianist and soprano are responsible for the tam-tams, and the soprano also plays finger cymbals. As shown by the arrows, all of the ensemble members, except the percussion, move to the positions indicated.

Example #374. Sydney Hodkinson: *November Voices* (1975).

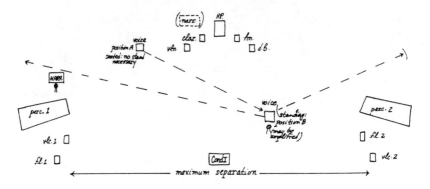

Percussion 1: Vibraphone; 1 Timpano; 2 Tom-toms; Crotales.

Percussion 2: 1 Timpano; Large Bass Drum; 2 Tom-toms; 2 Triangles; Crotales.

A "Ceremony for Voice, Narrator, and Instruments," as the composer labels the work, calls for three woodwinds, horn, harp, four strings, and percussion on stage. plus a brass septet off-stage. Surrounding the audience in the hall, or seated in the rear aisles or in the balcony, are so-called "Bell Percussion" extras—players who strike such metallic instruments as crotales, triangles, and Orff chimes.

Example #375. Joseph Pehrson: *De Rerum Natura* (1976).

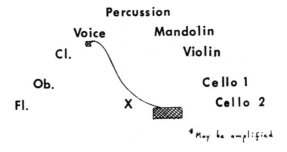

Percussion: 5 Cencerros; 2 Guïros; Crotales; Tambourine; Maracas; Slapstick; Temple Blocks; Indian Bells; Tam-tam; 2 Suspended Cymbals; Hand Cymbals; 2 Bongos; 3 Tom-toms; Claves; Chinese Woodblocks; Thundersheet.

A tenor voice is the soloist in this chamber work that includes three woodwinds and three strings, in addition to a fairly extensive percussion ensemble. As indicated, the voice may be amplified, the microphone and loudspeaker shown abstractly.

Example #376. Elliott Schwartz: *Chamber Concerto IV* (1981).

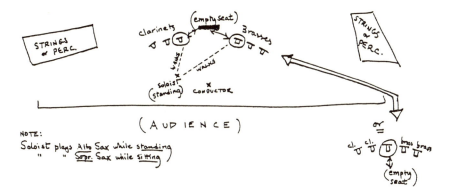

Percussion I: Glockenspiel; Tubular Chimes; Large Tam-tam; 4 Tom-toms; 1 Kettledrum.

Percussion II: Xylophone; 2 Kettledrums; Snare Drum; Triangle; Suspended Cymbal.

Percussion III: Vibraphone, 1 Kettledrum; Bass Drum; 3 Woodblocks; Suspended Cymbal.

Alternative seatings characterize this stage diagram; the string instruments or the three percussions may be situated at either stage left or stage right, and the brasses can be seated either on or off the platform, as shown by the arrow signs. The saxophone soloist is to walk from a standing position next to the conductor to the empty chairs as indicated. An intriguing comparison between this particular score of the composer and *Telly* (*See:* Example #465) again demonstrates Schwartz's fondness for unconventional platform set-ups, as well as an obvious predilection for a theatrical atmosphere permeating the unfolding of the composition.

Example #377. Azio Corghi: *". . . Promenade" dans l'île de la liberté* (1989).

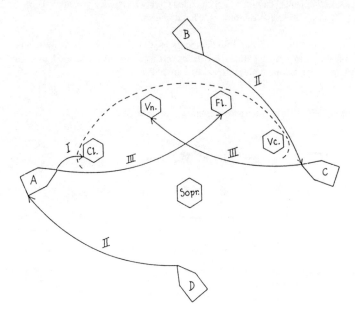

True to its title, Corghi's composition involves detailed movement of all the players save the cellist and the soprano soloist, shown by the arrows from *D* to *A, B* to *C, A* to *Cl.* and *Fl.*, *C* to *Vn.*

Orchestra or Symphonic Band

Pictographic procedures in the stage diagrams of late twentieth-century orchestra and symphonic band scores mainly duplicate those to be found in percussion and chamber music ensembles. That is to say, the percussion and keyboard instruments, and occasionally the harp, are depicted in visually recognizable terms, while the remaining forces are mostly identified by other means. These range from individual instrument names (Examples #381, #386, #391-393), sectional terms (Examples #395, #396), abstract symbols (Examples #388, #398), to a mixture of these various identifiers (Examples #378, #389, and #394)—all representing characteristic instances of these pictographic procedures.

Percussion Instrument(s) Only Representational

Example #378. Karel Husa: *Music for Prague* (1968).

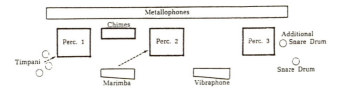

Metallophones and Percussion: 3 Timpani; Chimes; Marimba; Vibraphone; Xylophone; 3 Antique Cymbals; 3 Triangles; Cymbals; 3 Suspended Cymbals; Bass Drum; 3 Tam-tams; 3 Tom-toms; 2 or 3 Snare Drums.

There are two versions of this work, one for full orchestra and the other for concert band; both utilize identical stage set-ups for the percussion. The work calls for a minimum of five percussionists, although only three are shown in the diagram. Also, no pictogram is included for the xylophone among the four mallet instruments.

Example #379. Carlos Roqué Alsina: *Themen II* (1974).

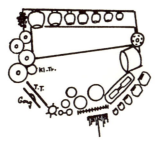

Percussion I: Almglocken; Vibraphone; Wood Windchimes; Sizzle Cymbal; Whistle; Bongos; Guïro; Temple Blocks; Cymbals; Tom-tom; Wood Drum; Sleighbells; Gong; Tam-tam; Bass Drum; Snare Drum; Off-stage Piccolo.

Themen II is scored for one percussionist and string orchestra. As shown, the percussion instruments form a tightly organized circle surrounding the player. It is not evident from the diagram whether the percussion ensemble is to be placed in front of or behind the group of string players. Nor are the components of the string ensemble itself included in the platform set-up; one surmises that the grouping of the members, wheter limited in number or extensive, is traditional in their placement.

Example #380. Donald Martino: *Ritorno* (1978).

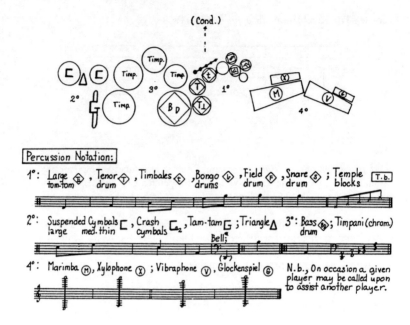

Ritorno is scored for a modest-sized orchestra, including celesta, harp, and a four-part percussion section. Only the latter is pictographically indicated in the score itself, the symbols identical to those used by Martino in some of his other works. (*See:* Examples #307, #421, and #422).

Keyboard Instrument(s) Only Representational

Example #381. Michael Tippett: *Concerto for Orchestra* (1963).

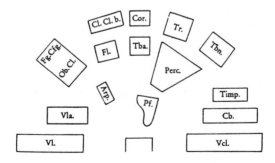

Percussion: Timpani; Triangle; Wood Drum; Cymbals; Tam-tam; Military Drum; Snare Drum; Bass Drum; Xylophone.

The piano in Tippet's work is not a solo instrument, even though it occupies a prominent place on the stage. It will be noted that the percussion section is situated in front of the brasses rather than behind them, as is customary. In the score itself all of the instruments do not appear in their normal order, but according to groups or small ensembles that remain unchanged for an entire movement of the composition.

Example #382. Carlos Roqué Alsina: *Schichten per orchestra da camera* (1971).

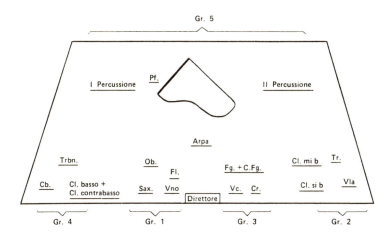

Percussion I: Marimba; 2 Bongos; 4 Tom-toms; 2 Tambourines; Bass Drum; Triangle; 2 Cymbals; Tuned Gong; Large Tam-tam; Crotale; Maracas; Temple Block; Windchimes.

Percussion II: 2 Timpani; 2 Bongos; 4 Tom-toms; Tambourine; Triangle; 2 Cymbals; Tam-tam; Crotale; Flexatone; Maracas; Temple Block; 3 Bells; 2 Small Bottles; Chains.

This is one more example of a composer's stage set-up in which the woodwind, brass, and string instruments are not grouped by section but are mixed together, here according to a five-part arrangement (Gr. 1—5). Each grouping, except Gr. 5, consists of four instruments, comprising soprano (Gr. 1), alto (Gr. 2), tenor (Gr. 3), and bass (Gr. 4) tessituras. The instruments in Gr. 5 (piano, harp, and percussion) provide an all-encompassing range that covers the entire gamut of available pitches.

Example #383. Joseph Schwantner: *Aftertones of Infinity* (1979).

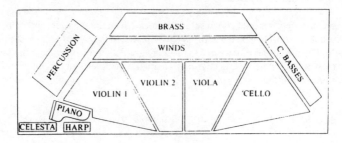

Percussion: Bell Tree; 3 Tom-toms; Small Suspended Triangle; Bass Drum; Tam-tam; Small Suspended Cymbal; 3 Timbales; 2 Small Gongs; 3 Japanese Temple Bells; Large Suspended Cymbal; Large Suspended Triangle; Large Bass Drum; Large Tam-tam; Tubular Bells; Glockenspiel; Marimba; Vibraphone; Crotales.

Included in the composer's listing of the woodwind instruments required in his score, is the stipulation that the oboist and English horn player are each to strike two crystal glasses, which are to be taped to small stools next to each player.

Example #384. John Downey: *Yad Vashem* (1994).

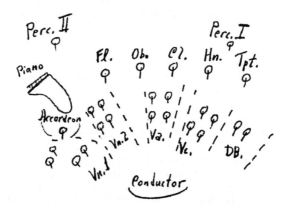

Percussion: Tambourine; Woodblocks; Bass Drum; 3 Tom-toms; Snare Drum; Maracas; Cowbell; 2 Anvils; Suspended Cymbal; Xylophone; Vibraphone; Triangle; Ratchet; 2 Sirens; Tenor Drum; Tubular Chimes; Orchestra Bells; Large Tam-tam; Glass and Metal Windchimes; 2 Timpani; Cymbal on Stand; Glockenspiel; 5 Crotales.

Yad Vashem is the name of the Holocaust Museum in Jerusalem, Israel. Called "An Impression for Chamber Orchestra" by its composer, the instrumentation is for a modest-sized string group plus three woodwinds and two brasses, an accordion, and the percussion listed above. The symbols used to depict the instrumentalists' positions seem to be unique to this composer. (*See also:* Example #352).

Percussion and Keyboard Instrument(s) Representational

Example #385. Karlheinz Stockhausen: *Gruppen für drei Orchester* (1957).

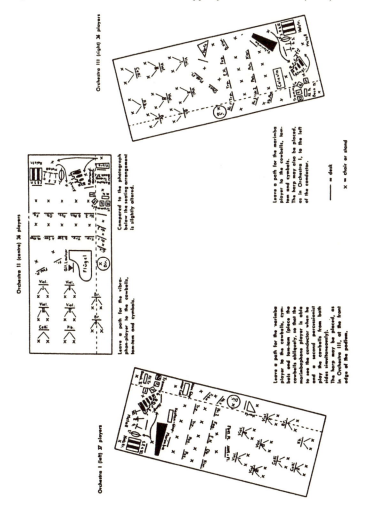

Percussion (Orchestra I): Marimbaphone; Tumba; Glockenspiel; Bongo; 5 Cowbells; Tam-tam; 3 Suspended Cymbals; 2 Wood Drums; Snare Drum; Tom-tom; Side Drum; Tambourine.

Percussion (Orchestra II): Vibraphone; Tumba; Tubular Bells; Bongo; 4 Cowbells; Tam-tam; 3 Suspended Cymbals; 2 Wood Drums; Snare Drum; Tom-tom; Side Drum; Tambourine; 2 Triangles; Ratchet.

Percussion (Orchestra III): Xylorimba; Tumba; 4 Cowbells; Bongo; 3 Suspended Cymbals; 2 Wood Drums; Snare Drum; Tom-tom; Side Drum; Tambourine; Tam-tam.

This pioneering composition for three orchestra, each with its own conductor, has one of the most elaborate and detailed performance diagrams to be found in contemporary score publications. It would be instructive to know whether subsequent performances of the work adhered to Stockhausen's plan used at the premiere. No doubt significant modifications were made by other conductors presenting the work to later audiences.

Example #386. Henri Dutilleux: *IIe Symphonie* (1959).

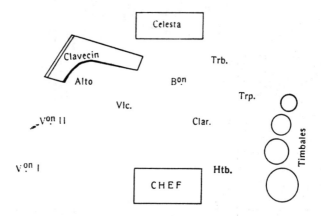

Called by its composer *Le Double*, Dutilleux's second symphony is for a large orchestra and a smaller ensemble of only twelve players, consisting of four strings, three woodwinds, two brasses, timpani, and two keyboards. The composer did not intend to write a modern concerto grosso but only to create a sense of reflected sound images between the two groups. The stage diagram concerns the chamber ensemble exclusively, in which only the clavecin (harpsichord) and timpani are given pictograms.

Example #387. Gilbert Amy: *Triade* (1967).

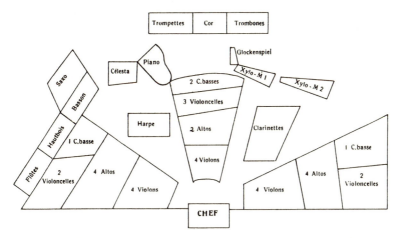

Inspired by a text of Henri Michaux, Amy's work uses no pictograms other than those for the piano and percussion. Of particular interest is the division of the string section into three parts and the separation of the clarinets from the other woodwinds.

Example #388. Girolamo Arrigo: *Infrarosso* (1967).

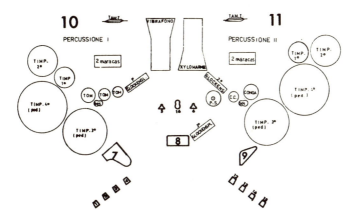

Percussion I: Tam-tam; 2 Maracas; 3 Tom-toms; Bongos; Glockenspiel; Vibraphone; 4 Timpani.

Percussion II: Tam-tam; 2 Maracas; Suspended Cymbal; Bongos; Snare Drum; Conga Drum; Glockenspiel; Xylomarimba; 4 Timpani.

Set-up Codes: 1) Flute (Piccolo); 2) Oboe (English Horn); 3) Clarinet (E-flat Clarinet); 4) Bass Clarinet (A Clarinet); 5) Horn; 6) Trombone; 7) Piano; 8) Celesta; 9) Harp; 10) Percussion I; 11) Percussion II; 12) Violin I; 13) Violin II; 14) Viola; 15) Violoncello; 16) Double Bass.

One might note the unorthodox positioning of the double bass in this stage diagram (16), not with the other strings (10—15) but placed between the horn (5) and trombone (6), presumably for acoustical reasons. Also the odd shapes of the vibraphone and xylophone invite speculation, their designs not duplicated in any other score examined.

Example #389. Henri Lazarof: *Ricercar* (1968).

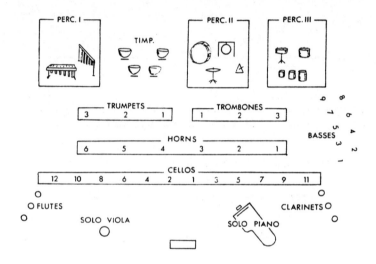

Percussion I: Chimes; Vibraphone.

Percussion II: Gong; Bass Drum; Triangle; Suspended Cymbal.

Percussion III: Snare Drum; Tenor Drum; 3 Tom-toms.

Lazarof's pictographs are precise and commendably consistent from one of his works to another. They provide a striking contrast to the impersonal numerals that identify the orchestral complement of the score. In the score itself, however, the composer relies on conventional terminology to identify both the percussion instruments and the various beaters required, a practice that many other orchestrators favor.

Example #390. Bernard Rands: *Wildtrack 1* (1969).

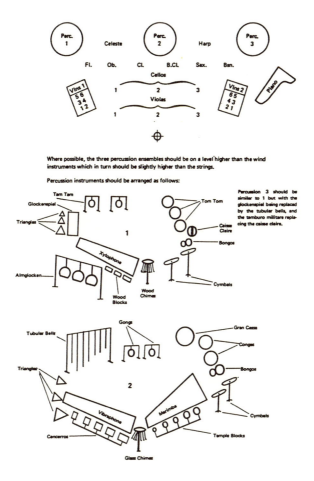

Percussion 1: 3 Triangles; 2 Sizzle Cymbals; 3 Almglocken; 2 Tam-tams; Glockenspiel; Wood Windchimes; 3 Woodblocks; Xylophone; Snare Drum; 2 Bongos; 3 Tom-toms.

Percussion 2: 3 Triangles; 2 Suspended Cymbals; 5 Cencerros; 2 Gongs; Vibraphone; Glass Windchimes; 5 Temple Blocks; Marimba; 2 Bongos; 2 Conga Drums; Bass Drum.

Percussion 3: 3 Triangles; 2 Sizzle Cymbals; 2 Tam-tams; Tubular Bells; Wood Windchimes; 3 Woodblocks; Xylophone; Tenor Drum; 2 Bongos; 3 Tom-toms.

Rands gives both a general seating diagram and set-ups for two of the three percussion ensembles called for, the third group being nearly identical with the first. It is specified that the woodwind players should be on a slightly higher elevation than the strings and the percussion higher still than the winds, including the celesta and harp. The curious shape of the piano symbol duplicates that seen in several previous diagrams (*See:* Examples # 264, #316, and #323, for instance).

Example #391. Gilbert Amy: *D'un espace deploye . . .* (1972).

The following arrangements of the orchestras can be used:

1) "Classical arrangement"

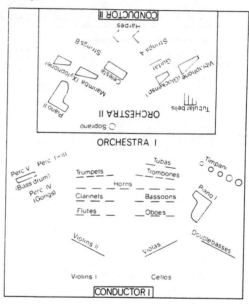

(Orchestra II will be on a higher level than Orchestra I. The conductors face each other.)

2) "Stereophonic" arrangement

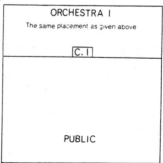

Percussion: 2 Woodblocks; 3 Temple Blocks; 2 Log Drums; Tenor Drum; Bass Drum; Triangle; 2 Anvils; Metal Claves; 3 Suspended Cymbals; 5 Chinese Gongs; 3 Tam-tams; 13 Tuned Gongs; Electronic Organ; Piano.

A unique aspect of this stage diagram is the opposing positions of the two orchestras, the players in Orchestra II (smaller chamber ensemble) having their backs to those in Orchestra I. Also unusual are the two suggested dispositions of the two orchestras, one the "classical," or standard arrangement of the instruments, the other a "stereophonic" layout. Presumably, the public faces both orchestral set-ups, so one is curious as to any difference in the massed sound reaching the audience.

The prevalence of abstract markings for *Orchestra I* other than for the piano and timpani, is in marked contrast to the more detailed symbols for *Orchestra II*, excluding the strings, guitar, and soprano soloist.

Example #392. Tibor Pusztai: *Folii* (1979).

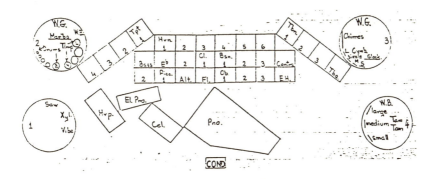

Percussion 1: Xylophone; Vibraphone; Saw.

Percussion 2: Marimba; 4 Timpani; 4 Drums; Bass Drum; Woodblock.

Percussion 3: Chimes; 3 Suspended Cymbals; Sizzle Cymbal; Glockenspiel.

Percussion 4: 3 Tam-tams.

Two unorthodox features of this set-up are the separation of the four percussionists and the trumpets and trombones, who are normally side by side. Two players seem to be required for the piano, celesta, and the electric piano.

Example #393. Steven Mackey: *Journey to Ixtlan* (1986).

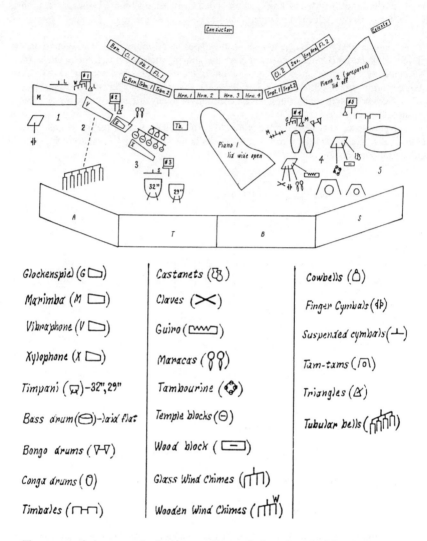

Glockenspiel (G ▭)	Castanets (🎭)	Cowbells (⌂)
Marimba (M ▭)	Claves (✕)	Finger Cymbals (⌀)
Vibraphone (V ▭)	Guiro (〰)	Suspended cymbals (⊥)
Xylophone (X ▭)	Maracas (♀♀)	Tam-tams (/o\)
Timpani (⌓)-32", 29"	Tambourine (◈)	Triangles (△)
Bass drum (⊖)-laid flat	Temple blocks (⊖)	Tubular bells (卅)
Bongo drums (∇∇)	Wood block (▭)	
Conga drums (0)	Glass Wind Chimes (卅)	
Timbales (冂⊣冂)	Wooden Wind Chimes (卅ᵂ)	

The score reader's perspective in this stage diagram is from the rear of the platform looking out to the audience area: choral voices at the back, then the percussion (five players), including the two pianos and celesta, the brasses at the front in a semi-circle, and finally the woodwinds in two groups, facing the conductor. The composer's list of his percussion is accompanied by very precise pictographs of each member. Also included are symbols for music stands and small tables for the hand-held instruments.

Keyboard Instrument(s) and Harp Representational

Example #394. Henryk Gorecki: *1st Symphony* (1959).

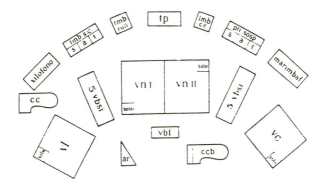

Percussion: Xylophone; 3 Snare Drums (without snares); Tenor Drum; Timpani; Snare Drum (with snares); 3 Suspended Cymbals; Marimbaphone; Vibraphone.

Gorecki's early symphony is for string orchestra and percussion. Included in the ensemble and given pictographic identification in the diagram are piano (cc), clavicembalo (ccb), and harp (ar).

Example #395. Milko Kelemen: *Sub Rosa* (1964).

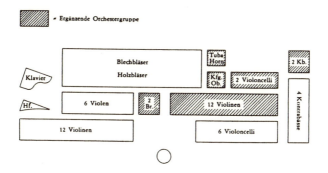

Shaded areas in this stage diagram indicate an additional, optional group of instruments. Not shown here are the two loudspeakers located in the auditorium that reinforce the volume of the final pages of music.

Example #396. George Crumb: *Echoes of Time and the River* (1967).

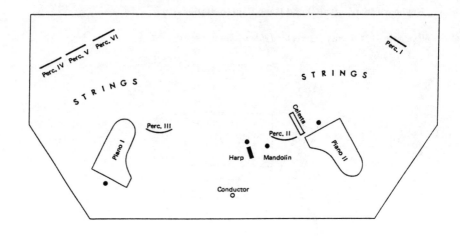

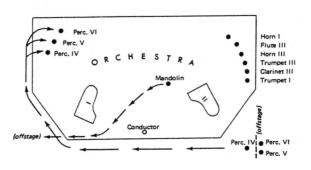

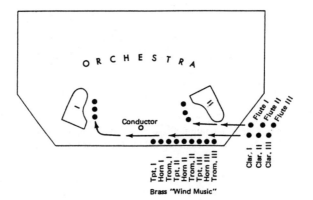

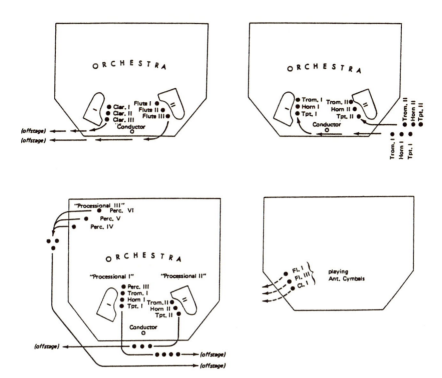

Percussion I: 2 Timpani; Medium Tam-tam; Glockenspiel; 2 Antique Cymbals; Small Suspended Cymbal; Bamboo Windchimes; Large Chinese Temple Gong.

Percussion II: Vibraphone; Large Tam-tam; 2 Antique Cymbals; Medium Suspended Cymbal; 2 Glockenspiel Plates; 2 Large Conga Drums; Glass Windchimes.

Percussion III: Small Tam-tam and Tub of Water; 5 Antique Cymbals; Large Suspended Cymbal; 2 Glockenspiel Plates; Bongos; Cowbells; Tubular Bells; Chinese Temple Bells.

Percussion IV: 2 Antique Cymbals; Small Suspended Cymbal; Pair of Finger Cymbals; Glass Windchimes; 2 Glockenspiel Plates; Sleighbells; Low-Pitched Bell.

Percussion V: 2 Antique Cymbals; Xylophone; 2 Glockenspiel Plates; 2 Timbales; Medium Suspended Cymbal; Glass Windchimes; Bass Drum.

Percussion VI: 2 Antique Cymbals; Very Small Tam-tam; 2 Glockenspiel Plates; Large Suspended Cymbal; Marimba; Glass Windchimes.

Perambulation by woodwind, brass, and percussion players is a prominent feature of Crumb's work, which he subtitled "Four Processionals for Orchestra." The movements of the players are clearly diagramed in the six accompanying platform set-ups for each of the four movements. It is stipulated that the music to be played during the processionals must be memorized, an obvious recognition of reality on the composer's part.

There are, of course, other 20th-century works that feature stage movements by some or all of the performers involved, both instrumental and vocal. Some of these requirements can be seen in Examples #266, #275, #309, #327, #331, #373, #377. #408, and #411. Perambulation is a compositional device that adds a theatrical element to the performance, in addition to modifying the direction, intensity, and timbre of the tones being played or sung. Obviously, there are physical limitations to the device as well as some very practical considerations to solve. The composer cannot very well ask the pianist, the harpist, or the timpanist, for example, to move about while playing! But any instruments easily carried and simultaneously played offer intriguing possibilities for the composer's soundscape.

Example #397. Patrice Mestral: *Relations (Périodes II)* (1967).

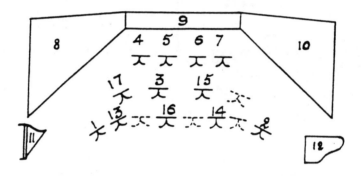

1) & 2): Flutes; 3): Oboe; 4) & 5): Trumpets; 6) & 7): Trombones; 8): *Percussion I:* Vibraphone; 12 Cowbells; 2 Bongos; Bass Drum; 3 Tom-toms; 2 Tumbas; 2 Tam-tams; 2 Suspended Cymbals; 9): *Percussion II:* Chimes; Glockenspiel; Woodblock; 4 Triangles; 5 Chinese Blocks; 2 Tumbas; 2 Timbales; 3 Gongs; 2 Tam-tams; Maracas; Claves; 10): *Percussion III:* Marimba; 2 Tom-toms; 2 Timbales; 2 Suspended Cymbals; 2 Tam-tams; Maracas; Claves; Guïro; Herd Bells; 11): Harp; 12): Piano: 13): Violin I; 14): Violin II; 15) Viola; 16): Violoncello; 17): Double Bass.

Though the composer keeps the brass instruments together in this suggested set-up, the three woodwind and five string instruments are mixed together. a device widely favored by many contemporary composers. The harp pictogram here is commendably accurate, even if somewhat simplified.

Example #398. Hans Werner Henze: *Compases para preguntas ensimismadas* (1970).

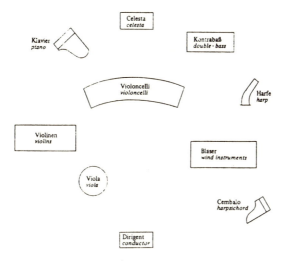

Wind Instruments: Recorder; Flute (Piccolo, Alto Flute); Oboe (English Horn); Clarinet (Bass Clarinet); Horn; Bassoon.

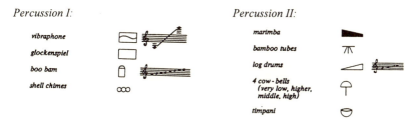

Although the harp is given its own symbol in this diagram, fanciful though it may be, it can hardly be regarded as a true pictogram as its shape in no way conforms to that of the instrument itself. Not shown in Henze's set-up is the positioning of the percussion instruments. Their pictograms, however (as shown here), are present throughout the score as a substitute for conventional terminology. Comparison of this particular diagram with others for Henze's works (such as Examples #1 and #303) demonstrates its relative simplicity and notable reduction of the number of instruments, together with their corresponding symbols required by the composer.

Example #399. Kazimierz Serocki: *Segmenti* (1970).

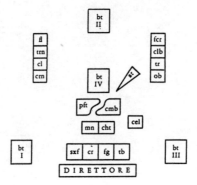

Orchestra: Flute (fl); also Piccolo (ott); Oboe (ob); E♭ Clarinet (cl); Alto Saxophone (sxf); Bass Clarinet (clb); Bassoon (fg); E♭ Cornet (crn); Trumpet (tr); Horn (cr); Trombone (trn); Saxhorn (fcr); Tuba (tb); Electric Mandolin (mn); Electric Guitar (cht); Cembalo (cmb); also Celesta (cel); Piano (pft); and Harp (ar).

Percussion I: Xylophone; Gong; Triangle; 2 Maracas; 2 Bongos; 2 Almglocken; Suspended Cymbals; Hi-hat Cymbal; 5 Temple Blocks.

Percussion II: Vibraphone; Bass Drum; Triangle; 2 Maracas; 2 Almglocken; Suspended Cymbal; Hi-hat Cymbal; 3 Snare Drums.

Percussion III: Marimba; Gong; Triangle; 2 Maracas; 2 Almglocken; Suspended Cymbal; Hi-hat Cymbal; 5 Chinese Blocks; 3 Timbales.

Percussion IV: Chimes; Guïro; Triangle; 4 Suspended Bottles; Deep Tam-tam; Sistrum; 3 Snare Drums; Tambourine; 2 Suspended Cymbals.

Segmenti is yet another example of the contemporary composer's fondness for alternating woodwind and brass instruments in groups, rather than always keeping each choir as a separate entity. The diagram is also notable for its pairing of piano/cembalo and mandolin/guitar. Serocki's composition also includes pictograms for five kinds of percussion mallets and beaters, and these appear throughout the score, while the instruments themselves are identified only by nomenclature.

Example #400. Robert Wittinger: *Costellazioni* (1971).

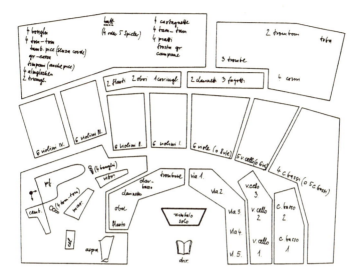

Percussion: 4 Bongos; 4 Tam-tams; Small Drum (without snares); Bass Drum; Timpani; 4 Almglocken; 2 Triangles; 4 Castanets; 4 Tom-toms; 4 Suspended Cymbals; Chimes; Large Slapstick.

In the majority of stage diagrams that show the position of a conductor, this is usually depicted either by terminology or by an abstract symbol. Here it appears as the open pages of a score, a clever device, and one that is present in Example #240, as well. The solo instrument located just in front of the conductor is a Hungarian cimbalon. It is accompanied by a chamber orchestra that includes piano, harpsichord, celesta, and harp (surrounding the soloist), with the full orchestra behind.

As is the frequent custom in many contemporary scores, the flutist also plays alto flute, while the pianist is responsible for the harpsichord part; the two instruments are shown closely joined together. Two of the percussionists also double on other instruments—the vibraphonist strikes bongos and the marimbaphonist plays on tom-toms. These auxiliary members are conveniently stationed behind the two mallet players. Wittinger specifies that four or five percussionists are required. He also indicates that the solo cimbalon is to be amplified at certain points in the composition.

Percussion, Keyboard Instrument(s), and Harp Representational

Example #401. Henri Lazarof: *Textures* (1970).

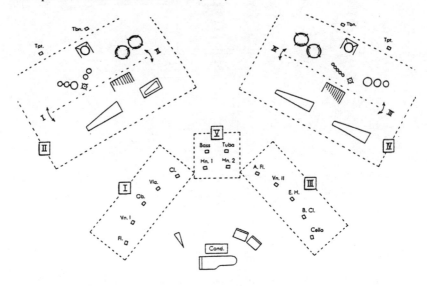

Percussion II: Tam-tam; 2 Timpani; 3 Tom-toms; Snare Drum; Tenor Drum; Chimes; Vibraphone; Xylophone; Glockenspiel; Suspended Cymbal.

Percussion IV: Tam-tam; 2 Timpani; 5 Temple Blocks; Suspended Cymbal; Snare Drum; Tenor Drum; Bass Drum; Chimes; Vibraphone; Xylophone.

Another elaborate stage diagram from this composer shows an unusual separation of the trumpets and trombones from the horns and tuba. Also, the alternation of woodwinds and strings in groups I and III is equally unorthodox in any orchestra set-up. As to be expected, harp, celesta, and harmonium are placed adjacent to the conductor's podium, the latter two instruments to be managed by one player. The pianist in *Textures* is, of course, the soloist with the entire ensemble. Unlike several other of Lazarof's depictions of the piano (refer to Example #365, for instance), its shape here conforms to actuality; it does not have the strange lefthand bulge to be observed in others of his stage diagrams.

No mallet or beater pictograms for the percussion show up in the score itself, nor does the composer indicate his preferences by means of standard terminology.

Example #402. Michael Colgrass: *Letter to Mozart* (1976).

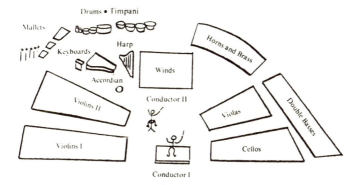

An amusing detail of this stage diagram is the stick figures of the two conductors, each are waving their baton. Conductor I is responsible for the tutti strings while Conductor II directs only the solo strings of the two-part chamber orchestra. The keyboards are piano and celesta (one player) and the mallets are glockenspiel, vibraphone, and xylophone. Other than the timpani depicted, the remaining percussion include chimes, woodblocks, mounted cowbells, temple blocks, suspended cymbal, snare drum, crotales, and crash cymbals.

All Instruments Non-representational

Many contemporary composers who advocate the presence of a stage diagram of instrumental seating in their scores, nonetheless have abandoned all references to pictographic representation of the instruments required in their works. Terminology or else simple abstract symbols merely indicate the relative positions of the various players. Perhaps the composers reasoned that a plethora of identifying pictograms would have unduly complicated their essential performance arrangements. For whatever justification by each of the composers whose stage diagrams are next cited, their set-ups vary widely in terms of complexity or absence thereof.

Non-representational can mean many things, of course, to many composers: some enclose the instrumental names within boxes or circles or other designs (Examples #407 and #414); others number the instrument locations (Examples #406, #409, #415, and #417), or else use simple abstract symbols such as in Examples #405 and #411. If accurate pictograms are not the objective, it matters little which method of identification the composer chooses.

Example #403. Vittorio Fellegara: *Variazioni (Frammenti II.) per orchestra da camera* (1961).

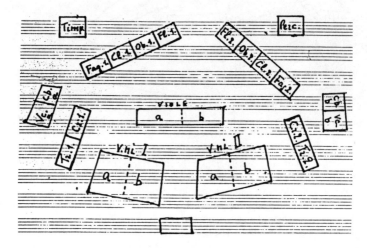

In addition to the timpani, separately indicated, the other percussion include 3 suspended cymbals, 3 snare drums, temple block, bass drum, and tam-tam, all played by one percussionist.

Example #404. Motohiko Adachi: *Konzert für Saiteninstrumenten* (1963).

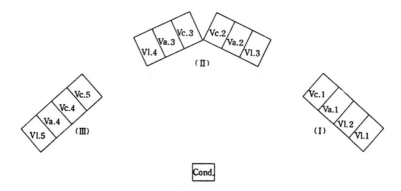

Example #405. Yasushi Akutagawa: *Music for Strings No. 1* (1963).

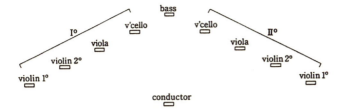

These two Japanese compositions for strings (Examples #404 and #405) employ the most basic of stage set-ups, and no further explication seems to be necessary.

Example #406. Friedrich Cerha: *Spiegel II* (1963).

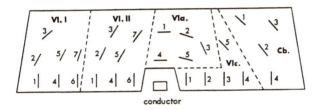

Cerha's diagram is unique in that it merely numbers the stands of the string players, indicating their angles one to another. Obviously, those players at some remove from the conductor must be able to see the conductor without hindrance.

Example #407. Gilbert Amy: *Diaphonies* (1965).

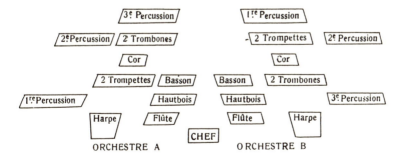

ORCHESTRA A:
 Percussion I: Xylomarimba; 3 Tam-tams; 2 Bongos; 3 Chinese Woodblocks;
 3 Maracas; Small Snare Drum.
 Percussion II: Vibraphone, 3 Tam-tams.
 Percussion III: Xylomarimba; 2 Gongs.

ORCHESTRA B:
 Percussion I: Xylomarimba; Suspended Cymbal; Low Tam-tam; Gong; 2 Pairs of
 Bongos; 3 Chinese Woodblocks; 3 Maracas.
 Percussion II: Vibraphone; Tam-tam; 2 Bongos.
 Percussion III: Xylomarimba; 3 Tam-tams; Deep Gong; Snare Drum; Temple Block.

Even though the composer has subtitled the work "For double ensemble of 12 instruments."
the forces constitute a two-part small orchestra of woodwinds, brasses, and percussion, plus
two harps. Amy requests that the two ensembles be separated as much as possible, not evident
in the diagram spacing.

Example #408. Harrison Birtwistle: *Verses for Ensembles* (1968).

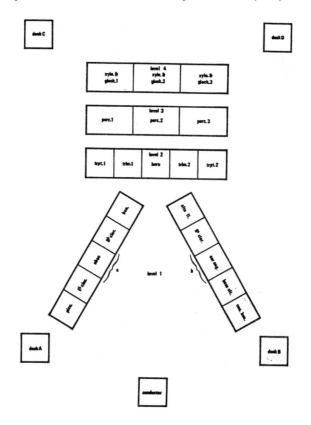

Percussion 1: Glockenspiel; Xylophone; 4 Bongos; 2 Conga Drums.

Percussion 2: Glockenspiel; Xylophone; 4 Cowbells; 4 Suspended Cymbals; 4 Timbales.

Percussion 3: Glockenspiel; Xylophone; 4 Temple Blocks; Side Drum; Tenor Drum; Large Timbale; Bass Drum.

Four different levels for his instrumental components are required in Birtwistle's score. Desks A to D are to be occupied at various times by soli woodwinds and brasses, their movements indicated by diagrams in the score itself.

Example #409. Friederich Cerha: *Mouvements I—III* (1968).

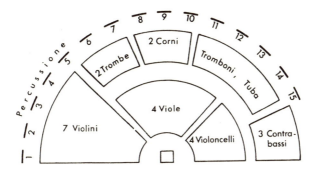

Percussion: 1) Whip; Maraca; Little Bells; 2) Small Whip; Claves; Triangle; 3) Maraca; Guïro; 4) Woodblock; Small Suspended Cymbal; Celesta; 5) Temple Block; Anvil; 6) Woodblock; Tambourine; Cowbell; 7) Ratchet; Bongo; Castanets; Cardboard Tube; 8) Xylophone; Cardboard Tube; Crotale; 9) Claves; Side Drum; Piano; 10) Toy Frog; Sleighbells; 11) Crotale; Violin; 12) Toy Frog; Glass Goblet; 13) Glockenspiel Bar; Piccolo; 14) Metal Block; Mandolin; 15) Temple Block; Guïro; Hammond Organ.

The numberings of the percussion instruments in the stage diagram are duplicated in the score, where the numbers relate to a single-line staff for each instrument.

Example #410. Betsy Jolas: *Quatre plages* (1968).

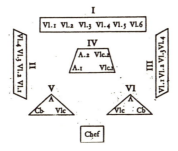

Jolas says that the six groupings of the string orchestra should be separated one from the other as far as possible. The members of groups II and III must turn sideways so as to face the conductor.

Example #411. Elliott Carter: *Concerto for Orchestra* (1969).

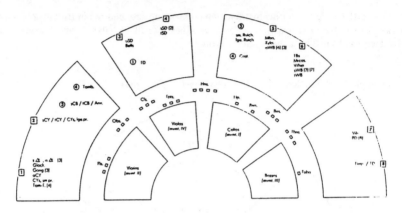

Metal Percussion: Glockenspiel (Tubophone); Tubular Bells; Vibraphone; 2 Triangles; 2 Cowbells; 3 Suspended Cymbals; Gong; Large Tam-tam; Tambourine; Anvil; Pair of Small Cymbals; Pair of Large Cymbals.

Wood Percussion: Marimba; Xylophone; 3 Woodblocks; 3 Temple Blocks; 2 Ratchets; Castanets; Slapstick (Whip); Maracas; Guïro.

Skin Percussion: 3 Snare Drums; Tenor Drum; Large Bass Drum; 5 Timpani.

"The listener will more easily grasp the composer's intent," writes Carter, "that of having the various strands of music heard from different directions surrounding the listener—if the distribution of players helps to emphasize the four separate instrumental groups indicated in the stereo seating diagram." The boxed numbers in the four percussion groups identify the positions of the eight players. The circled and bracketed numbers indicate locations to where certain players must move during the performance, from one group to another.

Example #412. Gunther Schuller: *American Triptych* (1969).

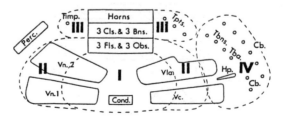

Percussion: Glockenspiel; Vibraphone; Snare Drum; Bass Drum; Woodblock; 4 Suspended Cymbals; Sizzle Cymbal; Hi-hat Cymbal; 2 Gongs; Tam-tam; Timpani.

Large Roman numerals designate the rotating orbits or tracks certain instruments are to follow during the first of the three movements that constitute Schuller's work. Each track has its own instrumentation: *I:* first two stands of Violin I, II, Viola, and Violoncello; *II:* the remaining stands of Violins I, II, Flutes, and Oboes; *III:* Clarinets, Bassoons, Horns, Trumpets, and Timpani; *IV:* Trombones, Tuba, and the remaining stands of Viola, Violoncello, and all Double basses. Only the percussion section lies outside of the stipulated orbits.

Example #413. Ib Nørholm: *Fluktuationen* (1974).

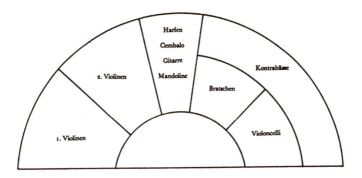

The layout for this score is straightforward and simple, minus any pictographic symbols. No signs are given for the contact microphones to be attached to the four plucked instruments at stage center, nor the location of loudspeakers and other electronic equipment.

Example #414. Oliver Knussen: *Symphony No. 3* (1979).

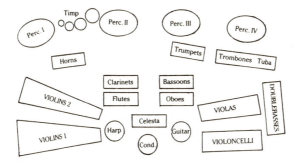

Percussion I: 4 Timpani; Crash Cymbals; Large Tam-tam; Small Anvil; Triangle; Tambourine; Crotales.

Percussion II: Small Suspended Cymbal; Hi-hat Cymbal; Small Bass Drum (with pedal); 2 Temple Blocks; Whip; Maracas; 2 Bongos.

Percussion III: Suspended Cymbal; Tambourine; Claves; Glockenspiel; Xylophone; Marimba.

Percussion IV: Side Drum; Tenor Drum; Large Bass Drum; Tubular Bells; Suspended Cymbal; Guïro; 2 Vibraslaps.

Although four percussionists (in addition to the timpanist) are indicated in this diagram, six players in all are required, according to the composer's performance directions. The orchestral layout is fairly standard, even to the positions of the celesta, harp, and guitar.

Example #415. Georgy Dmitriev: *"Ice Congealing, Ice Floating"* (1983).

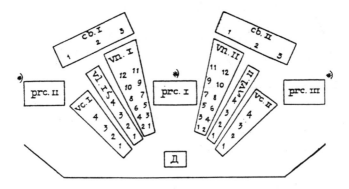

Percussion I: Bongo; 2 Tom-toms; 1 Timpano; Tambourine; Triangle; Cowbell; 3 Suspended Cymbals; Tam-tam; Marimba; Glockenspiel; Vibraphone; 2 Tubular Bells.

Percussion II: Bongo; Claves; 2 Tom-toms; Small Timpano; Triangle; Cowbell; 3 Suspended Cymbals; Tam-tam; Marimba; Vibraphone; 2 Tubular Bells.

Percussion III: Bongo; Claves; 2 Tom-toms; Large Timpano; Triangle; Cowbell; 3 Suspended Cymbals; Tam-tam; Marimba; Vibraphone; 7 Tubular Bells.

Duplication of instruments between the three percussion groups is a salient feature of this work. Also, the positioning of these ensembles in relation to the string orchestra is unorthodox, separated as they are by two string groups.

Example #416. Nicolaus A. Huber: *Go ahead* (1988).

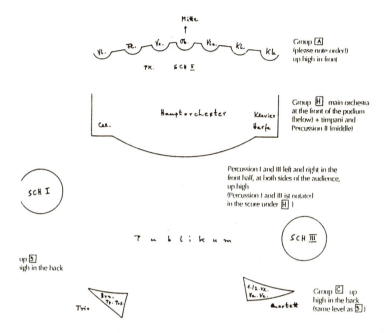

Huber's compositional essay is another example of a performer layout in which portions of the orchestra surround the audience. A trio of brass instruments and a string quartet are placed at the back of the hall and two percussion groups are at the sides, all four presumably in the balconies. Individual pictograms for the percussion are unnecessary here as the choice of instruments is up to the players, selected from the categories of wood, skin, and metal.

Example #417. John Corigliano: *Symphony No. 1* (1989).

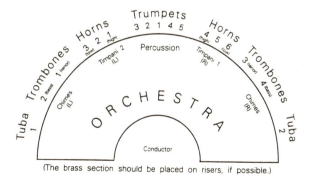

(The brass section should be placed on risers, if possible.)

Percussion: Glockenspiel; Vibraphone; Marimba; Xylophone; Crotales; 2 Sets of Chimes; Snare Drum; Field Drum; Tenor Drum; 3 Tom-toms; 3 Roto-toms; 2 Bass Drums; Suspended Cymbal; Finger Cymbals; Anvil; Metal Plate; Brake Drum; Tam-tam; Triangle; 3 Temple Blocks; Tambourine; Flexatone; Whip; Ratchet; Police Whistle.

Unorthodox in this seating chart is the positioning of the percussion ensemble in front of the brasses rather than behind them. Five or six players are required in addition to two timpanists, and the orchestra is a large one. Not shown in the diagram are either the piano or the harp, both important members of the orchestral forces.

Orchestra (or Symphonic Band) and Solo Instrument(s) or Voice(s)

Percussion Instrument(s) Only Representational

Example #418. Darius Milhaud: *Concerto for Percussion and Small Orchestra* (1930).

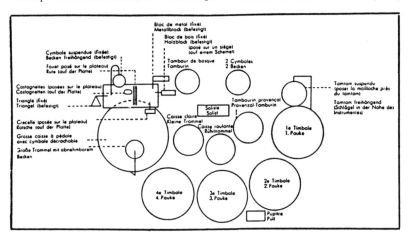

The orchestra in Milhaud's concerto consists of 2 flutes, 2 clarinets, trumpet, trombone, and a small string ensemble. His score represents the earliest use of a stage diagram uncovered by this researcher.

Example #419. Donald Martino: *Triple Concerto* (1978).

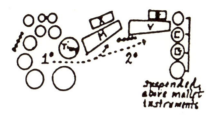

Percussion: Glass Windchimes: ●━━━━ Snare Drum: ○ Bongos: ⊙◯

Temple Blocks: ○ Timbales: ○ Tom-toms: ○

Medium-sized Bass Drum: ○ 2 Timpani: (Timp.) Marimba: [M]

Xylophone: [X] Vibraphone: [V] Glockenspiel: [G]

Suspended Cymbals: Ⓒ Tam-tams: Ⓖ

Martino's *Triple Concerto* is for soli soprano, bass, and contrabass clarinets, accompanied by a modestly-sized orchestra including piano and celesta. Neither of these two latter instruments, however, is included in the composer's suggested stage set-up.

Example #420. Robert Suderburg: *Concerto for Solo Percussionist and Orchestra* (1979).

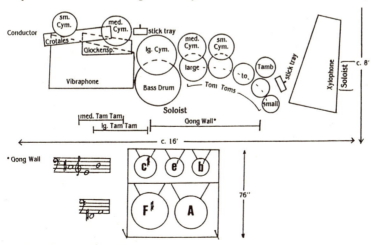

Other than conventional pictograms for the glockenspiel, vibraphone, and xylophone, the remaining percussion are depicted by the equally conventional O-symbol. Of special interest are the indicated dimensions of the stage layout, the width and depth in feet and the height of the gong wall in meters.

Example #421. Donald Martino: *The White Island* (1985).

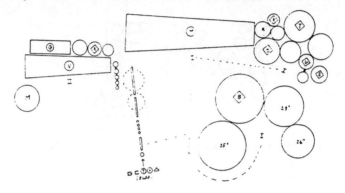

2 Percussion : 5 Temple blocks ⊡ ; Bass drum ⊗, 2 Tom-
toms ⟨T⟩, 2 Timbales ⟨L⟩, 2 Bongo drums ⟨b⟩, Military drum
⟨D⟩, Snare drum ⟨S⟩; medium and large Tam-tams **G**, medium
and large Cymbals **C**; 3 Timpani , 6 Roto-toms ⟨R⟩; Marimba ⟨M⟩, 4 Tubular chimes ⟨T⟩, 1 Tuned Gong ⊙, Vibraphone ⟨V⟩,
Glockenspiel ⟨G⟩, 2 Antique Cymbals △.

A full chorus is here accompanied by a chamber orchestra that includes piano, celesta (not indicated in the diagram), and 37 percussion instruments (two players). The exact dimensions of the three timpani is a practice not often seen in other scores by Martino.

Example #422. Donald Martino: *Concerto for Alto Saxophone and Orchestra* (1987).

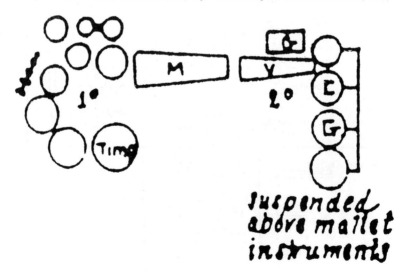

The solo saxophone in this work is accompanied by a fairly small orchestra: six woodwinds, five brass, piano, and strings in addition to the percussion shown in the stage diagram. The percussion pictograms in this stage diagram are nearly exact copies of those that appear in Martino's *Triple Concerto* (*See:* Example #419), thus confirming the consistency of this composer's practice of pictographic notation.

Example #423. James Currow: *Concertino for Solo Percussionist and Symphonic Band* (1988).

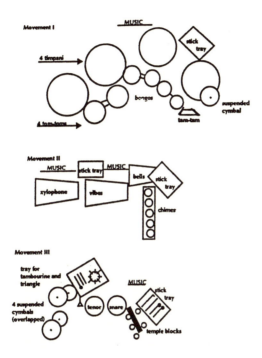

This is one of the very few works, researched by this writer, composed for a percussion soloist accompanied by symphonic band. The composer's stage diagram is distinguished by its different percussion set-ups for each of the work's three movements. It is also unique in that the various kinds of percussion beaters required are included in the stage set-up, these laid at hand on five stick trays. In addition the position of the necessary music stands are represented for each movement of the work.

Keyboard Instrument(s) Only Representational

Example #424. Francis Poulenc: *Concert pour 2 Pianos et Orchestre* (1932).

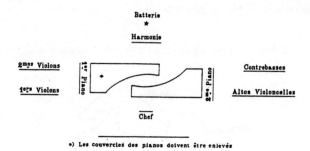

Harmonie (Woodwinds and Brasses): 2 Flutes; 2 Oboes; 2 Clarinets; 2 Bassoons; 2 Horns; 2 Trumpets; 2 Trombones; Tuba.

Batterie (Percussion): Snare Drum; Military Drum; Tenor Drum; Bass Drum; Tambourine; Castanets; Triangle.

This concerto is one of the earliest twentieth-century scores to include a stage diagram in its preliminary pages, coming as it does only two years after Darius Milhaud's *Concerto for Percussion and Small Orchestra (See:* Example #418). As in many other, subsequent works that include the piano, the composer has indicated that the piano lids be removed.

Example #425. Elliott Carter: *Double Concerto for Harpsichord and Piano with Two Chamber Orchestras* (1961).

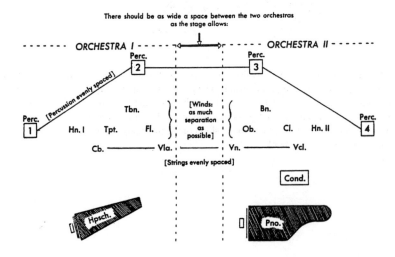

Percussion 1: Slapstick; Anvil; Cowbells; Woodblocks; Triangle; 2 Suspended Cymbals; Tambourine; Gong; Deep Tam-tam.

Percussion 2: 5 Temple Blocks; Triangle; Suspended Cymbal; Snare Drum; Tenor Drum; Tambourine; Tom-tom.

Percussion 3: Crotales; Claves; Maracas; Suspended Cymbal; 2 Snare Drums; Tenor Drum; Bass Drum.

Percussion 4: Crotales; 4 Bongos; 2 Tom-toms; Suspended Cymbal; Snare Drum; Guïro; Bass Drum.

A noteworthy feature of Carter's specifications is his stipulation of the spacings between the instruments in both orchestras, a directive not often encountered in other contemporary set-ups. An alternative position of the solo piano is suggested, with the player facing the conductor at stage center. Also, two conductors are recommended because of the occasional metric independence of the two orchestras. A distinctive requirement of the percussion is that the membranophones, metallophones; and lignophones (wood instruments), be arranged so as to form a continuous "scale" of pitches, from high to low.

Example #426. Paul Méfano: *Paraboles* (1964).

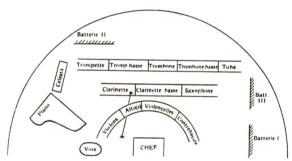

Percussion I, II, and III:
Version A: *Version B:*

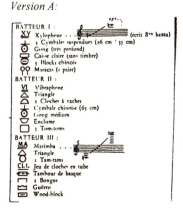

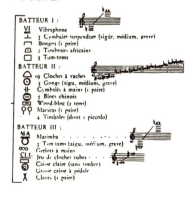

A dramatic soprano is the vocal soloist in Méfano's work. Curious is the disposition of the three percussion groups, with Batterie II widely separated from III and I. The composer is clear and succinct in his instrumental pictograms, which appear throughout the score pages in lieu of terminology. He states that the two versions of his work are equally feasible, *Version A* includes only the first two of the three vocal texts by Yves Bonnefoy, while *Version B* is restricted solely to the third poem.

Example #427. Donald Martino: *Concerto for Piano and Orchestra* (1965).

In arranging the orchestra the percussion ensemble must be in the position shown below, i.e., stage rear center. The orchestral pianist should be able to see both the soloist and the conductor but his instrument must not be visible to the audience. Since the percussion, harp, piano, celesta and mallet instruments frequently perform as a timbral unit, these instruments should be grouped together. Furthermore, their frequent use to double virtually every other instrument in the orchestra would suggest some central placement. In view of these considerations the following stage plan is proposed:

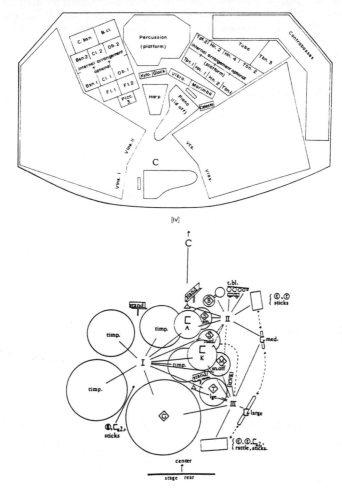

Percussion: 2 Claves: ©; 2 Tambourines: ⓣ; Guïro: ⓖ; 2 Woodblocks: ⓦⒷ; 2 Triangles: (△); Rattle; 2 Suspended Cymbals: [A, [K; 2 Gongs: (⊏G⊐); 5 Temple Blocks: ⊽⊽⊽, 2 Bongos: ⓑ ; 2 Snare Drums: Ⓢ ; Military Drum: Ⓜ ; Large Tom-tom: ⓣ ; Crash Cymbals: [a 2; 4 Timpani: O .

Two pictograms appear on the opening pages of Martino's score: one is for the entire orchestra and the soloist, the other for the required percussion ensemble. Only the two pianos, one in the orchestra and the other for the soloist, are depicted. Three of the listed percussion instruments do not appear as actual pictograms in the ensemble diagram—guïro, triangle, and rattle. In the score itself a combination of symbols and terminology identifies the percussion.

Example #428. Elliott Carter: *Piano Concerto* (1966).

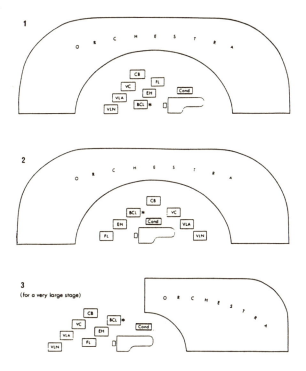

Not many composers specifically designate two or more alternative seating arrangements for their orchestra, as does Carter in his piano concerto. The boxed instrumental abbreviations are members of the "concertino" ensemble, while the orchestra proper serves as the "ripieno" group. Uncharacteristically for this composer, the percussive resources are limited to six pedal timpani, played by two percussionists.

Example #429. Knut Nystedt: *Lucis creator optime* (1968).

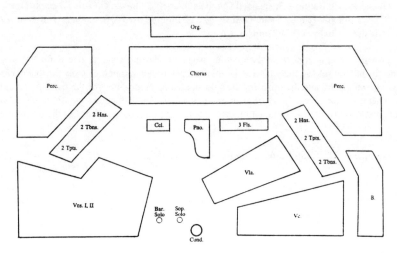

Percussion (Stage Right): 2 Timbales; Snare Drum; Tenor Drum; 2 Woodblocks; Glockenspiel; 3 Suspended Cymbals; Tam-tam; Xylophone.

Percussion (Stage Left): 2 Timbales; Snare Drum; Tenor Drum; 2 Woodblocks; Vibraphone; 3 Suspended Cymbals; Chimes; Gong.

The total resources of this composition comprise soli soprano and baritone voices, a chorus of mixed voices, and full orchestra. Three percussionists are needed for each percussion group, and the pianist also plays celesta. Stage right and left are from the orchestra's perspective looking out to the audience.

Example #430. Toru Takemitsu: *Asterism* (1968).

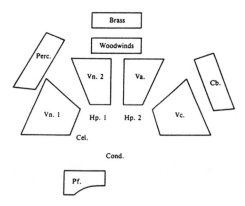

Percussion: Glockenspiel; Marimba; Vibraphone; Xylophone; Tubular Bells; 3 Suspended Cymbals; 3 Gongs; 2 Tam-tams; 5 Crystal Glasses or Small Metallic Bells or Bottles; Castanets; 4 Tom-toms; Tenor Drum.

Asterism is an astronomical term for a group of stars or a constellation. It also comes from cystallography, signifying the property of some cystallized minerals that show a star-like luminosity. The concept of the work is typical of Takemitsu's colorful imagination, but his stage diagram is exceedingly plain though entirely serviceable.

Example #431. Luciano Berio: *Concerto per due pianoforti e orchestra* (1973).

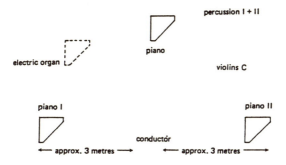

A full orchestra is required for Berio's concerto, with the violins divided into three parts (A, B, and C); only the third section is shown in the composer's diagram, for reasons left unexplained. The orchestral piano is treated coloristically as though it were a percussion instrument.

Example #432. Luciano Berio: *"points on the curve to find . . ."* (1974).

Berio's work is in reality a concerto for piano and thirty-two instruments—a chamber orchestra, in other words. Only the solo instrument receives pictographic representation in the composer's stage diagram.

Example #433. Luciano Berio: *Coro per voci e strumenti* (1976).

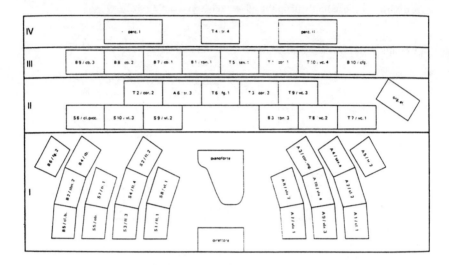

Percussion I: 5 Almglocken; 3 Tom-toms; 5 Tam-tams; Snare Drum; Chimes; Guïro; Sleighbells; Maracas; Crotales; Castanets; Ratchet.

Percussion II: 3 Woodblocks; 2 Bongos; 3 Tom-toms; 5 Tam-tams; Bass Drum; Tambourine; Guïro; Glockenspiel; Sleighbells; Crotales.

The composer stresses the fact that the four indicated levels for the instruments and singers are absolutely essential. Even though the piano occupies a prominent position on the stage, it is not a solo instrument as it was in the previous Berio composition.

Coro per voci e strumenti reveals a marked contrast in pictorial design to that found in certain others of Berio's scores; save for the piano. the orchestral entity is here depicted in almost neutral terms, quite unlike the elaborate and highly detailed diagrammatic layout for *Circles* (*See:* Example #275).

Example #434. Louis Andriessen: *Velocity* (1983).

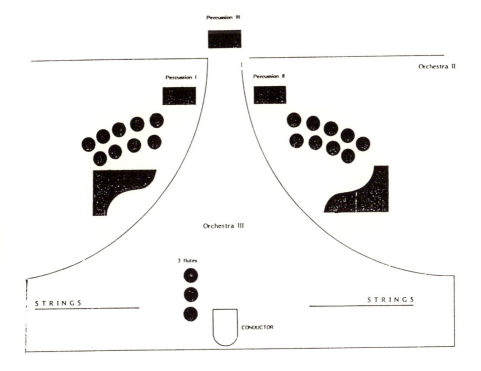

Percussion I: 4 Woodblocks, Piano.

Percussion II: Bass Drum; 2 Tom-toms.

Percussion III: 4 Woodblocks; Piano.

Three flutes are the soloists in this triple-orchestra score, the complement of Orchestra I and Orchestra II being identical. The genesis of the blackened symbols in the stage set-up will be recognized as the astronomical sign for the new moon, also utilized in Example #248.

Percussion and Keyboard Instrument(s) Representational

Example #435. Michael Colgrass: *Déjà vu* (1977).

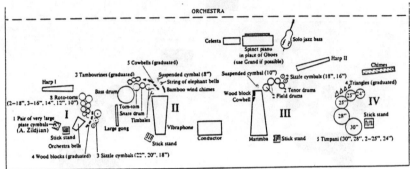

For solo percussion quartet with full orchestra, an interesting feature of this score is the substitution of a spinet piano for the normally expected oboes. As is the practice of many composers who devise elaborate pictographic stage diagrams for their percussion, the instruments themselves (in the score proper) are indicated by means of standard nomenclature.

Keyboard Instrument(s) and Harp Representational

Example #436. Warren Benson: *Helix* (1966).

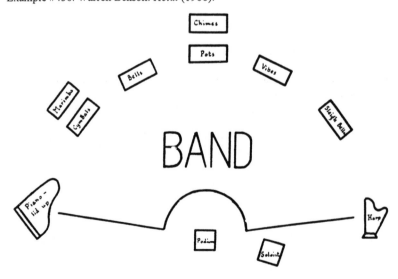

The soloist in Benson's work is a tuba player. Among the accompanying instruments only the piano and harp are represented pictographically. Percussion instruments are specified by their name and the band members not at all.

Example #437. Milko Kelemen: *Changeant for Violoncello and Orchestra* (1968).

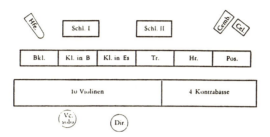

Schlagzeug (zwei Spieler):
I Röhrenglocken (es, cis, g, fis), Crotales (e, f, es, des, d), Becken (3), Kleine Trommel, Militär-Trommel, Rühr-trommel, Bongos (3), Woodblocks (5), Tempelblocks (5), 2 Steine, Almglocken (5), Triangel (3), Großer Gong, Gong mit Buckel, Lotosflöte

II Crotales (b, a, g), Xylophon, Becken (3), Congas (2), Tamtam, Eisenplatten (3), Glasflaschen (3), Steinplatten (3), Schellenbaum, Glaschimes, Kleine Kette, Messe-glöckchen, Flexaton, 2 Steine

Because this work is for violoncello with orchestra. Kelemen dispenses with a cello section, and the violas, as well. The same player manages both the cembalo and the celesta.

Percussion, Keyboard Instrument(s) and Harp Representational

Example #438. Maurice Ohana: *Synaxis* (1966).

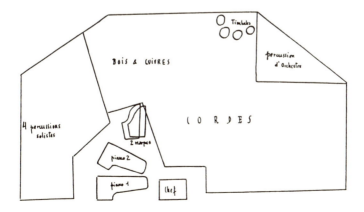

Solo Percussion 1: 7 Tuned Tom-toms; Snare Drum; Deep Tam-tam; 4 Tuned Chinese Cymbals; Crotales; Xylophone.

Solo Percussion 2: Tenor Drum; Tambourine; Tarole; Maracas; 2 Woodblocks; 2 Deep Gongs; 2 Crash Cymbals; Vibraphone.

Solo Percussion 3: 2 Timbales; 4 Temple Blocks; Maracas; Deep Tam-tam; Suspended Cymbal; Triangle; 2 Crash Cymbals; Low Woodblock; Xylomarimba.

Solo Percussion 4: 2 Bongos; 2 Saharan Drums; Bass Drum; 2 Deep Gongs; 3 Suspended Cymbals; 2 Crash Cymbals; Glockenspiel.

Of all the orchestral percussion required in Ohana's score, only the four timpani are depicted. Evidently the composer did not feel it was essential to specifiy the individual positions of the woodwind, brass, and string members of the orchestra, reserving pictorial representation only for the two pianos and the two harps.

Example #439. Henri Lazarof: *Spectrum* (1973).

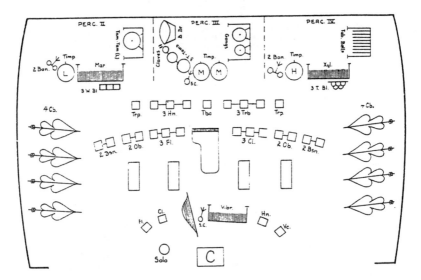

Percussion I: Vibraphone; Medium Suspended Cymbal.

Percussion II: Marimba; 2 Bongos; 3 Woodblocks; Large Tam-tam; 1 Timpano.

Percussion III: Bass Drum; 3 Tom-toms; 2 Timpani; Medium and Small Gongs.

Percussion IV: Xylophone; 5 Temple Blocks; 2 Bongos; Tubular Bells; 1 Timpano.

A detailed stage set-up characterizes this work for solo trumpet, orchestra, and tape. Pitted against the full woodwind and brass sections are a single cello, and eight double basses. The latter instruments are arrayed on two sides of the platform, while three wind members (flute, clarinet, horn), harp and several percussion face the conductor at the front.

All Instrument(s) Non-representational

The final group of citations for solo instrument, voice, or chorus with orchestra that display stage set-ups suggested by the composer, employ no pictographic symbols whatsoever. Visual representation of the solo and instrumental positions is accomplished by terminology and by a generalized sketch of the desired arrangement on the concert platform.

Example #440. Olivier Messiaen: *Trois petites liturgies de la présence divine* (1944).

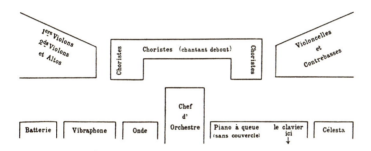

The *Choristes* in Messiaen's work comprise eighteen women's voices and the *Batterie* (percussion) consists of maracas, Chinese cymbal, and deep tam-tam. *Onde*, of course, is the *Ondes martenot* (called *ondes musicales* by its inventor Maurice Martenot), an electronic instrument beloved by French composers, especially Messiaen, who was one of the first to use the instrument in his scores.

Example #441. Oliver Messiaen: *Oiseaux exotiques* (1956).

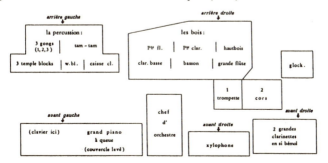

According to the composer, the piano part in this work is so important that it almost assumes the status of a concerto for the instrument. The piano's prominent position on the platform is shared by xylophone and a pair of clarinets, all three being of prime importance in creating the orchestral fabric of birdcalls. Although the five percussion instruments called for in this score are used extensively throughout the music, no indication is given by Messiaen as to the most suitable beaters for projecting their sounds through the consistently animated orchestration. What is prominent on every page are the birdcall identifiers, a literal ornthological catalogue of avian communication.

Example #442. Hans Werner Henze: *Antifone* (1960).

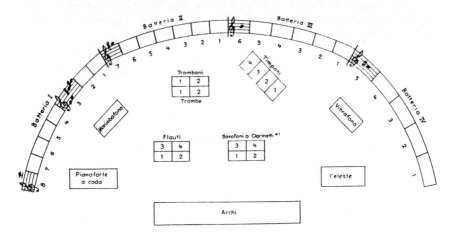

Percussion I: 8): Glockenspiel Plate; 7-4): Triangles; 3): Crotales; 2-1): Suspended Cymbals.

Percussion II: 7): Glockenspiel Plate; 6): Snare Drum; 5-4): Tom-toms; 3): Almglocken; 2-1): Tam-tams.

Percussion III: 6): Glockenspiel Plate; 5): Snare Drum; 4): Tenor Drum; 3): Suspended Cymbal; 2): Tom-tom; 1): Deep Tam-tam.

Percussion IV: 5): Glockenspiel Plate; 4): Bass Drum; 3): Large Suspended Cymbal; 2-1): Tam-tams.

Archi in Henze's composition are eleven solo strings. Although no percussion pictograms appear either in the stage diagram or in the score pages, various symbols for the percussion beaters are included in the separate instrumental listing and throughout the score.

Example #443. Witold Szalonek: *Concertino per flauto ed orchestra da camera* (1963).

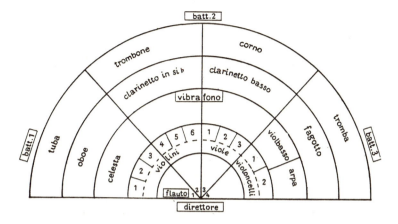

Percussion 1: Small Triangle; Gong; Small Cymbal; Large Glass Bottle; Snare Drum; Tenor Drum (with snares); 3 Woodblocks; Maracas.

Percussion 2: Medium Triangle; Medium Cymbal; Medium Glass Bottle; Medium Drum (with snares); Castanets; Timpani.

Percussion 3: Large Triangle; Tam-tam; Large Cymbal; Small Glass Bottle; Wood Drum; Small Drum (with snares); Tom-tom; 2 Bongos.

Woodwinds and brasses in the above score are single in number, and the strings are few in each section. The position of the vibraphone is curious, separated as it is from the three percussion groups.

Example #444. Theodore Antoniou: *Violinkonzert* (1965).

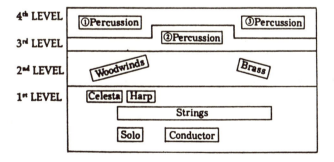

Percussion: Xylophone; Glockenspiel; Bass Drum; Side Drum; Large Tom-tom; Slit Drum; Tam-tam; 3 Suspended Cymbals; 3 Triangles; 3 Bongos; 3 Tom-toms; 3 Woodblocks; 3 Temple Blocks.

Although the composer indicates three percussion players in the stage layout of the orchestra, he does not specify which instruments each is to play. Presumably, it is up to the three percussionists to determine the arrangement of the required instruments. It will be noted that progressively higher platform levels are stipulated for the four choirs of instruments.

Example #445. Arrigo Benvenuti: *Polymérie (Versione I)* (1966).

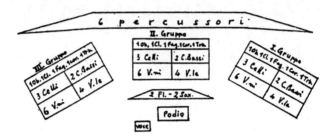

Percussion I: Timpani; 3 Bongos; Bass Drum; Tenor Drum; Claves; 2 Triangles; Whip.

Percussion II: Xylophone; Vibraphone; Cowbells; 2 Sanctus Bells.

Percussion III: Guitar; Maracas; 2 Sanctus Bells.

Percussion IV: Piano; Organ.

Percussion V: Celesta; Glockenspiel; 2 Tumbas; Small Sleighbells; 2 Electric Bells.

Percussion VI: 3 Gongs; Cymbals; 2 Suspended Cymbals; 3 Drums; 2 Tom-toms; 2 Temple Blocks; 2 Woodblocks; 2 Guïros; Large Tam-tam.

Polymérie is for solo voice and a three-part orchestral ensemble. The large number of percussion instruments required in this score evidently made it impractical to provide pictographs for each member of the six ensembles.

Of the six percussionists called for here (actually, only five, as the players of the piano and organ can hardly be thought of as percussionists), *No. VI* has the largest number of instruments, and *No. III* the fewest. A two-page preliminary listing of performance techniques in the score includes symbols for five kinds of percussion beaters—soft wool, hard wood, metal, wirebrush, and a hammer. Also indicated are the customary symbols for using the handles of the various sticks (shown in Example #524).

Example #446. George Crumb: *Star-Child* (1977).

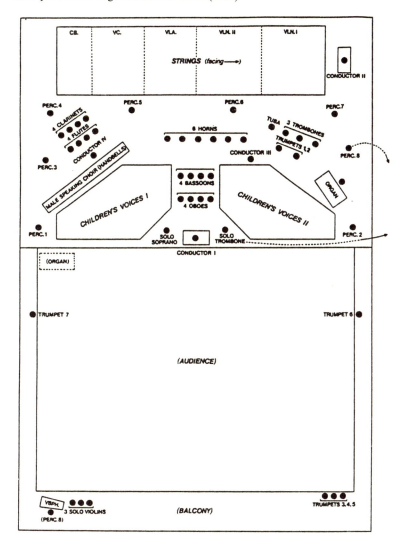

Percussion 1: Small Tam-tam; Large Suspended Cymbal; 4 Crotales; Sleighbells.

Percussion 2: Medium Tam-tam; Large Suspended Cymbal; 4 Crotales; Sleighbells.

Percussion 3: Large Tam-tam; 3 Timpani; Cymbal (to lay on Timpano head); Bass Drum; 2 Suspended Cymbals; Tambourine; Crotale; Claves; Glockenspiel; Tubular Bells.

Percussion 4: Large Tam-tam; Small Log Drum; Iron Chain; 4 Tom-toms; Sizzle Cymbal; Xylophone; Glockenspiel; Vibraphone; Flexatone; Bongo; Wind Machine.

Percussion 5: Large Tam-tam; Maraca; Sizzle Cymbal; Sleighbells; Large Suspended Cymbal; Mounted Tambourine; 4 Tom-toms; Crotales; Claves; Flexatone; Tubular Bells; Thunder Sheet.

Percussion 6: Maraca; Medium Tam-tam; Sleighbells; Sizzle Cymbal; Tenor Drum; 4 Tom-toms; Medium Suspended Cymbal; Conga Drum; Claves; Tubular Bells; Thunder Sheet.

Percussion 7: Large Log Drum; Iron Chain; Sizzle Cymbal; Bass Drum; Small Tam-tam; 4 Tom-toms; 4 Pot Lids; Medium Tam-tam; Glockenspiel; Flexatone; Conga Drum; Tenor Drum; Claves.

Percussion 8: 3 Timpani; Cymbal (to lay on Timpano head); Bass Drum; Tambourine; Large Tam-tam; Low-pitched Bell; Crotale; Snare Drum; Large Suspended Cymbal; Flexatone; Claves; Vibraphone.

There are a number of unusual aspects to this work. First is the placing of five trumpets, three solo violins, and a vibraphone in the rear balcony of the hall. Next is the scattering of the eight percussion groups around the circumference of the stage, and finally, the requirement that there be three conductors to coordinate the contributions of all the instruments, the male speaking choir, the two choruses of children's voices, and the solo soprano voice and trombone—a daunting task for any performance aggregation of players and singers.

Example #447. Bernard Rands: *Aum* (1977).

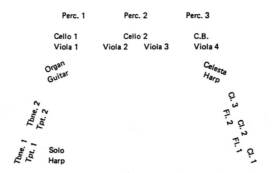

Percussion 1: Bongos; 3 Almglocken; Marimba; Glockenspiel; Tam-tam; Medium Suspended Cymbal; Tenor Drum; 2 Tom-toms; 2 Gongs.

Percussion 2: Bongos; Small Suspended Cymbal; Military Drum; Conga Drums; Vibraphone; Tam-tam; 2 Gongs.

Percussion 3: Large Suspended Cymbal; Marimba; Tubular Bells; 5 Temple Blocks; Snare Drum; Tam-tam; 2 Tom-toms; 2 Gongs; Bongos.

This is a prime example of a stage diagram reduced to its bare essentials. The instruments are designated only by nomenclature, while showing their desired positions on the platform. An interesting comparison might by made with its extreme opposite—the very elaborate and detailed pictographic stage diagrams to be seen in Examples #333 and #390.

Example #448. John Harbison: *Concerto for Double Brass Choir and Orchestra* (1989).

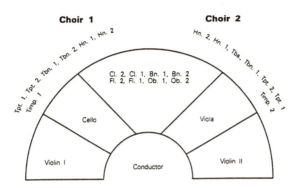

The double choir of brasses are placed in the normal position of these instruments in any orchestral set-up, at stage rear rather than at the front as one might expect for solo members. Presumably, this is because of their overpowering sonic contribution to the music.

Electronic Components

A unique phenomenon of the mid to late twentieth century is the presence of electronic components among the aggregate of sound resources required in a composer's score. This modern technology has made an impact on contemporary music in the area of pictographic notation no less than in the realm of computer generated composition. Quite a few recently-published scores have included specific indications of microphone, tape deck, amplifier, mixer console, and loudspeaker positionings in their prefatory stage diagrams. Some composers have been very detailed and precise in their directions for the electronic set-up in their work and often quite literal in their pictographic depictions of the required components. (*See:* Examples #450 and #472). Others have been less literal in the visual aspect of microphones, loudspeakers, and other equipment, relying on simplified, almost abstract, symbols to show the desired position of these components, as in Example #455, for instance.

To illustrate the extent and variety of pictographic representations of the various electronic constituents in recent compositions, the examples are grouped according to their total resources: 1) Percussion Ensemble(s) (including keyboard instrument[s]); 2) Chamber Music Ensemble; 3) Orchestra; 4) Choral Ensemble; 5) Solo Instrument(s). Within each category the citations are listed chronologically. as they were in all the previous sections of this compendium.

Percussion Ensemble

Example #449. Roman Haubenstock-Ramati: *Jeux 2 for Two Percussionists* (1963).

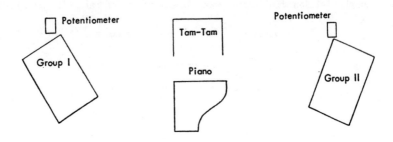

Group I and Group II: As large a number of instruments as possible. *Metallophones:* Tam-tams; Gongs; Cymbals; Hi-hat Cymbals; Metal Sheets; etc.; *Membranophones:* Timpani; Bongos; Tom-toms; Conga Drums; Drums (from small to large); etc.; *Idiophones:* of Metal; Wood; Glass; Plastic; Cardboard; etc.

Several unusual specifications distinguish this work for a duo of percussionists. Each player is to select as extensive an array of instruments, as possible, from the three indicated categories, and each is responsible for controlling the output of a potentiometer (volume control) placed near at hand. Both the piano and the oversized tam-tam are to be provided with contact and directional microphones (not shown in the diagram), and the piano is to have its lid removed and the sustaining pedal fastened down. Thus, the maximum of timbral volume and variation is assured in any performance of this composition.

Typical of many twentieth-century foreign publications, Haubenstock-Ramati's score comprises fourteen pages of preliminary, detailed performance instructions in both German and English. There are many columns of pictograms and other symbols explaining unorthodox methods of striking various of the percussion instruments and of playing in the piano interior directly on the strings. The score. itself, consists of but a single sheet, divided into grids, each occupied by one of the illustrated pictograms. The page can be read in any direction, a device common to many experimental works of our time.

Example #450. Lejaren Hiller & G. Allan O'Connor: *Computer Music for Percussion and Tape* (1963).

SUGGESTED SET-UP FOR MOVEMENTS I AND III

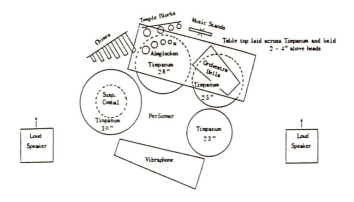

SUGGESTED SET-UP FOR MOVEMENT II

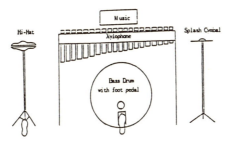

As most present-day composers know, the combining of pre-recorded electronic sound materials with live performance, whether solo, ensemble, or orchestra, began in the early 1950's; the *Rhapsodic Variations for Tape and Orchestra* (1953-54) by Otto Luening and Vladimir Ussachevsky was one of the very earliest such examples. It was not until a decade later, however, that composers began to include the positioning of their electronic equipment in any stage diagrams prefacing their scores. In the example above, pictographic reference to the electronic components is limited to the two required loudspeakers, non-representational though they be. No indication is given by the composers as to the location of the necessary tape machine and/or amplifier for relaying the recorded sound to the speakers; one assumes they are to be located off-stage.

Example #451. Lejaren Hiller: *Machine Music* (1964).

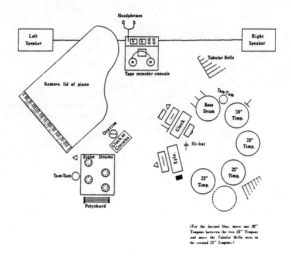

Percussion: 2 Tam-tams; 3 Triangles; 4 Brake Drums; Polychord; Ocarina; 2 Glockenspiels; Ratchet; 2 Cymbals; Tubular Bells; Bass Drum; 4 Timpani; Xylophone; Hi-hat Cymbal; Guïro; Woodblock; Suspended Cymbal; Snare Drum; 2 Slit Drums; Alarm Clock.

Hiller's pictorial renditions of the 2-channel tape recorder central to this work, as well as the headphones to be worn by its operator, are authentically depicted. Curiously, however, the pictograms for certain of the percussion instruments shown in this stage diagram do not agree with those in Hiller's listing of the instruments on a facing page. For example:

Instrument:	Diagram:	Listing:
Polychord:		
Bass Drum:		
Timpani:		
Tubular Bells:		
Glockenspiel:		
Xylophone:		

Neither the ratchet or the alarm clock included in the listing are identified with pictograms in the stage plan.

Example #452. Jacob Druckman: *Animus II* (1969).

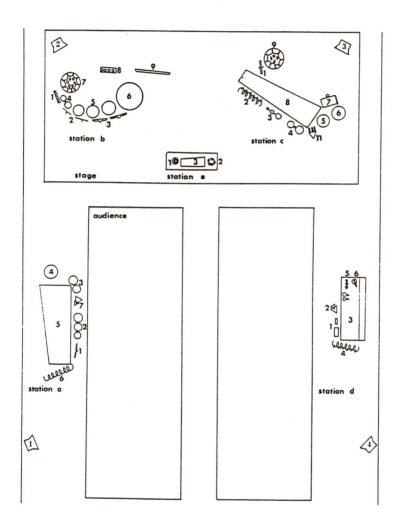

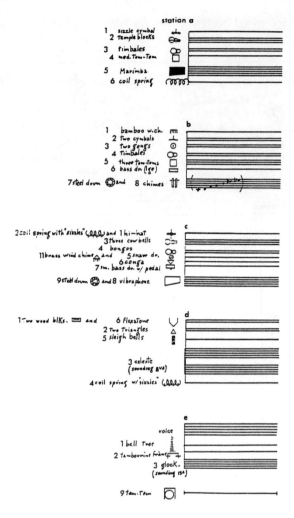

For female singer and two male percussionists, the subject matter of Druckman's work, according to the composer, is "The sensuality of ensemble playing amplified to the point of eroticism." The singer's stage position is not indicated as she is to move about freely during the performance. The percussionists are to move between the five indicated stations, *station a* to *station e*. The four numbered loudspeakers are placed as indicated in the diagram. Not shown, however, are such essentials as tape deck, mixer or amplifier, and microphones.

Example #453. Cristobal Halffter: *Noche Pasiva del Sentido* (1970).

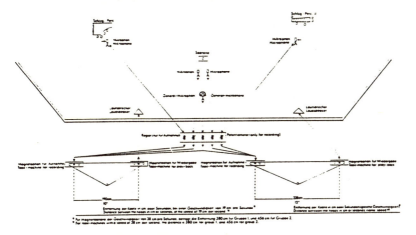

Percussion I: Gong; Tam-tam; 2 Suspended Cymbals; Tumbler; Sizzle Cymbal; Hand Bell.

Percussion II: Vibraphone; 3 Antique Cymbals; 2 Gongs; 2 Tam-tams; Tubular Bells; 2 Suspended Cymbals; Hand Bell; Sizzle Cymbal; Tumbler; Triangle.

For solo soprano voice and two percussionists, the stage diagram for this work is very explicit in showing both the location and the interconnections of the composer's electronic components. There are four microphones assigned to the singer and the percussionist (⌐⌐) and a general microphone (⌐⌐) that picks up the sounds from all three performers as well as what emanates from the pair of loudspeakers (⌐⌐). Four tape decks (⌐⌐) are required, two to record the sounds and two for their playback. A potentiometer (amplifier with volume control) modifies the miked sounds and relays them to the two loudspeakers.

Example #454. George Crumb: *Music for a Summer Evening* (1974).

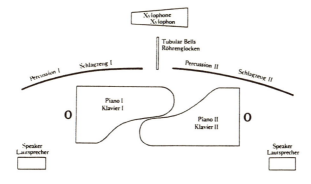

Percussion I: 3 Japanese Temple Bells; Large Tam-tam; 2 Maracas; Small Tam-tam; Glass Windchimes; Large and Small Suspended Cymbals; Claves; 3 Woodblocks; Sleighbells; Glockenspiel; Large Timpano; Slide Whistle; Thunder Sheet; Crotales; Quijada (Jawbone of an Ass); African Log Drum; Sizzle Cymbal; Bass Drum; 2 Tom-toms; Sistrum; Tibetan Prayer Stones; Bell Tree; Tubular Bells; Xylophone.

Percussion II: Vibraphone; Bamboo Windchimes; 5 Temple Blocks; Sizzle Cymbal; Large Suspended Cymbal; Slide Whistle; 2 Tom-toms; Large and Small Tam-tams; 2 Tom-toms; Bongos; Jug; 2 Triangles; Bongos; Bell Tree; Sleighbells; Tubular Bells; Xylophone; Guïro; African Thumb Piano.

Both pianos in Crumb's composition are amplified by means of conventional microphones suspended above the bass strings of each piano. As shown, two loudspeakers (⊏⊐) on either side of the platform relay the keyboard sounds out to the audience. As the composer's complement of percussion instruments is quite extensive, including such exotica as slide whistle, quijada, Tibetan prayer stones, and African thumb piano, it is obvious that individual pictograms for each instrument would have unduly complicated the visual aspect of this stage diagram.

Example #455. Roger Reynolds: *". . . From Behind the Unreasoning Mask"* (1975).

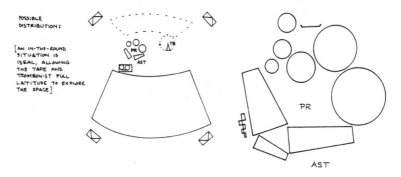

Percussion: Glockenspiel; Vibraphone; Xylophone; 2 Bass Drums; 3 Tom-toms; Suspended Cymbal; Small Gong; 5 Temple Blocks; Claves; 2 Flexatones; 5 Pairs of Castanets; Glass Windchimes; Wood Windchimes.

Reynold's composition is for trombone solo, one percussionist, with an assistant, and a 4-channel tape. Two stage pictographs are presented, one showing the positions of the trombonist, percussion set-up and tape deck (▭▯▭) and the four loudspeakers (◩◪). The other diagram pinpoints the locations of the individual percussion members. The assistant not only performs on various of the percussion but controls the volume of the tape recorder, as well.

Example #456. William Kraft: *Soliloquy for Solo Percussionist and Tape* (1975).

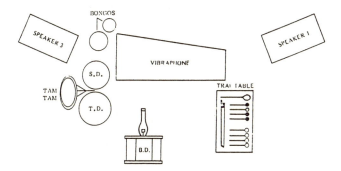

Noted for his many works for percussion ensemble, Kraft has indicated the instruments here in simple yet clear terms, including the sticks and mallets required. Unaccountably, the diagram does not show the location of the second of the three loudspeakers specified, nor are any of the other electronic components represented.

Chamber Ensemble

Example #457. Paul Méfano: *Lignes* (1968).

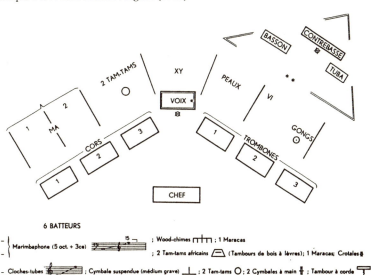

"Pour voix de basse noble" is Méfano's directive for the vocalist in this work. The vocalist is to be provided with a contact microphone (☒), as is the double bass. Soloist and the three instruments shown at the right rear of the stage are to be elevated above the other players. In the score the composer identifies the percussion instruments both with pictograms and with nomenclature; the logic of this practice is unclear.

Example #458. Claudio Santoro: *Intermitencias II* (1969).

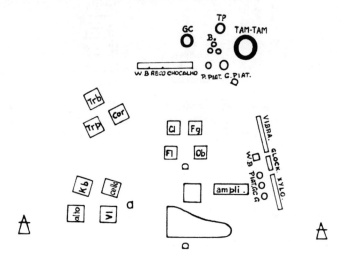

Percussion I: Woodblocks; Bongos: Suspended Cymbals; Snare Drum; Bass Drum; Tam-tam; Chinese Gong; Guïro; Rattle.

Percussion II: Glockenspiel; Xylophone; Vibraphone; Woodblocks; Suspended Cymbal.

Only the percussion and the piano receive pictographic representation in Santoro's score, in addition to the required amplifier and the two loudspeakers (⟁).

Example #459. Gilbert Amy: *Cette étoile enseigne à s'incliner* (1970).

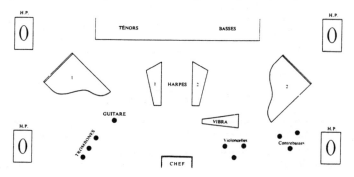

Vibraphone, pianos, and harps only are identified with pictograms in Amy's work, the remaining ensemble members located by abstract symbols. Four loudspeakers (   ) are placed in the four corners of the performance platform; they transmit the sounds from a pre-recorded tape, the tone control console being situated in clear view of the conductor.

Example #460. István Anhalt: *Foci* (1970).

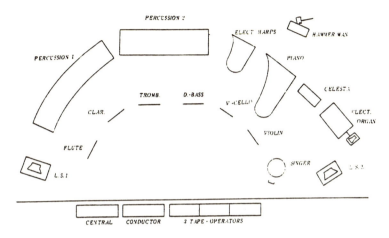

Percussion 1 & 2: Glockenspiel; Vibraphone; Tubular Bells; Crotales; Tam-tams; 3 Javanese Gongs; Small Indian Bell; 3 Triangles; Middle-sized Elephant Bell; 3 Suspended Cymbals; Small Rivet Cymbal; Sleighbells; Water Gong; 1 Timpano; 2 Bongos; Conga Drum; Bass Drum; 2 Tom-toms; 3 Timbales; Tenor Drum; 5 or 6 Tunable Small Drums; Tambourine; Pair of Sandblocks; Castanets; Glass Washboard; Guïro; 2 Claves; 2 Marimbas; 2 Sets of Temple Blocks; Ratchet; 4 Maracas; Bamboo and Glass Windchimes; Cardboard Box (filled with peas); Heavy Wooden Hammer; About 5 lbs. Of Broken Glass; Brick-lined Shallow Box.

This work requires three 2-channel tape decks (▭), each with its own operator, and six loudspeakers (◁), only two of which are shown. At the left of the conductor is the central volume control (amplifier) with its own operator. Two keyboard players are needed for the electric harpsichord/piano and the celesta/organ, all of which are given visual identification. The soprano is to be amplified, her microphone represented as:⌐___┘ . The three tape operators as well as all the instrumentalists walk on stage, one by one, at the outset of *Foci*, accompanied by heavy blows from the Hammer-Man (upper stage left corner).

There are no pictograms for either the percussion instruments or their beaters present in the score pages; occasionally the stick types suggested by the composer are indicated by terminology, although Anhalt is not consistent with such directives.

Example #461. George Crumb: *Ancient Voices of Children* (1970).

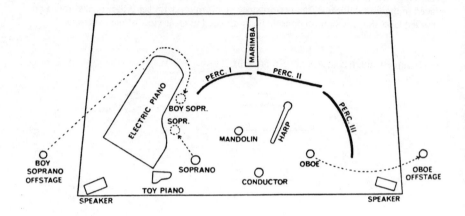

Percussion I: Large Tam-tam; Pair of Finger Cymbals; 2 Maracas; Antique Cymbal; Tambourine; 1 Timbale; Marimba.

Percussion II: Medium-sized Tam-tam; 4 Tunable Tom-toms; Tenor Drum; Large Suspended Cymbal; 2 Maracas; Tubular Bells; Sleighbells.

Percussion III: Small Tam-tam; Pair of Tibetan Prayer Stones; Claves; Vibraphone; 1 Mounted Glockenspiel Plate; Sleighbells; 1 Large Timpano; 2 Antique Cymbals; 2 Maracas; Large Suspended Cymbal; 5 Japanese Temple Bells.

The electric piano in Crumb's score is to have contact microphones taped to its soundboard, the sounds relayed to a stereo amplifier (off-stage) and then to two loudspeakers (⬚) on opposite sides of the concert platform. Clearly marked by dotted lines are the movements of the soprano, the boy soprano, and the oboist, the latter two performers from off-stage to positions on the platform.

Example #462. Werner Heider: *Kunst-Stoff* (1971).

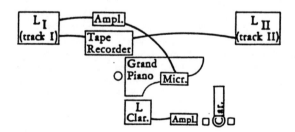

The interconnections of tape recorder, amplifier, and loudspeakers are carefully indicated here, as is the special microphone for the prepared piano. The clarinet is amplified by means of a vibration pickup plus a volume control foot pedal; its timbre is to be altered by such devices as "fuzz" distortion, wah-wah pedal, and "octavoice." The piano is prepared as follows: a "tinkling" effect in the top register, achieved by placing something like a small study score on the strings; a "clatter" effect in the middle range by means of a chain laid across the strings; and a "rattle" effect effectuated by placing a heavy cardboard on the low-range strings.

Example #463. Joseph Ott: *Matrix VII* (1971).

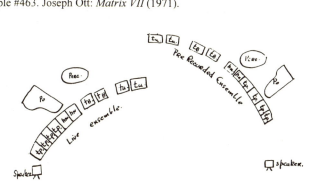

Percussion: Xylophone; Marimba; Timpani; Bass Drum; Suspended Cymbal; Triangle; Temple Blocks; Gong.

A singular aspect of this composition is the presence of two separate but equal ensembles, each comprising ten brass instruments, percussion, and piano. One ensemble is live, the other pre-recorded, the tape output relayed to the two loudspeakers located on both sides of the stage apron. Only the two pianos receive visual representation, and the location of the tape deck and/or amplifier is not shown.

Example #464. Vinko Globokar: *Airs de voyageur vers l'interieur* (1972).

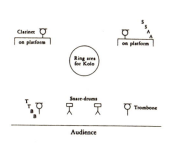
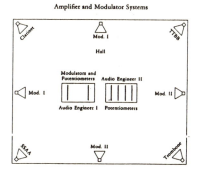

Two stage diagrams are required for this experimental work; the first shows the positioning of the five instruments and the two groups of mixed voices, together with the microphones (   ) for each. The second diagram relates only to the electronic equipment needed for the work, including which sounds are to emanate from which loudspeakers (   ).

Example #465. Elliott Schwartz: *Telly* (1972).

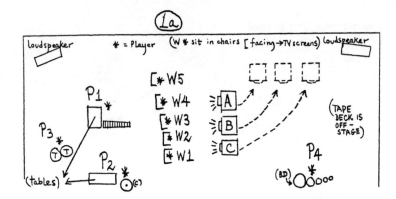

Percussion 1: Xylophone or Marimba; Maracas; Cowbell; Ship's Bell; Indian Bell.

Percussion 2: Suspended Cymbal; 2 Woodblocks or Temple Blocks; Triangle; Tambourine.

Percussion 3: 2 Timpani; Small Transistor Radio.

Percussion 4: 3 Drums; Bass Drum; Small Transistor Radio.

This chamber work for five wind or brass players, ad libitum (W1—W5) and four percussionists (P1—P4), is augmented by three television sets (A, B, C) and two transistor radios, the latter "played" by two percussionists (P3 and P4). A tape deck (not shown) records the sound made by all the performers, its volume as well as that of the TV sets manipulated at will by the players as the sounds pour forth from the pair of loudspeakers at the back of the platform. Because the wind or brass players must be mobile during the music, the composer suggests that *very large* instruments be avoided. As shown, the TV sets are moved from their initial position to where their screens can be seen by the audience.

Telly is yet another work in our survey that features a transistor radio among its percussion components. An earlier example was shown in *Aeolian Partitions* of Pauline Oliveros (*See:* Example #317), demonstrating that at least two present-day composers favor the unpredicable contribution to their sonic entity by this ubiquitous purveyor of recorded sound, whether talk or music.

Example #466. Raymond Zupko: *Fixations* (1974).

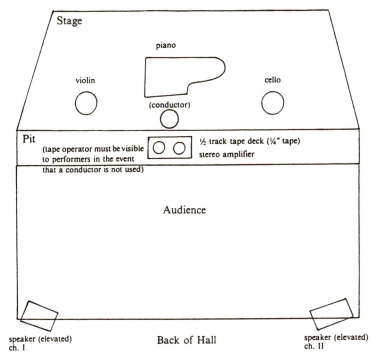

The operator of the tape deck in Zupko's trio for violin, cello, and piano, who is positioned in the orchestra pit but visible to the players, not only varies the tape playback level but starts and stops the tape four times during the performance. The composer's stage diagram is very precise in designating the location of his electronic components, including the pair of loudspeakers (⊏⊐) at the rear of the hall that are to be elevated.

Example #467. Eugene E. Bowen: *Jewelled Settings* (1980).

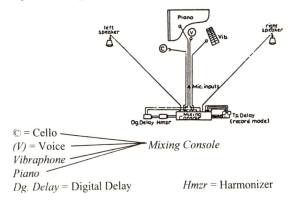

Ⓒ = Cello
(V) = Voice
Vibraphone   } *Mixing Console*
Piano
Dg. Delay = Digital Delay   *Hmzr* = Harmonizer

As shown in this composer's diagram, the microphones (o) for the quartet of performers are connected to a mixing console comprising a harmonizer, digital delay, and tape recorder. The modified resultant sounds are then relayed to the two loudspeakers (⬱) set on opposite sides of the stage.

Example #468. Frank Brickle: *Stolen Kisses* (1983).

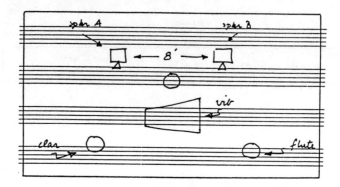

Although a piano is an essential part of the composer's resources, it is not included in the stage diagram. The two loudspeakers, set eight feet apart, are to be elevated three feet, pointed directly to the audience. No indication is given of the nature of the two-channel tape required in the work.

Example #469. Lyle Mays: *Somewhere in Maine* (1988).

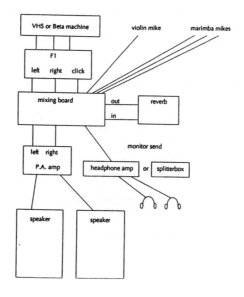

This stage diagram is unique in that it is only concerned with the electronic components essential to the work. Written for violin and marimba duo, each player is supplied with a microphone, their combined sounds going through an elaborate process of timbral modification before coming forth from a pair of loudspeakers. It is curious that the only electronic item here given visual representation are the two sets of headphones to be worn by the operators of the equipment.

Orchestra

Example #470. Richard Hoffman: *Orchestra Piece* (1961).

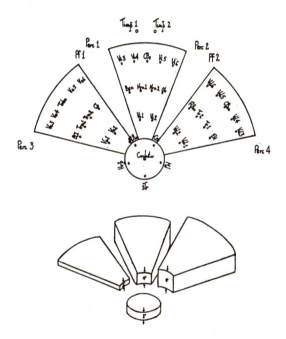

Percussion 1: Vibraphone; Chimes; High Gong.

Percussion 2: Glockenspiel; Xylophone; Suspended Cymbal.

Percussion 3: Bass Drum; Tambourine; Suspended Cymbal.

Percussion 4: Snare Drum; Triangle; Low Gong.

Timpani 1 and 2: 4 drums each.

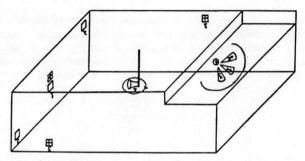

A stereophonic effect is clearly the resultant of Hoffmann's very detailed stage set-up for this symphonic work. Individual microphones (o) are indicated for all the players in each of the three orchestral sections, the sounds relayed to five loudspeakers (· ☐ and 🔊) located at the sides and rear of the auditorium, shown in the second diagram. In addition there is a non-directional microphone (not depicted) hanging above the circle of five soloists; this relays their sounds to a continuously revolving loudspeaker (🔊 ·) in the center of the audience space.

Example #471. Arne Mellnäs: *Aura* (1964).

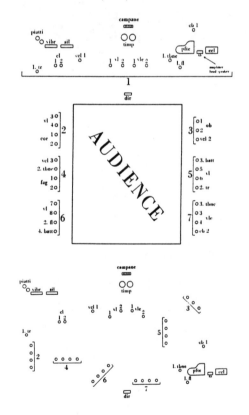

Not shown in this stage diagrammatic set-up are twelve hanging bottles to be struck with spoons and fourteen inflated balloons attached to music stands to be exploded with pins; these actions are carried out by certain woodwind, brass, and string players. Two possible stage arrangements are provided by the composer, one in which groups 2 to 7 surround the audience, and one in which they entirely occupy the concert platform. Amplifier and loudspeaker relate only to a single double bass, which is fitted with a contact microphone.

Example #472. Karlheinz Stockhausen: *Mixtur* (1964).

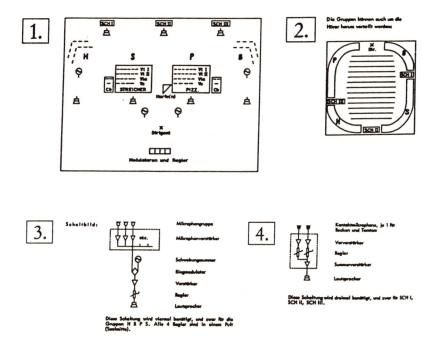

Stockhausen's orchestra is divided into five parts (*See:* Diagram 1.): *SCH* (Percussion); *H* (Woodwinds); *B* (Brass); *P* (Pizzicato—half of the strings plus harp); and *S* (Strings, the other half). The three percussionists wear contact microphones connected to three loudspeakers (⏚). Directional microphones hang above the other groups and all microphones are linked up to amplifiers, oscillators, ring-modulators, potentiometers, and loudspeakers (*See:* Diagram 3.). An alternative arrangement of the set-up of the orchestra is shown in Diagram 2. Finally, the electronic components for the percussion are detailed in Diagram 4.

Example #473. Luc Ferrari: *Société II* (1967).

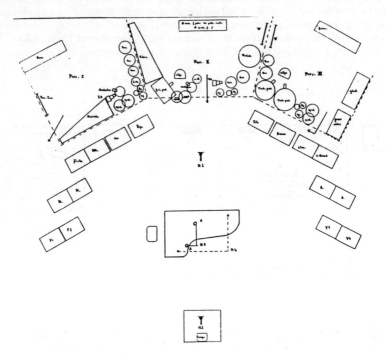

Percussion I: Marimba; 3 Temple Blocks; Bongos; Conga Drum; 3 Tom-toms; Tenor Drum; Triangle; 2 Suspended Cymbals; Guïro; Charleston Cymbal; Tam-tam; Hand Cymbals; Claves; Crotales; Tambourine; Sleighbells.

Percussion II: Vibraphone; 3 Temple Blocks: Bongos; Conga Drum; 2 Tom-toms; Snare Drum; Bass Drum (with foot pedal); Hand Cymbal; 2 Suspended Cymbals; Charleston Cymbal; Low Timbale; Tam-tam; Claves; Tambourine; Whip; Castanets.

Percussion III: Keyed Glockenspiel; Bongos; Conga Drum; Whip; 2 Tom-toms; Very Large Bass Drum; Triangle; Hand Cymbals: 2 Suspended Cymbals; 2 Timpani; Tam-tam; Claves; Woodblock; Maracas.

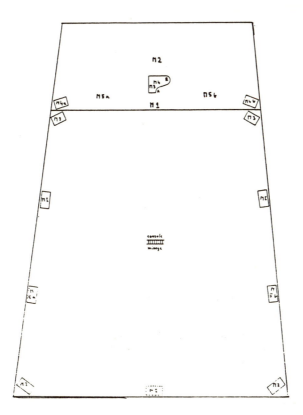

Société II is designed for four soloists (piano and three percussionists) and sixteen additional instrumentalists (four woodwinds, three brasses, and nine strings). Two pictograms are presented by the composer: the first shows the layout of the electronic components and the second details the three percussion ensembles. Microphone placements are shown by M1—M5 and instructions are provided for the exact locations of the two microphones for the piano. The mixing console is set in the exact center of the hall. Two loudspeakers are specified for the piano and four apply to the orchestral instruments.

Divided into "suites," at several points Ferrari has included a supplementary stage diagram showing the movements of the percussionists from one position to another, mainly adjacent to the piano so as to enable them to play on the interior strings with various beaters. These items are not indentified with pictograms but by means of standard nomenclature.

Example #474. Heinz Holliger: *Siebengesang* (1967).

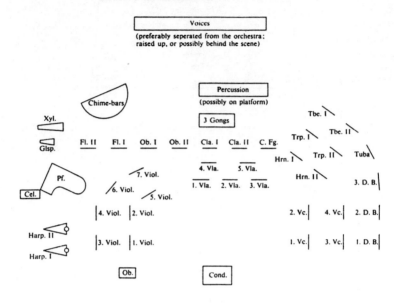

Percussion: Xylophone; Glockenspiel; 13 Chime Bars; 3 Gongs; 2 Woodblocks; 2 Temple Blocks; 4 Bongos; 3 Tom-toms; 2 Maracas; Small Snare Drum; Large Bass Drum; 3 Suspended Cymbals; 3 Tam-tams.

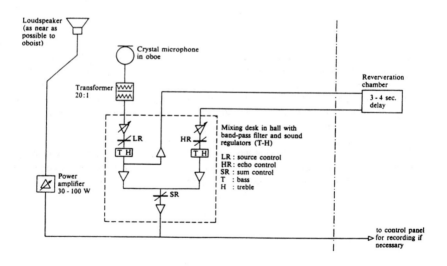

This "Seven Song" is for oboe, orchestra, chorus, and a loudspeaker next to the oboist. The electronic set-up is detailed in a separate diagram, pinpointing the interactions of the oboist's crystal microphone, and the transformer, amplifier, mixing desk, reverberation chamber, control panel for recording, and loudspeaker. This diagram must surely be a sound technician's dream come true.

Example #475. Zbyněk Vostřák: *Pendel der Zeit* (1967).

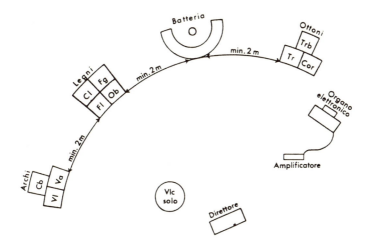

Percussion (Wooden): Woodblocks; Temple Blocks; Wood Drums; Xylophone.

Percussion (Membrane): Bongos; Tumbas; Conga Drums; Small Drums; Tom-toms; Bass Drums; Timpani.

Percussion (Metal): Cymbals; Gongs; Tam-tams; Chimes; Vibraphone.

The only electronic equipment required in this work is an amplifier attached to the electronic organ; the position of a loudspeaker is not shown. Not pertinent to the electronic aspect of this score, but of interest nonetheless, is a directive to the percussionist to choose at least six instruments from each of the three listed categories so as to create a row of "pitches" within each group. In the stage diagram the composer has indicated the desired minimum distances between the string, woodwind, and the brass groups; these should be two meters (roughly seven feet) in length. Furthur, Vostřák suggests that the organ should be a Hammond, "best suited," he says, "to the proper rendering of the part."

Example #476. Heinz Holliger: *Pneuma* (1970).

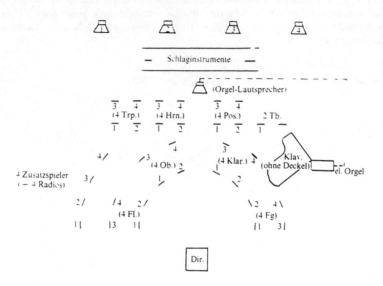

Percussion: 2 Suspended Cymbals; Sizzle Cymbal; 2 Tom-toms; 2 Conga Drums; 4-8 Triangles; 2 Metal Blocks; 2 Maracas; Guïro; Glass and Bamboo Windchimes; 2 Sandpaper Blocks; 2 Switches; 4 Bongos; Whip; 2 Tam-tams; Snare Drum; Bass Drum; Flexatone; 3 Timpani.

Circuit Diagram

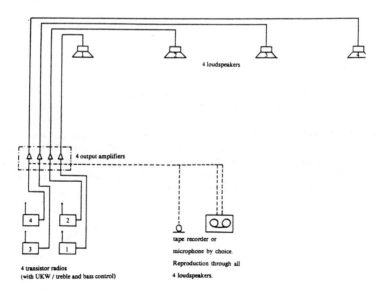

For this work there are four general loudspeakers (⟨⟩) and a separate speaker for the electronic organ. Connected to these components are four amplifiers, four transistor radios, and a tape recorder (⟨OO⟩). A circuit diagram supplements the stage layout suggested by the composer.

Example #477. Friedholm Döhl: *Klang-Szene II* (1971).

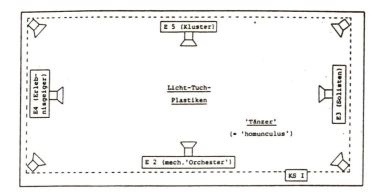

Obviously a staged work, involving a dancer with lighting and electronic effects, this "Sound-Scene" utilizes eight loudspeakers—four general and four related to specific sound sources, as indicated within the appended boxes.

Example #478. Cristobal Halffter: *Planto por las victimas de la Violencia* (1971).

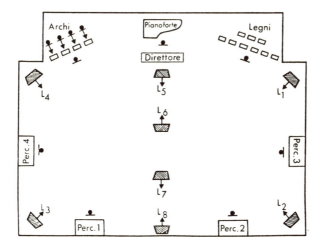

Percussion 1: Vibraphone; Marimbaphone; 2 Suspended Cymbals; 2 Gongs; 2 Tam-tams; 3 Bongos; 5 Tuned Glasses.

Percussion 2: Xylophone; Glockenspiel; 2 Crotales; 2 Gongs; 2 Suspended Cymbals; 2 Triangles; 3 Woodblocks; Thunder Sheet; 5 Tuned Glasses.

Percussion 3: Vibraphone; Marimbaphone; 2 Suspended Cymbals; 2 Crotales; 2 Gongs; 3 Tom-toms; 5 Tuned Glasses; Hand Bell.

Percussion 4: Xylophone; Keyed Glockenspiel; Tubular Bells; 2 Suspended Cymbals; 2 Gongs; Bass Drum; 5 Tuned Glasses.

Halffter is very precise here in showing the desired positions of the seven general microphones (⚫), four contact microphones (🔲), and eight numbered loudspeakers required for his *Planto*. Not shown pictographically, however, are such components as filters, ring-modulators, or electronic gates. Among the orchestral instruments only the piano is given a pictogram.

Example #479. Bronislaw Kazimierz Przybylski: *In honorem Nicolai Copernici* (1972).

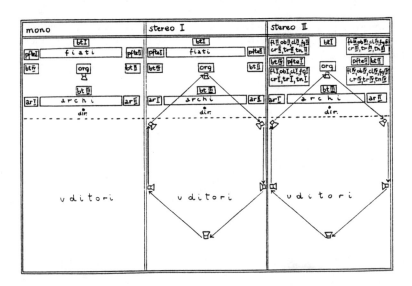

Percussion I: Claves; Maracas; 5 Tom-toms; 4 Timpani.
Percussion II: Xylophone; Chimes; Triangle; Cowbells; Small Cymbal; 4 Temple Blocks.
Percussion III: Glockenspiel; Cymbal; Bamboo Shaker; Wood Drum; 2 Bongos.
Percussion IV: Vibraphone; Large Cymbal; Guïro; Snare Drum; Bass Drum.

Two aspects of this composition set it apart from most of the other scores cited in this section. First of all, the composer's suggested stage diagram outlines three performance possibilities for this work. All three involve the electronic organ, but only one version is designed for a single loudspeaker (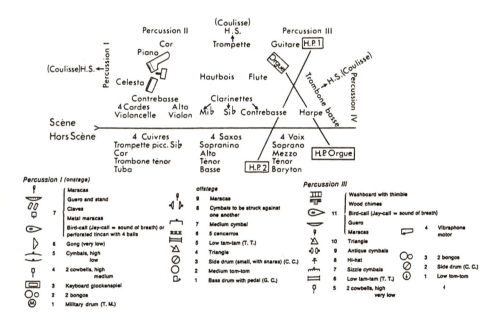) through which to direct the organ sounds out to the audience. The two other versions connect the organ output to five speakers located at the sides and rear of the auditorium, and one version (Stereo II) re-arranges the seating of the woodwind, brass, percussion, and keyboard instruments. The position of the two harps and string section remains the same for all three performance possibilities.

An interesting technical manipulation occurs in the fourth movement of this work: the organ output begins with the stage loudspeaker and then makes its way around the speakers surrounding the audience, the rotation of the sound steadily increasing in velocity.

Example #480. Francis Miroglio: *Tremplins* (1973).

Miroglio's orchestra in this work is divided into two parts; a large contingent of instruments (five woodwinds, three brass, four percussion ensembles, piano, celesta, organ, harp, guitar, and four strings) on the stage platform and a smaller ensemble consisting of four saxophones, four brass, and four vocalists) off-stage (*Hors Scène*). Three loudspeakers (H.P.) are indicated, one for the electric organ and two for the guitar, one on-stage and one off-stage. All four percussion groups are given elaborate listings with individual pictograms, but only those for *Percussion I* and *Percussion III* are included here as those for groups *II* and *IV* are very similar, with a great deal of duplication of symbols. As shown, only the piano and the celesta are pictured on stage, the percussion sections merely indicated by name, as are the remaining instruments.

Chorus

Example #481. Cristobal Halffter: *Gaudium et Spes (Beunza)* (1973).

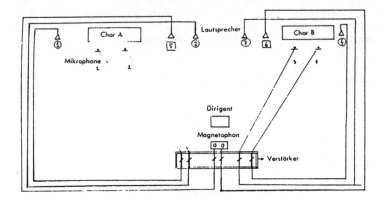

Four microphones (▬●▬) in Halffter's composition, which are positioned in front of Choruses A and B, direct the vocal sounds to a tape recorder ⌈O O⌉ and amplifier (*Verstärker*). These technical devices in turn relay the sounds to six loudspeakers (⅄) located on either side of the two choral groups.

Example #482. Brian Ferneyhough: *Time and Motion Study III* (1974).

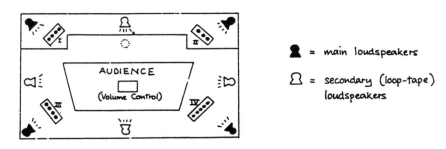

Soprano I: (Claves); *Alto I:* (Claves); *Tenor I:* (Claves; Large Suspended Cymbal); *Bass I:* (Claves; Tam-tam); *Soprano II:* (Bamboo Windchimes; Sandblocks); *Alto II:* (Glass Windchimes; Sandblocks); *Tenor II:* (Jingle Windchimes; Chimes; Gong); *Bass II:* (Tom-tom; Tam-tam); *Soprano III:* (Maracas); *Alto III:* (Maracas; Small Suspended Cymbal); *Tenor III:* (Bongos); *Baritone I:* (Darrabucca Drum); *Mezzo-Soprano:* (Maracas); *Alto IV:* Maracas; Tam-tam); *Tenor IV:* (Bongos); *Baritone II:* (Darrabucca Drum; Suspended Cymbal).

An unusual requirement: the sixteen solo voices in this work also play the indicated percussion instruments in addition to their vocalizing. Their stage positions surrounding the audience are shown in abstract terms, with only the loudspeakers being given representational pictograms. The conductor's position is indicated by the small dotted circle, although the composer says that this can be changed, if desired.

Solo Instruments or Voice

Example #483. José Maria Mestres-Quadreny: *Three Canons in Homage to Galileo* (1968).

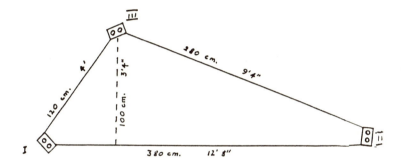

Tape recorder I always records.
Tape recorders II and III always play back.

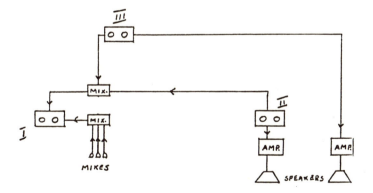

There are two versions of this work, one for solo piano, the other for percussion. Both use an identical set-up of electronic equipment: three tape recorders placed as shown in the diagram, with a 26-foot length of magnetic tape running through all three recorders. As all the sounds are pre-recorded, no instruments appear in the composer's diagrammatic plan.

Example #484. Mario Davidovsky: *Syncronisms No. 6 for Piano and Electronic Sounds* (1970).

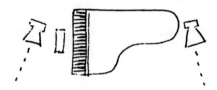

In the composer's words, "The electronic segment should perhaps not be viewed as an independent polyphonic line, but rather as if it were inlaid into the piano part." And, further: "It is highly desirable to locate both loudspeakers very close to the piano in order to concentrate, as much as possible, the projection of the sound."

Example #485. Maki Ishii: *Sen-Ten* (1971).

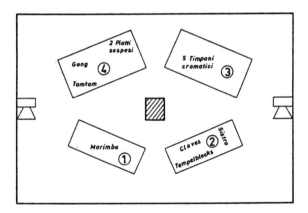

This work is designed for one percussionist and electronic sounds. Two tape recorders are required (not shown), one for ordinary percussive effects and one for traditional Japanese instrumental sounds; both are connected to the pair of loudspeakers located at the sides of the stage. Circled numerals within elongated boxes indicate the types of instruments that may be added, ad libitum, to those specified by the composer: (1): other mallet instruments; (2): miscellaneous small percussion; (3): other membranophones; (4): other metal idiophones.

Example #486. Olly Wilson: *Sometimes* (1976).

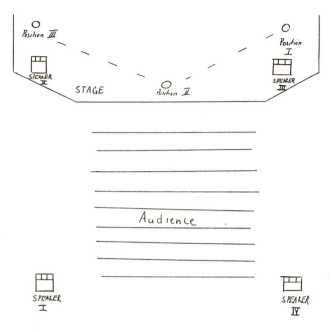

The tenor soloist in this work occupies three positions on stage, as indicated by the dotted lines. Four loudspeakers relay pre-recorded tape sounds to the audience, two on stage and two situated at the rear of the auditorium. Not shown in the diagram are tape deck, amplifier, or other electronic equipment.

Example #487. Vinko Globokar: *Introspection of a Tuba Player* (1983).

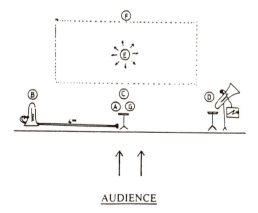

A unique work and one that is highly characteristic of this composer, *Introspection* requires an unusual electronic component set-up. At stage center is a stool (⟍⟋) for positions (A), (C), and (G). To its left is a tuba (B) stood upright on its bell and connected to a plastic tube fitted with a mouthpiece (⟹◁). At stage right is another tuba and stool (D), the tuba connected to an amplifier and the player facing towards position (B). During the music the tuba player moves from one position to another, these movements coordinated with elaborate stage lighting effects.

There is little doubt that depictions of electronic set-ups in the stage diagrams of future scores will provide intriguing variations on those previously illustrated. They may be infinitely more complicated and extensive in their stipulations or, to the contrary, they may be significantly more simplified, reflecting the increasing sophistication and simplicity of advanced sound reproduction. It will be rewarding for composers interested in electronic music to make personal comparisons between past, present, and future requirements in this field of musical endeavor.

It may very well be that by this time the interested reader of this compendium of pictographic score notation may feel literally overwhelmed by the sheer number and variety of the stage diagrams illustrated on the previous pages. Ranging as they have from simplistic, "bare bones" depictions of a stage layout to elaborately detailed and meticulously designed arrangements of the composers' forces involved, these examples have at the very least demonstrated convincing proof of the validity of this particular aspect of contemporary notation. It is one that has engaged the attention of many composers of our time, creators of percussion ensemble, chamber music, and orchestral works from the patently conservative to the notably experimental in compositional outlook. It will, one thinks, be enlightening to chart the future development of this particularized aspect of modern musical notation and, as well, to hazard a guess as to where it might lead the composers of the future.

III. PICTOGRAPHIC PERFORMANCE DIRECTIVES

In addition to their penchant for devising stage diagrams in certain scores—elaborately detailed, notably simplistic, and all degrees between—contemporary composers have been equally fruitful in inventing symbols for methods of obtaining special effects from their instruments, whether wind, brass, keyboard, percussion, or string. First and foremost are the pictographic signs for the many and varied agents for striking the members of the percussion section, whether these are constructed of metal, wood, or skin. And the agents themselves, being made of different materials, have suggested a bewildering variety of shapes and sizes, as the following pages will verify.

It will be noted, once again, that there exists little consensus among our composers as to the best, and final, choice among the extensive array of symbols used in present-day publications. Whether such agreement will ever be reached is certainly open to question. The odds do not favor this ever happening, at least in the foreseeable future.

Percussion Instruments

Beater, Mallet and Stick Symbols

Example #488. *Bamboo Sticks*:

Example #489. *Bass Drum Mallet (hard)*:

Example #490. *Bass Drum Mallet (medium)*:

Example #491. *Bass Drum Mallet (soft)*:

Example #492. *Bass Drum Mallet (two-headed)*:

Example #493. *Beater (with flexible handle)*:

Example #494. *Beater (soft; material unspecified):*

Example #495. *Beaters (medium, material unspecified):*

Example #496. *Bows (Double bass or Violoncello):*

Example #497. *Brass Beater:*

Example #498. *Bundle of nails:*

Example #499. *Cane Stick:*

Example #500. *Carpet Beater:*

Example #501. *Chime Mallet:*

Example #502. *Chime Mallet (padded):*

Example #503. *Clave:*

Example #504. *Clothes brush:*

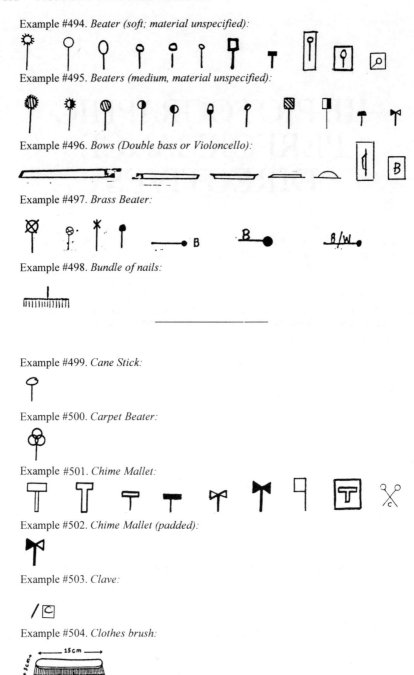

Example #505. *Cluster Stick:*

Example #506. *Comb:*

Example #507. *Double Beaters/Mallets/Sticks:*

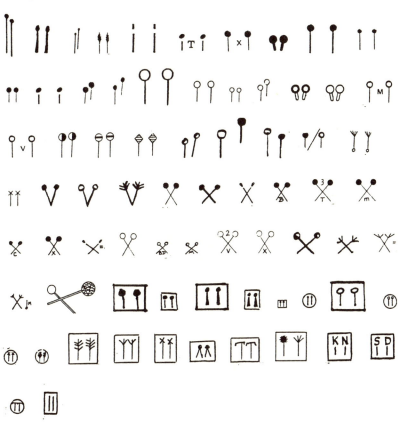

Example #508. *Drum Stick (type unspecified):*

Example #509. *Drum Stick (end):*

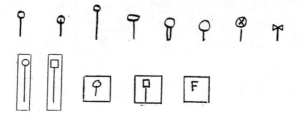

Example #510. *Felt Stick (degree unspecified):*

Example #511. *Felt Stick (hard):*

Example #512. *Felt Stick (medium):*

Example #513. *Felt Stick (soft):*

Example #514. *File:*

Example #515. *Fingernails:*

Example #516. *Fingertips:*

Example #517. *Fist (strike with):*

Example #518. *Glockenspiel Mallet:*

Example #519. *Gong Mallet:*

Example #520. *Guïro Scratcher:*

Example #521. *Hairbrush:*

Example #522. *Hammer:*

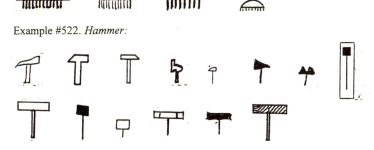

Example #523. *Hand (strike with):*

Example #524. *Handle of Beater or Mallet:*

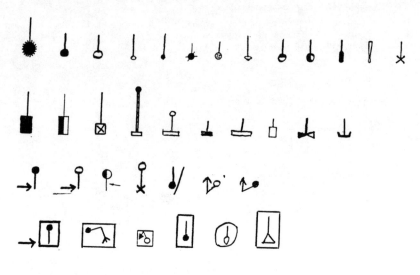

Example #525. *Knife-blade:*

Example #526. *Knitting Needles:*

Example #527. *Leather Stick:*

Example #528. *Marimba Mallet:*

Example #529. *Marimbula Mallet:*

Example #530. *Metal Beater:*

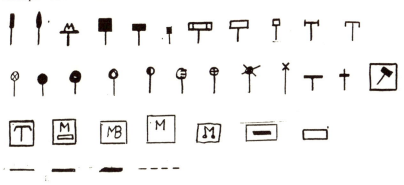

Example #531. *Pick or Plectrum (hard):*

Example #532. *Pick or Plectrum (soft):*

Example #533. *Plastic Beater:*

Example #534. *Plastic Ruler:*

Example #535. *Porcelain Beater:*

Example #536. *Quadruple Beaters/Mallets/Sticks:*

Example #537. *Rattan Beater:*

Example #538. *Rubber Beater (degree unspecified):*

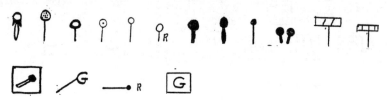

Example #539. *Rubber Beater (hard):*

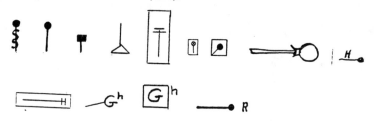

Example #540. *Rubber Beater (medium):*

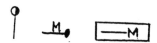

Example #541. *Rubber Beater (soft):*

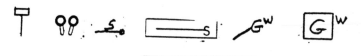

Example #542. *Scraper-stick:*

●●●●●●●●●●

Example #543. *Screwdriver:*

Example #544. *Snare Drum Sticks:*

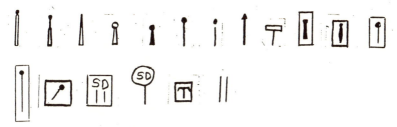

Example #545. *Sponge Mallet:*

Example #546. *Steel (Hard) Brush:*

Example #547. *Steel Rod:*

Example #548. *Stick (hard, material unspecified):*

Example #549. *Superball Mallet:*

Example #550. *Switch:*

Example #551. *Table Knife:*

Example #552. *Tam-tam Beater:*

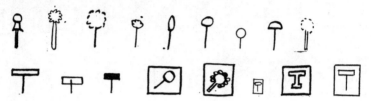

Example #553. *Thimble:*

Example #554. *Thin Metal Stick:*

Example #555. *Thin Wood Stick:*

Example #556. *Thumb (strike with):*

Example #557. *Timpani Mallet (degree unspecified):*

Example #558. *Timpani Mallet (hard):*

Example #559. *Timpani Mallet (medium):*

Example #560. *Timpani Mallet (soft):*

Example #561. *Timpani Stick (small hard felt):*

Example #562. *Toothbrush:*

Example #563. *Triangle Beater:*

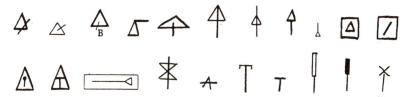

Example #564. *Triple Beaters/Mallets/Sticks:*

Example #565. *Tuning Fork:*

ψ ψ Ψ

Example #566. *Vibraphone Mallet:*

Example #567. *Wirebrush (Jazz Brush):*

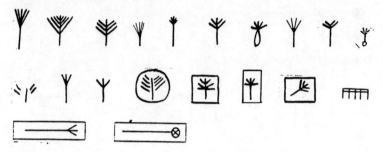

Example #568. *Wooden Hammer:*

Example #569. *Wooden Stick:*

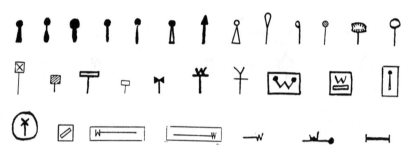

Example #570. *Wool Beater:*

Example #571. *Xylophone Mallet:*

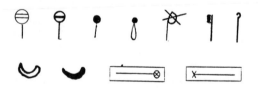

Example #572. *Xylophone Plate:*

Example #573. *Yarn Mallet (degree unspecified):*

Example #574. *Yarn Mallet (hard):*

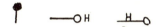

Example #575. *Yarn Mallet (medium):*

Example #576. *Yarn Mallet (soft):*

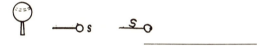

Attack Symbols (methods of striking)

Striking on Metal Instruments

Example #577. Strike dome of suspended cymbal with stick:

Example #578. Strike dome of suspended cymbal with soft beater:

Example #579. Strike dome of suspended cymbal with tip of snare drum stick:

Example #580. Soft stick in left hand on cymbal dome and in right hand on edge:

Example #581. Strike dome of cymbal at the edge:

Example #582. Strike dome of cymbal at designated areas:

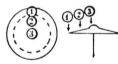

Example #583. Slide with soft stick on suspended cymbal dome from center to edge:

Example #584. Enclose rim of suspended cymbal with slapstick before striking:

Example #585. Separate wires of wirebrush on rim of suspended cymbal:

Example #586. Strike edge of cymbal with handle of stick:

Example #587. Sweep in a circular motion around the cymbal surface with a comb:

Example #588. With left hand enclose rim of suspended cymbal with two sponge sticks:

Example #589. Attach a strand of bow hair or a thin piece of thread to the cymbal stand. Pull stand taut over cymbal rim with left hand. With right hand move strand back and forth along its length:

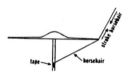

Example #590. Strike instrument with a sponge beater and wire brush in left hand and with flat right hand:

Example #591. Strike bottom of cowbell with a violoncello or double bass bow:

Example #592. Roll with soft stick on inside of almglocken:

Example #593. Strike tam-tam with cowbell:

Example #594. Strike crotales and triangles with hard beaters:

Example #595. Hold side of special beater firmly against rim of bell while moving it in a circular motion:

Example #596. Rapidly rub the lower bar of the triangle with the beater:

Striking on Membranophones

Example #597. Strike side of drum:

Example #598. Place cymbal on the timpani head:

Example #599. Strike cymbal laid on timpani surface with a soft beater:

Example #600. Strike center of drum or cymbal with a hard stick:

Example #601. Play on the rim of the drum:

Example #602. Move in irregular cycles with two wire brushes on the head of the snare drum:

Example #603. Rub on the surface of the timpani with a hairbrush:

Keyboard Instruments

Prepared Piano

Example #604. Toshiro Mayuzumi: *Pieces for Prepared Piano and Strings* (1957).

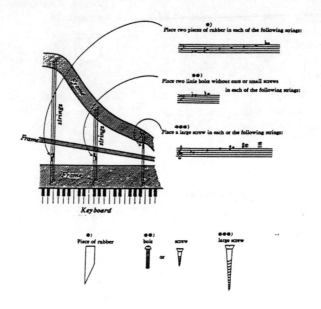

Example #605. Donald Erb: *The Seventh Trumpet* (1969).

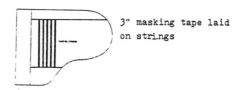

3" masking tape laid
on strings

Example #606. Kazimierz Serocki: *Swinging Music* (1970).

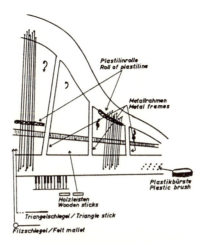

$\begin{cases} \text{°} \\ \text{°} \end{cases}$ - Diskantlage / Upper range

$\begin{cases} \text{°} \\ \text{°} \end{cases}$ - Obere Mittellage / Upper middle range

$\begin{cases} \text{°} \\ \text{°} \end{cases}$ - Untere Mittellage / Lower middle range

$\begin{cases} \text{°} \\ \text{°} \end{cases}$ - Baßlage / Bass range

Klassifizierung der vier Tonhöhenbereiche analog der Einteilung durch Metallrahmen im Inneren des Instruments / For the sake of definition, the compass of the instrument will be divided into four ranges, according to the divisions of the metal frame inside the instrument

Interior Effects

Example #607. Extraneous objects on the strings.

Hair Brush: Thimbles:

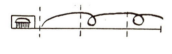
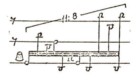

Example #608. Roger Reynolds: *Blind Men* (1966).
Strings plucked with two types of metal picks: with slightly rounded edge; with sharp edge.

Exterior Effects

Example #609. Actions on piano keyboard.

Closed hand (fist):   Fingertips:

Open hand: Specific finger(s):

Edge of hand (sideways on keys):   Knuckle:

Flat hand (palm):   Forearm:

Mound of the palm: Forearm and hand:

Glove on hand:

With thimbles on two fingers

Example #610. Roger Reynolds: *Blind Men* (1966).

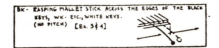

Example #611. John Cage: *The Wonderful Widow of Eighteen Springs* (1942).

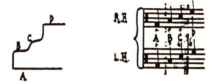

Grand piano completely closed.
A = underside of piano; B = front of keyboard lid; C = back of lid and front of keyboard; D = top of piano.

Plucked Instruments

Example #612. Harp Effects:

Holding tuning key by shank, place handle across strings:

Hold tuning key by shank, strike strings:

Brush strings left to right with fingertips:

Rub strings with drum and metal sticks:

Strike strings with hard and soft sticks: Tap strings with open hand:

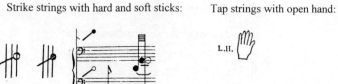

L.II.

Example #613. Guitar Effects:

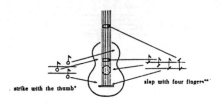

strike with the thumb*   slap with four fingers**

Woodwind Instruments

Example #614. *Amplification:*

Air microphone

Contactmic.

Example #615. *Duffalo Effect:*

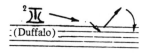

:(Duffalo)

Brass Instruments

Example #616. *Mute Symbols:*

Cup: Plunger:

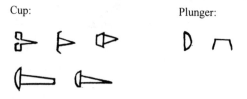

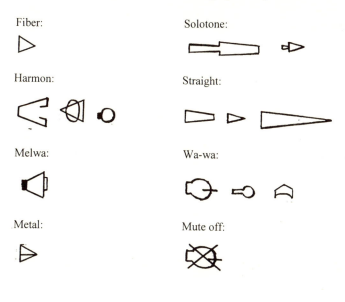

Fiber:

Solotone:

Harmon:

Straight:

Melwa:

Wa-wa:

Metal:

Mute off:

Example #617. *Percussive Effects:*

Tap with fingers or nails on trombone bell:

Beat with finger ring or thimble on edge of trombone bell:

Beat on trombone mouthpiece with palm:

Tap on mouthpiece of trombone with palm:

Beat two mouthpieces together:

String Instruments

Example #618. *Bowing Symbols:*

At the point of the bow:

At the frog (nut) of the bow:

Bowing directly over the bridge:

Bowing on the bridge:

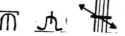

Bowing at the side of the bridge:

Bowing near the bridge:

Bowing behind the bridge:

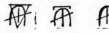

Bowing on the mute:

Bowing against the mute:

Eliptical motions with the bow:

Moving the bow vertically on the string:

Tap on instrument body where indicated:

Example #619. *Mute Symbols.*

Mute on:

Mute off:

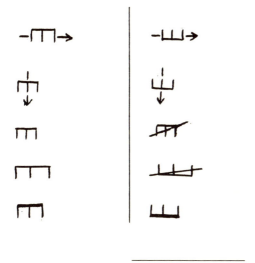

For reasons not at all self-evident, contemporary composers in general have seemingly not been as committed to pictorializing their specific directives concerning percussion effects, keyboard and harp special techniques, or woodwind, brass, or string idiomatic devices as they have been in stipulating the stage diagrams that show the desired layout of the forces in their works. Certainly, there is amply opportunity for orchestrators to indulge in fanciful instrumental directive pictographs to the same extent as when portraying their desired platform arrangements. On the other hand, many late twentieth-century scores are replete with newly designed, often strikingly unique symbols for producing all kinds of unconventional effects on instruments; these symbols, however, are usually not true pictograms when they appear to be completely non-representational. And when even this kind of abstract notation is not present in the scores, the composers must rely on standard terminology and nomenclature. Thus this notation is set entirely apart from the procedures that have been catalogued throughout this compendium. In the end the composer must thoughtfully evaluate both the undeniable virtues and the obvious drawbacks of pictographic notation—and then to use or not use the technique according to one's personal interest and conviction.

BIBLIOGRAPHY

Adler, Samuel. *The Study of Orchestration.* New York: W.W. Norton & Company, 1982. pp. 329-360, 383-85.

Anderson, Shirley. *A Standard System of Symbols, Notation, and Nomenclature for Percussion Instruments.* Philadelphia: Curtis Publishing Co., 1963.

Bajzak, Dieter. *Percussion: An Annotated Bibliography.* Metuchen, NJ: Scarecrow Press, 1988.

Blades, James. *Percussion Instruments and Their History.* New York: Frederick A. Praeger, Publishers, 1970. pp. 438-39.

Caskel, Christoph. "Notation for Percussion Instruments." *Percussionist*, Vol.8, No.3, 1971. pp. 80-84.

Centazzo, Andrea. *Guid ogli Strumenti a Percussione: Storia e Uso.* Padua: Franco Muzzio & Co., 1979. pp. 209-210.

_____. *Percussion—New Techniques.* Milan: G. Ricordi, 1983.

Cope, David. *New Music Notation.* Dubuque, IA: Kendall/Hunt Publishing Co., 1976. pp. 76-80, 83-85.

Galm, John. "The Need for Using Symbols in Percussion Notation." *NACWPI Journal*, Fall, 1972. pp. 46-49.

Leach, Joel T. "The Use of Cymbals in Multiple Percussion." *Brass and Percussion*, No.1/2. 1973.

Karkoschka, Erhard. *Notation in New Music.* Translated by Ruth Koenig. New York: Frederick A. Praeger, Publishers, 1972.

Kennan, Kent and Donald Grantham. *The Technique of Orchestration.* Fourth Edition. Englewood Cliffs, NJ: Prentice-Hall, Inc., 1990. pp. 268-271.

Kotonski, Wlodzimierz. *Schlaginstrumente in modernen Orchester.* Mainz: B. Schott's Söhne. 1968.

McCarthy, Frank. *Notational Standards for Percussion. Percussion Anthology*, Third Edition, 1984. pp. 468-470.

_____. "Symbols for Percussion Notation." *Percussionist*, Vol.18, No.1, 1980. pp. 8-19.

Meyer, Ramon. *Percussion Ensemble Floor Plans. Percussion Anthology*, Third Edition, 1984. pp. 299-301.

O'Neill, John C. "Recent Trends in Percussion Notation." *Percussionist*, Vol.18, No.1, 1980. pp. 20-55.

Peinkofer, Karl and Fritz Tannigel. *Handbook of Percussion Instruments.* Translated by Kurt and Elsa Stone. Mainz: B. Schott's Söhne, 1969. pp. 17-18, 180-182.

Rastell, Richard. *The Notation of Western Music.* New York: St. Martin's Press, 1982. pp. 259-261.

Reed, H. Owen and Joel T. Leach. *Scoring for Percussion.* Englewood Cliffs, NJ: Prentice-Hall, Inc., 1969. pp. 37, 124.

Risatti, Howard. *New Music Vocabulary.* Urbana, IL: University of Illinois Press, 1975. pp. 76-77, 83, 95-110, 133, 148, 159-60.

Smith Brindle, Reginald. *Contemporary Percussion.* London: Oxford University Press, 1970. pp. 12-15, 19.

Stone, Kurt. *Music Notation in the Twentieth Century.* New York: W.W. Norton & Co., 1980. pp. 206-213.

PUBLISHER LIST

L-1   Lang Percussion Co.
       Leduc (*See:* A-4)
       Litolff (*See:* H-3)

M-1   Margun Music, Inc.
       Marks (*See:* E-8)
M-2   MCA Music
M-3   Media Press, Inc.
M-4   Meredith Music Publ.
M-5   Merion Music, Inc.
M-6   Mills Music, Inc.
M-7   Mitchell Peters Publ.
M-8   MLC Publications
M-9   M.M. Cole Publ. Co.
       Modern (*See:* E-1)
M-10   Moeck-Verlag
M-11   Ms (Manuscript)
M-12   Music for Percussion, Inc.
       Musica (*See:* E-5)
       Musicales (*See:* A-6)

N-1   Norruth Music, Inc.

O-1   Ongaku No-Tomo Sha
O-2   Oxford University Press

P-1   Peer International
       Peters, C.F. (*See:* C-3)
       Peters, Mitchell (*See:* M-7)
P-2   Polskie Wydawnictwo Muzycne
P-3   Pomorze Budapest

P-4   Prentiss-Hall, Inc.
       Presser, Theodore (*See:* T-1)

       Reimers (*See:* E-3)
R-1   Remo Belli Percussion Library
       Ricordi (*See:* G-1)
R-2   Rouart, Lerolle et Cie.

       Salabert (*See:* E-4)
S-1   Sam Fox Publ. Co., Inc.
S-2   Samfundet til Udgivelse af Dansk
       Musik
       Schirmer, G. (*See:* G-2)
       Schott's (*See:* B-9)
S-3   Seesaw Music Corp.
S-4   Smith Publications
S-5   Sonic Arts Publications
S-6   Soundings Press
S-7   Source: Music of the Avant-Garde
S-8   Southern Music Co.
S-9   Studio 4 Productions

T-1   Theodore Presser Co.

U-1   United Music Publ., Ltd.
U-2   Universal Edition, A.G.

W-1   Western International Music, Inc.
W-2   Wilhelm Hansen Edition
W-3   World Library of Sacred Music

       Zerboni (*See:* E-7)

INDEX

(Refer to *Publisher's List* for codes that follow work titles in parentheses)

About the Author

GARDNER READ is Professor Emeritus and Composer-in-Residence at the School of Music, Boston University. A respected expert in the field of music composition, he has written numerous books and articles on composition theory including the *Compendium of Modern Instrumental Techniques* (Greenwood, 1993), which received the *Choice* Outstanding Academic Book Award in 1994.

ISBN 0-313-30469-6

90000>

HARDCOVER BAR CODE